ENGLISH CATHOLICISM
1680–1830

Volume 2

ENGLISH CATHOLICISM
1680–1830

Edited by
Michael Mullett

Volume 2

English Catholic Writings on Devotion, Prayer, Liturgy,
Instruction, Hagiography and Church History 1686–1755

LONDON AND NEW YORK

First published 2006 by Pickering & Chatto (Publishers) Limited

Published 2016 by Routledge
2 Park Square, Milton Park, Abingdon, Oxon OX14 4RN
711 Third Avenue, New York, NY 10017, USA

Routledge is an imprint of the Taylor & Francis Group, an informa business

© Taylor & Francis 2006

BRITISH LIBRARY CATALOGUING IN PUBLICATION DATA
English Catholicism, 1680–1830
1. Catholic Church – In literature 2. Catholic Church – England – History
– 18th century – Sources 3. Christian literature, English – Catholic authors
– Sources 4. Christian literature, English – Catholic authors – History and
criticism 5. Christianity and literature – England – History – 18th century
– Sources 6.England – Church history – 18th century – Sources
I. Mullett, Michael A.
820.9'38282

ISBN-13: 978-1-85196-824-4 (set)

Typeset by P&C

Facsimile preparation by Free Range
Book Design & Production Ltd, UK

Contents

Robert Parsons, *A Christian Directory, Guiding Men To Their Eternal Salvation. Divided into Three Books: The first whereof appertaining to Resolution, is onely contained in this Volume, divided into Two Parts, and set forth now again with many Corrections and Additions. There is added also, A Method for the Use of all: With two Tables* (London, 1687), pp. 586–610

Just as the benign climate of James's reign created opportunities for Catholic controversial publishing, so there also arose a demand for devotional works, supplied, in this case, by recourse to an earlier source. This 775-page volume was published openly in London in 1687 and bore the imprint 'Henry Hills, Kings printer, for the King and Matthew Turner'. The printer, Henry Hills, Sr (*c.* 1625–88/9), was a former Baptist and Cromwellian, turned Catholic after James II's accession.

The work's author, the Jesuit Robert Parsons (or Persons), was born in Somerset in June 1546, entered St Mary's Hall, Oxford, in 1564 and in 1566 moved to Balliol, taking his Bachelor of Arts in May 1568 and in 1569 becoming a full Fellow of that College. He began to lecture in Rhetoric in 1571, was made college bursar in 1572, took his Master of Arts in December 1572 and became Dean of Balliol in 1573. In 1574, however, this steady succession of distinctions was drastically interrupted when Parsons, showing signs of a drift towards Catholicism, was accused of financial malpractice. He was compelled to resign his Fellowship and left Oxford for London.

Having visited Rome, he became a Jesuit postulant in July 1575, studied at the Society's Roman College and was ordained in July 1578. By the beginning of the 1580s he was appointed at the head of an English Jesuit mission to England, in which Edmund Campion (1540–81) also took part. Parsons, in disguise as a military officer, arrived in London in June 1580 and threw himself into the work of the Mission, travelling in the West Country and the Midlands, meeting Catholic leaders and setting up a Catholic press, which was however, confiscated in 1581. Campion was arrested and executed, while Parsons set off for France.

In Rouen in 1582 he published what has been described as his most influential work, *The First Book of the Christian Exercise, Appertayning to*

Resolution, re-titled in later editions *The Christian Directory*. Then, in 1582 Parsons became involved in plans for an invasion of Scotland in support of the Catholic dynastic claims of Mary Queen of Scots (1542–87). He entered into a collaboration with Philip II of Spain (1527–98), staying in that kingdom until May 1583. Increasingly optimistic about the good prospects of an invasion, Parsons, with William Allen (1532–94), drew up plans for a conquered and re-Catholicized England. Parsons also published a defence of Spanish war aims. Despite the failure of the Armada of 1588, his hopes were re-ignited by Spanish invasion attempts in 1592 and 1596. He remained on Spanish soil through the years 1589–96, acting as spokesman for the English Catholic refugees and supplicating Philip's financial aid for English Catholic educational initiatives.

During Elizabeth's declining years, Parsons became increasingly preoccupied with the issue of the succession to her throne, and in what was probably his own work, *Conference about the Next Succession to the Crowne* (1593), he argued that religion as well as blood descent should be the criterion for succeeding, while in his 1596 work, *Memorial for the Reformation of England*, he set out his radical vision of a Catholic England of the future. At the same time, the increasing likelihood, if not inevitability, of the succession to the English throne of James VI of Scotland (1567–1625) saw Parsons busy with attempts to get the King to pre-engage himself to relief for English Catholics. In 1597 he was installed as rector of the English College, Rome, a position he held for the remainder of his life. He continued to be embroiled in the heated disputes within the English Catholic community about the nature of its own governance. He also remained involved in controversies with Protestants about such issues as the legitimacy of the English Reformation. The writings which resulted from this included his *Certamen ecclesiae Anglicanae* (1599).

The accession of James VI as James I of England, followed by the 1605 Gunpowder Conspiracy and its consequences, forced Parsons to confront in polemical writings the issue of Catholic loyalty, particularly the oath of allegiance of 1606. Though his own wish was to expand the *Christian Directory*, he was heavily involved in intra-Catholic controversy as well as adversarial work against Protestants. Shadowed by ill health from 1608, he died in the English College in April 1610 and was buried alongside Cardinal Allen. Widely regarded as a dangerous and, indeed, treasonable, political meddler, Parsons was, especially within the seventeenth century, a devotional writer of wide influence both within his own Church and beyond. His popular approach becomes evident in the present work in his use of scriptural sources rather than academic or patristic authorities, and in his ready recourse to English translations of any Latin texts cited.

The *Christian Directory* was enlarged for publication in 1585 and was also published in 1607, 1650, 1660, 1683 and 1696, and again, in 1753 (Dublin) and 1820 (New York). While it was a mainstay of Catholic devotional literature – it was translated into Welsh in 1591, followed by French, Italian and German versions, as amended by the Calvinist Edmund Bunny (1540–1618) and bearing the original title, *A Book of Christian Exercise*; it also became an admired manual of Christian piety beyond the confessional divide.[1]

1. See Brad S. Gregory, 'The "True and Jealouse service of God": Robert Parsons, Edmund Burry and *The First Booke of the Christian Exercise*', *Journal of Ecclesiastical History*, 45 (1994), pp. 235–68.

A
CHRISTIAN
Directory
GUIDING MEN
TO THEIR
Eternal Salvation.

Divided into Three B o o k s :
The firſt whereof appertaining to Reſolution, is
onely contained in this Volume, divided into
Two Parts, and ſet forth now again with
many Corrections and Additions.

There is added alſo,

A METHOD for the USE of all :
With two TABLES.

By the R. F. *ROBERT PARSONS*,
Prieſt of the Society of J E S U S.

Pſal. 4. v. 3.
Filii hominum ut quid diligitis vanitatem.
You children of men, why love you vanity.
Luke 10. v. 42.
Porro unum eſt neceſſarium. But one thing is neceſſary.

L O N D O N:
Printed by *Henry Hills*, Printer to the King's Moſt Excellent
Majeſty for His Houſhold and Chappel; and for him and
Matt. Turner at the *Lamb* in *High-Holbourn.* 1 6 8 7.

CHAP. IV.

*The Fourth and greateſt Impediment of all other,
that hindereth Reſolution; to wit, the love
and reſpect which men bear to the Pleaſures,
Commodities, and Vanities of this World.*

AS the former impediments which now by Gods
grace we have removed, be in very deed
great ſtays to many men, from the Reſolution we
talk of; ſo this that preſently we take in hand, is
not onely of it ſelf a ſtrong impediment and let,
but alſo a general cauſe and (as it were) a common
ground to all other impediments that be, or may
be. For if a man could touch the hidden pulſe of all
ſuch as refuſe, or neglect, or do defer to make this
Reſolution, he ſhould find the true cauſe and ori-
gen thereof, to be the love and reſpect which they
bear unto this world, whatſoever other excuſes they
pretend beſides. The Noble-men of *Jewry* pretended fear to be the cauſe, why they could not reſolve to confeſs *Chriſt* openly; but St. *John* that
felt their pulſes, and knew their diſeaſe, uttereth
the true cauſe to have been *for that they loved the
glory of men, more than the glory of God.* *Demas* that
forſook St. *Paul* in his bands, even a little before his
death, pretended another cauſe of his departure to
Theſſalonica; but St. *Paul* ſaith it was, *Quia diligebat
hoc ſæculum:* For that he loved this world. So that
this world is a general and univerſal impediment,
and more largely diſperſed in mens hearts, than
outwardly appeareth; for that it bringeth forth divers other excuſes, thereby to cover it ſelf in the people, where it abideth.   **2.** This

*The world,
the ground
of all other
impediments*

John 12.

1 Tim. 4.

Lib.1. Part 2. *Againſt the love of the World.* **587**

2. This may be confirmed by that moſt excel- Mat. 13. Mark 4. Luk. 8. lent *Parable* of our Saviour *Chriſt*, recorded by three Evangeliſts, concerning the three ſorts of men which are to be damned, and the three cauſes of their damnation; whereof the third and laſt, and moſt general (including as it were both the two former) is the love of this World.　For the firſt ſort of men there mentioned, are compared to a *High-way*, wherein all ſeed of life that is ſown, either wither- eth preſently, or elſe is eaten up by the birds of the air; which is (as *Chriſt* expoundeth it) by the Devils, in ſuch careleſs men, as contemn whatſoever is ſaid unto them; ſuch are Infidels, Hereticks, and other like obſtinate and contemptuous people. The ſecond ſort of reprobate people are compared to rocky grounds, in which, for lack of deep root, the feed that falleth continueth not: And by this are ſignified light and inconſtant perſons, that now are fervent, and by and by key-cold again; and ſo in time of temptation, they are gone, ſaith *Chriſt*. The third ſort are compared to a field, wherein the ſeed of life groweth up, but yet there are ſo many thorns about the ſame (which *Chriſt* our Saviour expoundeth to be the cares, troubles, miſeries, and deceivable vanities of this life) *as the good corn is choaked up, and ſo bringeth forth no fruit at all.*　By which laſt words he ſignifieth, that whereſoever his Doctrine is taught and groweth up, and yet bringeth not forth due fruit; that is to ſay, whereſoever his Faith is planted, received and profeſſed (as among Chriſtians it is) and yet bringeth not forth vertu- ous life, holy converſation, good works, and due ſervice of God, correſpondent to this ſeed: there the principal cauſe is, for that it is choa- ked with the love and care of this preſent world.

1.
The Expo- ſition of the Parable of the feed, and of four ſorts of people ſignified therein.

2.

3.

3. This

The impor-
portance of
this Parable,
and circum-
ſtance there-
of.
Mat. 13.

3. This is a Parable of marvellous great importance, as may appear ; both for that *Chriſt* after
the recital thereof, cryed with a loud voice, *He that
hath ears to hear, let him hear :* as alſo, for that he
expounded it himſelf in ſecret only to his Diſciples :
and principally, for that before the expoſition thereof, he uſed ſuch a ſolemn Preface, ſaying, *To you
it is given to know the myſteries of the kingdom of Heaven, but to others, not : for that they ſeeing, do not ſee ;
and hearing, do not hear, nor underſtand.* Whereby our
Saviour ſignifieth, that the underſtanding of this Parable above others, is of ſingular importance , for
conceiving the true myſteries of the Kingdom of
Heaven ; and that many are blind which ſeem to
ſee, and many deaf and ignorant, that ſeem to hear
and know ; for that they underſtand not well the
myſteries of this Parable. For which cauſe alſo his
Divine Wiſdom maketh this concluſion , before he
begins to expound the Parable : *Happy are your eyes
that ſee, and bleſſed are your ears that hear.* After which
words, he beginneth his expoſition with this admonition : *Vos ergo audite Parabolam.* Do you therefore
hear and underſtand this Parable , that are made
worthy thereof.

Six princi-
pal points of
this chapter.

4. And for that this Parable doth contain and
touch ſo much indeed, as may, or is needful to be
ſaid, for removing of this great and dangerous impediment of worldly love againſt the ſervice of
God : I mean to ſtay my ſelf onely upon the expli-
cation thereof in this place ; and will declare the
force and truth of certain words here uttered by
Chriſt, concerning the world and worldly vanities,
and how warily they are to be uſed by us. And for
ſome order and method, I will draw all to theſe ſix

I.

principal points or heads that do enſue. Firſt, how,
and in what ſence , all this whole world and commodities thereof are meer vanities in themſelves,
and

and of no value, as *Chriſt* here ſignifieth ; and conſequently ought not be an impediment to let us
from ſo great a matter, as the Kingdom of Heaven,
and ſerving of God, is. Secondly, how they are
not only vanities and trifles, but alſo *Deceptions*, as
the words of *Chriſt* are ; that is to ſay, deceits and
fallacies, not performing to us indeed thoſe little
trifles which they do promiſe, and we ſo highly
eſteem. Thirdly, how they are *ſpinæ* ; that is to
ſay, *pricking-thorns*, as our Saviour affirmeth ; albeit, they ſeem to worldly men to be moſt ſweet
and pleaſant for a time, and to be flowers rather
than thorns. Fourthly, how they are *Ærumnæ* ;
that is to ſay, miſeries and afflictions, according
to our Saviours meaning and ſpeech. Fifthly, *Quo-
modo ſuffocant*, how they do ſtrangle or choak
their poſſeſſours, in the ſence which our Saviour the
Son of God, in this Parable avoucheth. Sixthly,
how we may uſe them, notwithſtanding, without
theſe dangers and evils, to our great comfort, gain,
and preferment, if we will, and do take the right way
therein.

2.

3.

4.

5.

6.

SECT. 1.

How all the world is vanity.

5. ANd now for the Firſt: Albeit I might ſtand
upon many reaſons and demonſtrations ;
yet do I not ſee how briefly and pithily it may
be better declared, that all the pleaſures and goodly ſhews of this world are meer vanities, as *Chriſt*
here ſignifieth ; than to alledge the teſtimony
and proof of ſome, which have taſted and proved them all ; that is to ſay, of ſuch an one, as ſpeak-
eth not onely by ſpeculation, but alſo of his own
expe-

1.

590 *Christian Directory.* **Chap 4.**

2 Par. 9.
The worldly
profperity of
King *Solo-*
mon. experience and practice. And this is the wise and mighty King *Solomon*, of whom the Scripture reporteth wonderful matters, touching his peace, prosperity, riches, and glory in this world: As for example, *That all the Kings of the Earth desired to see his face, for his wisdom and renowned felicity: That all the Princes living besides, were not like him in wealth: That he had six hundred sixty and six talents of Gold (which is an infinite sum) brought him in yearly, besides all other that he had from the Kings of* Arabia, *and other Princes : That silver was as plentiful with him as heaps of stones, and not esteemed , for the great store and abundance he had thereof: That his Plate and Jewels had no end: That his Seat of Majesty , with stools, lions, to bear it up, and other furniture, were of Gold, passing all other kingly Seats in the world: That his precious Apparel and Armour was infinite: That he had all the Kings, from the River of the* Philiftims, *unto* Egypt, *as his servants : That he had forty thousand Horses in his Stables to ride, and twelve thousand Chariots, with horses and other furniture ready to them for his use. That he had two hundred Spears of Gold born before him, and six hundred Crowns of Gold bestowed upon every Spear ; as also three hundred Bucklers, and three hundred Crowns of Gold bestow'd in the gilding of every Buckler : That he* * 30. cori
fimilæ, &
60 cori fa-
rinæ, & eve-
ry corus is
21 quarters
and odd. *spent every day in his House, a thousand* * *nine hundred thirty and seven quarters of meal and flour ; thirty Oxen, with an hundred Wethers, beside all other flesh : That he had seven hundred Wives, as Queens, and three hundred other, as Concubines.* 3 Reg. 4.
3 Reg. 11. All this, and much more doth holy Scripture report of *Solomon*'s worldly Wealth, Wisdom, Riches, Prosperity ; which he having tasted, and used to his fill, pronounced yet at last this Ecclef. 1. sentence of it all: *Vanitas vanitatum, & omnia vanitas :* Vanity of vanities, and all is vanity. By *vanity of vanities,* meaning (as St. *Hierom* interpre- In cap. 1.
Ecclef. teth) the greatness of this vanity, above all other vanities that may be devised. **6. Nei-**

6. Neither onely doth King *Solomon* affirm this thing in word, but doth prove it alſo by examples of himſelf: *I have been King of* Iſrael *in* Jeruſalem, (ſaith he) *and I purpoſed with my ſelf, to ſeek out by wiſ-dom all things ; and I have ſeen that all under the Sun are meer vanities and affliction of ſpirit. I ſaid in my heart, I will go and abound in all delights, and in every pleaſure that may be had ; and I ſaw that this was alſo vanity. I took great works in hand, builded houſes to my ſelf, planted Vineyards, made Gardens, and beſet them with all kind of trees ; I made my fiſh-ponds to water my trees. I poſſeſſed Servants and Hand-maids, and had a great Family, great herds of Cattel, above any that ever were before me in* Jeruſalem. *I gathered together Gold and Silver, the Riches of Kings and Provinces. I appoin-ted to my ſelf Muſicians and Singers, both men and wo-men, which are the delights of the children of men : Fine Cups alſo to drink wine, and whatſoever my eyes did de-ſire, I denied it not unto them ; neither did I let my heart from uſing any pleaſure, to delight it ſelf in theſe things which I had prepared. And when I turned my ſelf to all that my hands had made, and to all the labours wherein I had taken ſuch pains and ſweat ; I ſaw them* all vanity and affliction of mind.

Solomon's ſaying of himſelf, Ecclef.

Cap. 2. Ibid.

7. This is the teſtimony of *Solomon*, upon his own proof, in theſe affairs : And if he had ſpoken it upon his wiſdom onely (being ſuch as it was) we ought to believe him ; but much more, ſeeing he affirmeth it of his own experience. But yet, if any man be not moved with this, let us bring yet another witneſs out of the New Teſtament, and ſuch a one as was privy to the opinion of our Saviour *Chriſt* herein ; and this is, the holy Evangeliſt and Apo-ſtle St. *John,* who maketh an earneſt exhortation to all wiſe men, never to entangle themſelves with the love of worldly affairs, uſing this reaſon for the ſame : *Mundus tranſit, & concupiſcentia ejus :* The world

The teſtimo-ny of S. John 2.

1 John 2.

world is tranſitory, and all that is to be deſired
therein; that is to ſay, it is vain, fleeting, uncertain, and not permanent.   And then coming to
ſhew the ſubſtance of this tranſitory vanity, he re-
duceth them all to three general heads or branches,

The gene-
ral branches
of worldly
vanities.
ſaying, *Whatſoever is in this world, is either concupiſcence of the fleſh, or concupiſcence of the eyes, or pride of
life.*   By the firſt he compehendeth all ſenſualplea-
ſures uſed in the cheriſhing and pampering the fleſh:
by the ſecond, all beauty and bravery of riches: by
the third, he ſignifieth the vanity of ambition in
worldly honour and eſtimation.

Three prin-
cipal vani-
ties.
8. Theſe then are three general and moſt principal vanities of this life, wherein worldly men do
weary out their brains; to wit, *Ambition, Covetouſneſs,* and *carnal Pleaſure.*   Whereunto all other leſ-
ſer vanities are addreſſed, as to their Superiours.
And therefore it ſhall not be amiſs to conſider of
theſe three in this place, together with their dependents; for that every one of theſe three have divers
branches depending of them; eſpecially the firſt,
which here I will handle, called by St. *John, Ambition and pride of life,* whereunto belong theſe ſix members that enſue.

2.
Vain-glory.
9. Firſt, Vain-glory, which is a certain diſordinate deſire to be well thought of, well ſpoken of,
praiſed and glorified of men.   And this is as great a
vanity (though it be common to many) as if a man
ſhould run up and down the ſtreets after a feather
flying in the Air, toſſed hither and thither with the
blaſts of infinite mens mouths. For as this man might
weary out himſelf before he got the thing which he
followed, and yet when he had it, he had gotten
but a feather; ſo a vain-glorious man may labour a
good while, before he obtain to the praiſe which he
deſireth.   And when he hath it, it is not worth three
chips, being but the breath of a few mens mouths,
                                                    that

Lib. 1. Part 2. *Againſt the love of the World.* 593

that doth alter upon ever light occaſion , and now maketh him great, now little, now good, now bad, now nothing at all. *Chriſt* himſelf may be an example of this, who was toſſed to and fro in the ſpeech of men. Some ſaid he was a *Samaritan,* and had a Devil ; others ſaid, he could not be a Prophet, or of God, for that he kept not the Sabbath-day : others asked, if he were not of God, how he could do ſo many Miracles ? ſo that there was a ſchiſm or diviſion among them about this matter, as St. *John* affirmeth. Finally, upon *Palm*-Sunday they received him into *Jeruſalem* with triumph of *Hoſanna,* caſting their apparel under his feet : but the Thurſday and Friday next enſuing, they cry'd *Crucifige* againſt him; and preferred the life of *Barrabas,* a wicked Murderer, before his.

Mar. 27.
John 8.

John 9.
Mat. 21.
Mar. 11.
Mark 27.
Luke 23.

10. Now my Friend, if they dealt thus with the Saviour of the world, which was a better man than ever thou wilt be ; and did more glorious Miracles than ever thou wilt do , that in reaſon might have purchaſed him Name and Honour among the people : why doſt thou ſo labour and beat thy ſelf about this vanity of vain-glory? Why doſt thou caſt thy travels into the wind of mens mouths? Why doſt thou put thy riches in the lips of mutable men, where every flatterer may rob thee of them ? Haſt thou no better a cheſt to lock them up in ? St. *Paul* was of another mind, when he ſaid , *I eſteem little to be judged of you, or of the day of man.* And he had reaſon : for what careth he that runneth at the Tilt, if the ignorant people that ſtand by, do give ſentence againſt him , ſo the Judges give it with him ? If the blind man in the way to *Jericho,* had depended of the liking and approbation of the goers by , he had never received the benefits of his ſight ; for that they diſſwaded him from running and crying ſo vehemently after

The miſery of depending on other mens mouths

1 Cor. 4.

Luke 12.

Q q *Chriſt.*

Chriſt. It is a miſerable thing for a man to be a Wind-mill, which grindeth not, nor maketh Meal, but according as the blaſt endureth. If the gale be ſtrong, he ſcourgeth about luſtily ; but if the wind be ſlack, he relenteth preſently : ſo if you praiſe the vain-glorious man, he will run ; but if he feel not the gale blow, he is out of heart.

Dan. 31. He is like the Babylonians, who with a little ſweet muſick, were made to adore any thing whatſoever.

Prov. 27.   12. The Scripture ſaith moſt truly, *As ſilver is tried in the fire by blowing it, ſo is a man tried in the*

A fit ſimili-   *mouth of him that praiſeth.* For as ſilver, if it be
tude.   good, taketh no hurt thereby ; but if it be evil, it goeth all into fume : ſo doth a vain man, by praiſe and commendation. How many have we ſeen puffed up with mens praiſes, and almoſt put beſides themſelves for joy thereof ; and yet afterward brought down with a contrary wind and driven full

Pſal. 9.   near to deſperation by contempt ? How many do we ſee daily (as the Prophet did in his days) commended in their ſins, and bleſſed in their wickedneſs ? How many palpable and intolerable flatterries do we hear, both uſed and accepted dai-

Pſal. 140.   ly, and no man crieth with good King *David, A-*
Pſal. 39.   *way with this oil and ointment of ſinners, let it not come upon my head?* Is not all this vanity? Is it not madneſs, as the Scripture calleth it? The glorious Angels in Heaven ſeek no honour unto themſelves, but all unto God ; and thou, poor Worm of the Earth, deſireſt to be glorified? The four and twenty El-

Apoc. 4.   ders in the Apocalyps, took off their Crowns and caſt them at the feet of the Lamb ; and thou wouldſt pluck forty from the Lamb to thy ſelf, if thou couldeſt. O fond creature ! how truly ſaith

Pſal. 84.   the Prophet, *Homo vanitati ſimilis factus eſt :* A man is made like unto vanity, that is, like unto his own vanity,

vanity, as light as the very vanities themselves; which he followeth.   And yet the Wise man more *Eccl. 2?,* expresly, *In vanitate sua appenditur:* The sinner is weighed in his vanity; that is, by the vanity which he followeth, is seen how light and vain a sinful man is.   And is there any man who will leave to resolve to serve God, and seek his own salvation, for fear what the World will say or think of him?   What importeth it thee (dear Brother) in the next life, what they all say of thee here?   Think then upon this, and esteem it as a vanity indeed

12. The second vanity that belongeth to Ambi- **2.** tion, is desire of worldly honour, dignity, and pro- W?r ?ly motion.   And this is a great matter in the sight of honour and promotion. a worldly man; this is a Jewel of rare price, and worthy to be bought with any labour, travel, or peril whatsoever.   The love of this letted the great *John 11.* men that were Christians in *Jewry,* from confes- *John 19.* sing *Christ* openly.   The love of this, letted *Pilate* from delivering *JESUS,* according as in consci- ence he saw he was bound.   The love of this, letted *Agrippa* and *Festus* from making themselves *Acts 26.* Christians, albeit they esteemed St. *Pauls* Do- ctrine to be true.   The love of this, letteth infinite men daily from embracing the means of their sal- vation.   But (alas) these men do not see the va- nity hereof.   St. *Paul* saith, not without just cause, *1 Cor. 14.* *Nolite esse pueri sensibus:* Be you not children in un- derstanding.   It is the fashion of children to esteem more of a painted Table, than of a rich Jewel. And such is the painted Dignity of this World, gotten with much labour, maintained with great care and sollicitude, and lost with intolerable grief and sorrow.   For better conceiving whereof, pon- der a little with thy self (gentle Reader) any state of dignity that thou wouldst desire, and think how many have had that, or the like before thee.   Re-

Qq 2   member

member how many have mounted up, and how they
have deſcended down again: and imagine with
thy ſelf which was greater, either the joy in getting,
or the ſorrow in loſing it.   Where are now all thoſe
Emperours, thoſe Kings, thoſe Princes and Pre-
lates, which rejoyced ſo much once at their own
advancement? Where are they now, I ſay? who
talketh or thinketh of them? Are they not forgotten, and caſt into their Graves long ago? and do
not men boldly walk over their heads now, whoſe
faces might not be looked on, without fear in their
life? What then have their Dignities done them
good?

The vanity
of worldly
Honour.

13. It is a wonderful thing to conſider the vanity
of this worldly Honour.   It is like a mans own ſhadow, which the more a man runneth after, the more
it flyeth; and when he flyeth from it, it followeth him again; and the onely way to catch it, is
to fall down to the ground upon it.   So we ſee that
thoſe men which deſired Honour in this world,
are now forgotten; and thoſe which moſt fled from
it, and caſt themſelves loweſt of all men, by humility, are now moſt of all honoured: honoured (I ſay)
moſt, even by the world it ſelf, whoſe enemies
they were whilſt they lived.   For who is honoured
more now, who is more commended and remembred than St. *Paul*, and his like; which ſo much de-

Phil. 3.

ſpiſed worldly honour in this life, as he made leſs
account thereof than of common dung? Moſt vain
then is the purſuit of worldly Honour, which neither contenteth the mind, nor eaſeth the pained
body, nor continueth with the poſſeſſor, nor lea-
veth behind it any benefit or contentation, and
conſequently ought not to prevail with any man,
againſt this great Reſolution, of which here we
treat.

14. The

14. The third vanity that belongeth to ambition or pride of life, is Nobility of fleſh and bloud ; a great pearl in the eye of the world, and indeed to be eſteemed, when it is joyned with Vertue, and accompanied with the fear of God ; but otherwiſe both in it ſelf, and in the ſight of Almighty God, a meer trifle and vanity. Which holy *Job* well underſtood (albeit he were of Noble parentage) when he wrote theſe words: *I ſaid unto rottenneſs, thou art my father ; and unto worms, you are my mother and ſiſters.* He that will behold the Gentry of his Anceſtors, let him look into their Graves, and ſee whether *Job* ſaith truly or no. True Nobility was never begun but by Vertue ; and therefore, as it is a teſtimony of Valour and Vertue in the Predeceſſors ; ſo ought it to be a ſpur to the ſame in the Succeſſors. And he which holdeth the Name thereof by deſcent onely, without ſubſtance of Vertue, is a meer Alien, in reſpect of his Anceſtors ; from whom he degenerateth, and hath nothing of theirs, but the bare outward ſhew onely. Of which ſort of men, God ſaith by one Prophet, *They are made abominable, even as the things which they love,* &c. *Gloria eorum à partu, ab utero, & à conceptu :* Their glory is from their birth, from the belly, and from their conception only. That is to ſay, they vaunt and glory of their Anceſtors, Progenitors, and noble Birth, whereas having no Vertue in them correſpondent to their birth, but following their ſenſual appetites, and ſetting their affections on wicked and abominable delights ; they are made in like manner abominable, and contemptible both to God and man. And in this ſence it is a fond vanity to beg credit of dead men, whereas we deſerve none our ſelves ; to ſeek up old titles of honour from our Anceſtors, we being utterly incapable thereof, by our own baſe manners and behaviour. *Chriſt* clearly confounded this

3. The vanity of worldly Nobility.

Job 17.

Oſee 9.

Qq 3   vanity,

Mat. 8. 20.
34. 26.

vanity, when being deſcended himſelf of the greateſt Nobility and race of Kings that ever was in
the World; and beſides that, being alſo the Son of
God (a much higher title) yet called he himſelf

John 10.

ordinarily by the name of *The Son of man*; that is
to ſay, the Son of the poor Virgin *Mary*, (for o-
therwiſe he was no Son of man:) And further
than this alſo, he called himſelf a Shepherd, which

1 R'g. 9.
1 Reg. 16.

in the World is a name of contempt. And when
long before his Incarnation he was to make a King
firſt in Iſrael, he did not ſeek out the ancienteſt
bloud, but took *Saul*, of the baſeſt Tribe of Jews,
(to wit, of *Benjamin*) and after him *David*, the
pooreſt Shepherd of all his Brethren. And when
he came into the World, he ſought not out the no-

Mat. 4.
Pſal. 49.
1 Cor. 1.

bleſt men to make Princes of the Earth, that is, to
make Apoſtles; but took of the pooreſt and ſimpleſt,
thereby to confound (as one of them ſaith) the
fooliſh vanity of this World, in making ſo great account of the pre-eminence of a little fleſh and bloud
in this life, where merit of vertue is not found;
though yet on the other ſide, where worldly Nobility and Gentry is furniſhed with ſpirit and vertue, it is (no doubt) an excellent Ornament, and
may do ſingular much good in Gods ſervice, and
is highly reſpected by him, as by many examples
may be proved : but in no wiſe is it a ſufficient motive to let any man from the reſolution of Gods ſervice, for that he is noble ; for that in this reſpect it
is a meer trifle indeed.

4.
The vanity
of worldly
wiſdom.
1 Cor. 1.
3 Reg. 9.

15. The fourth vanity that belongeth to ambition or pride of life, is worldly wiſdom ; whereof
the Apoſtle ſaith, *The wiſdom of this world is folly
with God*. If it be folly, then it is great vanity (no
doubt) to delight and boaſt ſo much in it, as men
do, eſpecially againſt the wiſdom of God and his
Saints. It is a ſtrange and wonderful thing to behold

hold, how contrary the Judgments of God are to the Judgments of worldly men. Who would not think, but that the wiſe men of this World were the fitteſt to be choſen to do *Chriſt* ſervice in his Church? Yet St. *Paul* ſaith, *Non multi ſapientes, ſe-* *cundum carnem:* God hath not choſen many wiſe men, according to the fleſh. Who would not think but that a worldly wiſe man might eaſily alſo make a wiſe Chriſtian? yet St. *Paul* ſaith no; except firſt he become a fool: *Stultus fiat, ut ſit ſapi-* *ens:* If any man ſeem wiſe amongſt you, let him become a fool to the end he may be made wiſe. Vain then, and of no account is the wiſdom of this World, except it be ſubject to the wiſdom of God. And whoſoever in this worldly wiſdom, and for worldly reſpects never ſo important in his own ſight, and according to the World, ſhall condemn them that condemn the World, and do reſolve them-ſelves to Gods ſervice; his wiſdom is folly in this behalf, and his prudence meer vanity: and ſo will he confeſs it one day, when he ſhall come to cry with thoſe of his condition in the next life, *Nos in-* *ſenſati vitam illorum æſtimabamus inſaniam:* We ſenſeleſs and fooliſh worldly wiſe men did think the life of Saints to be meer madneſs; but now we come to ſee that they were wiſe indeed, and we onely fools. And this is to be underſtood, when humane worldly wiſdom contradicteth ſpiritual wiſdom, and not otherwiſe.

1 Cor. 3.

1 Cor. 3.

Sap. 9.

16. The fifth vanity belonging to pride of life, is corporal beauty; whereof the Wiſe man ſaith, *Vain is beauty, and deceivable is the grace of a fair countenance.* Whereof alſo King *David* underſtood properly, when he ſaid, *Turn away my eyes (O Lord) that they behold not vanity.* This is a ſingular great vanity, dangerous and deceitful. Beauty is com-pared by holy men, to a painted Snake, which is

5.
The vanity of beauty.
Prov. 31.
Pſal. 118.
Pſal. 4.

Qq 4   fair

fair without, and full of deadly poiſon within. If a man did conſider what infinite ruines and deſtructions have come by over-light liking thereof, he would beware of it. And if he remembred what foul droſs lieth under a fair skin, he would little be in love therewith, ſaith one holy Father. God hath imparted certain ſparkles of beauty unto his Creatures on Earth, thereby to draw us to conſideration and love of his own beauty, whereof the other is but a ſhadow; even as a man finding a little iſſue of water, may ſeek out the fountain thereby; or happening upon a ſmall vain of gold, may thereby come to the head-Mine it ſelf. But we, like babes, delight our ſelves onely with the fair cover of the Book, and never do conſider what is written therein. In all fair creatures that man doth behold, he ought to read this leſſon, ſaith one Father, that if God could make a piece of Earth ſo fair and lovely, by imparting unto it ſome little ſpark of his beauty; how infinite fair is he himſelf, and how worthy of love and admiration! And how happy ſhall we be, when we ſhall come to enjoy his beautiful preſence, whereof now all creatures do take their beauty!

A leſſon to be read in the beauty of all creatures.

17. If we would exerciſe our ſelves in this manner of cogitations, we might eaſily keep our hearts pure, chaſte, and unſpotted before God, in beholding the beauty of his Creatures upon Earth. But for that we uſe not this paſſage from the Creature to the Creator, but do reſt onely in the external appearance of a deceitful face, letting go the bridle to our foul cogitations, and ſetting wilfully on fire our own concupiſcences; hence it is, that infinite people do periſh daily, by occaſion of this fond vanity of an alluring viſage. I call it fond, for that ever child may deſcry the deceit and vanity thereof. For, take the faireſt face in the world.

Lib. 1. Part 2. *Againſt the love of the World.* **601**

world, wherewith infinite fooliſh men fell in love upon the ſight thereof, and raſe it over but with a little ſcratch, and all the matter of love is gone : let there come but an Ague for ſome four or five days, and all this goodly beauty is deſtroyed : let the Soul depart but one half hour from the Body, and this loving face is ugly to look on : let it lie but two days in the grave, or above-ground dead, and thoſe who were ſo earneſtly in love with it before, will ſcarce abide to behold, or come near it. And if none of theſe things happen unto it, yet quickly cometh on old age, which riveleth the ſkin, draw-eth in the eyes, ſetteth out the teeth, and ſo disfigu-reth the whole viſage, as it becometh more con-temptible and horrible now, than ever it was beau-tiful and alluring before. And what then can be more vanity than this? what more madneſs than either to take a pride thereof, if we have it our ſelves, or to endanger our Souls for the ſame, if we behold it in others? How miſerable are thoſe peo-ple, who beſtow ſo much labour in procuring or pre-ſerving this corporal beauty, as though all their hap-pineſs conſiſted therein ; yea, many do make it the chief obſtacle of their reſolution to ſerve God, and the principal occaſion of their downfal and damna-tion.

18. The ſixth vanity belonging to pride of life, **6.** is the glory of fine Apparel, againſt which the Scri- pture ſaith, *In veſtitu ne glorieris unquam* : See thou never take glory in apparel. Of all vanities, this is the greateſt, which yet we ſee ſo common among men and women of this world, as nothing more ; but conſider the vanity. If *Adam* had never fal- len, we had never uſed apparel ; for that apparel was deviſed to cover our ſhame of nakedneſs, and other infirmities contracted by that Fall. Wherefore, we that take pride and glory in apparel,

do

do as much as if a beggar fhould glory and take pride of the old Clouts that do cover his fores: St.*Paul* faid unto a Bifhop, *If we have wherewithal to*
1 Tim. 6. *cover our felves, let us be content.* And *Chrift* touched deeply the danger of nice Apparel, when he
Mat. 3. 11. commended fo much St. *John Baptift* for his coarfe
Luke 7. and auftere Attire, adding for the contradictory, *Qui mollibus veftiuntur in domibus Regum funt :* They which are not like *John*, but go clothed in foft and delicate Apparel, are in Kings Courts; *i. e.* in Kings Courts of this World, but not in the Kings Court of Heaven. For which caufe in the defcription of the rich man damned, this is not omitted by our
Luke 16. Saviour, *That he was apparelled in purple and filk ;* as though this alfo had been fome help to him towards his damnation: as on the contrary, the Scripture fetting down the fingular fanctity of *Elias* the
4 Reg. 1. Prophet, nameth alfo his poor Apparel, *That his reins were covered with hair-cloth,* &c. It is a wonderful thing to confider the different proceeding of God, and of the World in this affair, God himfelf
Gen. 3. was the firft Taylor that ever made Apparel in this World, and he made it for the moft noble of all our Anceftors in Paradife; and yet he made it but
Heb. 12. of Beafts-skins. And St. *Paul* teftifieth of the nobleft Saints of the old Teftament, that they were covered onely with Goats-skins, and with the hairs of Camels. What vanity is it then for us to be fo curious in Apparel, and to take fuch pride therein as we do ? We rob and fpoil all fort of creatures upon earth, to cover our backs, and adorn our bo-
The ex- dies. From one, we take his wool; from ano-
treme vani- ther, his skin ; from another his hair and furr: and
ty and po- from fome other, their very excrements, as the
verty of filk, which is nothing elfe but the excrements of
man. Worms. Nor yet content with this, we come to Fifhes, and do beg of them certain Pearls to hang about

about us. We go down into the ground for Gold and Silver; and turn up the ſands of the Sea for Precious Stones: and having borrowed all this of other creatures far more baſe than our ſelves, we jet up and down, provoking men to look upon us, as if all this now were our own. When the ſtone ſhineth upon our finger, we will ſeem (forſooth) thereby to ſhine. When Silver, Gold, and Silks do gliſter on our backs, we look big, as if all that beauty came from us. When Cats-dung doth ſmell in our Garments, we would have men think, that we Pſal. 77. ſend forth ſweet odours from our ſelves. And thus (as the Prophet ſaith) we paſs over our days in vanity, and do not perceive our own extreme folly. And yet is this folly ſo ſtrong and potent with many, as not to want this vanity of gay Apparel is a ſufficient motive to ſtay them from the reſolution we propoſe of Gods ſervice, and their own everlaſting good.

19. And thus much now may ſuffice, for decla- The ſecond head of worldly vanities. ration of the firſt general head of worldly vanities, termed by St. *John, Pride of life.* There followeth the ſecond, which he calleth *Concupiſcence of the eyes;* Concupiſcence of the eyes. whereunto the ancient Fathers have referred all vanities of riches, and wealth of this World. Of this St. *Paul* writeth to *Timothy : Give commandment* 1 Tim. 6. *to rich men of this world, not to be high minded, nor to put confidence in the uncertainty of their riches.* The reaſon of which ſpeech is uttered by the Scripture in another place, when it ſaith, *Riches ſhall not pro-* Prov. 11. *fit a man in the day of revenge;* that is, at the day of death and judgment. Which thing the rich men of this World do confeſs themſelves, though too late, now being in torments: *Divitiarum jactantia* Sap. 5. *quid nobis contulit ?* What hath the bravery of our riches profited us? All which doth evidently declare the great vanity of worldly riches which can

do

604   *Chriſtian Directory.*   **Chap.** 4.

do the poſſeſſor no good at all, when he hath moſt
Pſal. 75.   need of their help.   *Rich men have ſlept their ſleep,*
(ſaith the Prophet) *and have found nothing in their*
hands : that is, rich men have paſſed over this life,
as men paſs over a ſleep, imagining themſelves to
have golden Mountains and Treaſures wherewith
to help themſelves in all needs that ſhall occur ;
and when they awake (at the day of their death)
they find themſelves to have nothing in their
hands that can do them good. In reſpect whereof, the Prophet *Baruch* asketh this queſtion : *Where*
Bar. 3.   *are they now, which heaped together gold and ſilver,*
and which made no end of their ſcraping together ?
And he anſwereth himſelf immediately, *Extermi-*
nati ſunt, & ad inferos deſcenderunt : They are now
rooted out, and are gone down unto Hell. To
Jam. 5.   like effect ſaith Saint *James : Now ye rich men, do*
ye weep, and wail, and houl in your miſeries that come
upon you ; your riches are rotten, and your gold and ſil-
ver is ruſty ; and the ruſt thereof ſhall be in teſtimony a-
gainſt you : it ſhall feed upon your own fleſh, as if it were
fire ; you have hoarded up wrath to your own ſelves in
the laſt day.

A compari-   20. All this, and much more, is ſpoken by the
ſon,   Holy Ghoſt, to ſignifie the dangerous vanity of
worldly wealth, and the folly of thoſe men who
labour ſo much to procure the ſame unjuſtly, or having them, do uſe the ſame to vanity, and not to
the profit of their own Souls. And ſurely, if ſo
many skilful Phyſicians, as I have here alledged holy Scriptures, ſhould agree together, that ſuch or
ſuch meats were unwholſome and perilous : I think
few men would give the adventure to eat thereof,
though otherwiſe in ſight, ſmell, and taſte, they
appeared ſweet and pleaſant. How then cometh
it to paſs, that ſo many earneſt admonitions of
God himſelf, ſtay us not from the diſordinate love of
the this

Lib.1.Part 2. *Againſt the love of the World.* 605

this dangerous vanity ? *Nolite cor apponere,* ſaid God Pſal. 61.
by the Prophet: that is, Set not your hearts upon
the love of riches. *Qui diliget aurum, non juſtifica-* Eccl. 31.
bitur, ſaith the Wiſe man : He that loveth gold, ſhall
never be juſtified. *I am angry greatly upon rich na-* Zach. 1.
tions, ſaith God by *Zachary. Chriſt* ſaith, *Amen di-* Mat. 19.
co vobis, quia dives difficile intrabit in regnum cœlorum :
Truly, I ſay unto you, that a rich man ſhall hardly
get into the Kingdom of Heaven. And again, *Wo*
be to you rich men, for that you have received your con-
ſolation in this life. Finally, St. *Paul* ſaith generally Luke 6.
of all and to all, *They which will be rich, do fall into* 1 Tim. 6.
temptations, and into the ſnares of Sathan, and into ma-
ny unprofitable and hurtful deſires, which do drown them
in everlaſting deſtruction and perdition.

21. Can any thing be ſpoken more effectually, The pre-tence of Wife and Children, r.futed.
to diſſwade from the love of riches ? Muſt not here
now all covetous men of the World condemn themſelves in their own Conſciences? Let them excuſe
themſelves as much as they will, by the pretence of
Wife, and Children, and Kinsfolk, as they are wont,
ſaying, they mean nothing elſe but to provide for
their ſufficiency. But doth *Chriſt* our Saviour admit this excuſe? He asked the rich man that had
filled his Barns, who ſhould have thoſe riches ? for
ſo much, as that very night they were to take his
Soul from him: And he might have anſwered, his
Wife, Children, and Kindred ; but he durſt not,
for that the interrogation began with *Stulte,* Thou
fool : and indeed, it is great folly, if we conſider
it well: For tell me (dear Chriſtian Brother) what
comfort may it be to an afflicted Father in Hell, to
remember that by his means his Wife and Children
do live wealthily in Earth, and that by his eternal
wo, they enjoy ſome few years pleaſures ? No, no,
this is vanity, and a meer deceipt of our ſpiritual
enemy. For within one moment after we are
dead

dead, we ſhall care no more for Wife, Children, Father, Mother, or Brother, in this matter, than we ſhall for a meer ſtranger ; and one penny given in alms whiles we lived, for Gods ſake, ſhall comfort us more at that day, than thouſands of pounds beſtowed upon our Kindred for the natural love we bear unto our own fleſh and bloud. The which one point would *Chriſt* all worldly men could conſider, and then (no doubt) they would never take ſuch care for Kindred as they do, and be ſo ſparing in doing good to themſelves, eſpecially upon their Deathbeds, whence preſently they are to depart to that place where fleſh and bloud holdeth no more priviledge, nor riches have any power to deliver ; but onely ſuch as were well beſtowed in the ſervice of God, or given to the Poor for his Names ſake. In which reſpect onely a rich man is happy, if he know how to uſe his happineſs whilſt he hath time, which few do. And this ſhall be ſufficient for this point of riches.

The third head, of worldly vanities. 22. The third branch of worldly vanities is called by St. *John, Concupiſcence of the fleſh* ; which containeth all pleaſures and carnal recreations of this life ; as, are banquetting, laughing, playing, and ſuch other delights, wherewith our fleſh is much comforted in this World. And albeit in this kind there is a certain meaſure to be allowed unto the godly for the convenient maintenance of their health, (as alſo in riches it is not to be reprehended) yet that all theſe worldly ſolaces are not onely vain, but alſo dangerous in that exceſs and abundance, as worldly wealthy men ſeek and uſe them , appeareth plainly by theſe words of Luke 6. *Chriſt : Wo be unto you who do now laugh, for you ſhall weep. Wo be unto you that now live in fill and ſatiety, for the time ſhall come when you ſhall ſuffer hunger.* And again, in St. *John's* Goſpel, ſpeaking to his Apoſtles

poſtles, and by them to all other, he ſaith, *You ſhall* John 16. *weep and mourn, but the world ſhall rejoyce :* Making it a ſign diſtinctive between the good and the bad, that the one ſhall mourn this life, and the other re-joyce and make themſelves merry.

23. The very ſame doth *Job* confirm both of Job 21. the one and the other ſort : for of Worldlings he ſaith, *That they ſolace themſelves with all kind of mu-ſick, and do paß over their days in pleaſure, and in a very moment do go down into hell.* But of the godly, he ſaith in his own perſon, *That they ſigh before they* Job 5. *eat their bread.* And in another place, *That they* Job 9. *fear all their works, knowing that God ſpareth not him which offendeth.* The reaſon whereof the Wiſe man yet further expreſſeth, ſaying, *That the works* Eccl. 9. *of good men are in the hands of God, and no man know-eth whether he be worthy of love or hatred at Gods hands : but all is kept uncertain for the time to come.* And old *Tobias* inſinuateth yet another cauſe, when he ſaith, *What joy can I have or receive,* Tob. 5. *ſeeing I ſit here in darkneß ?* ſpeaking literally of his corporal blindneſs ; but yet leaving it alſo to be underſtood of ſpiritual and internal dark-neſs.

24. Theſe are then the cauſes (beſides exter- Why good men are ſad nal affliction which God often ſendeth) why the in this life. godly do live more grave, ſad, and fearful in this 1 Cor. 2. life, than wicked men do, according to the counſel 2 Cor. 7. of St. *Paul* ; and why alſo they ſigh often and weep, Job 2. as *Job* and *Chriſt* do affirm ; to wit, for that they remember oftentimes the ſevere Juſtice of Almigh-ty God ; their own frailty in ſinning ; the ſecret Judgment of his predeſtination uncertain to us ; the vale of miſery and deſolation wherein they live here ; which made even the very Apoſtles them-ſelves to groan, as St. *Paul* affirmeth, albeit they Rom. 8. had much leſs cauſe than we have. In reſpect Epheſ. 4. Mat. 24. whereof

2 Cor. 5.
& 7.

Eccl. 7.

Prov. 28.

Mich. 6.

John 10.

Luke 19.

whereof we are willed to paſs over this life in care-fulneſs, watchfulneſs, fear, and trembling. In re-gard whereof alſo, the Wiſe man ſaith, *It is better to go to the houſe of ſorrow, than to the houſe of feaſt-ing.* And again, *Where ſadneſs is, there is the heart of wiſe men: but where mirth is, there is the heart of fools.* Finally, in conſideration of theſe things, the Scripture ſaith, *Beatus homo qui ſemper eſt pavidus:* Happy is the man which always is fearful. Which is nothing elſe, but that which the Holy Ghoſt com-mandeth every man by *Micheas* the Prophet: *So-licitum ambulare cum Deo:* To walk carefully and diligently with God, thinking upon his Command-ments; how we keep and obſerve the ſame; how we reſiſt and mortifie our Members upon Earth; how we beſtow our time, talents, and riches lent unto us; how we labour in good works for the gaining of Heaven, what account we could yield, if preſently we were to die, *&c.* Which cogita-tions, if they might have place with us, would cut off a great many of thoſe worldly paſtimes, where-with the careleſs ſort of ſinners are overwhelmed; I mean, of thoſe good-fellowſhips in eating, drink-ing, laughing, ſinging, diſputing, and other ſuch vanities that diſtract us moſt. Hereof *Chriſt* gave us a moſt notable advertiſement, in that he wept oftentimes: as for example, at his nativity, at the reſuſcitation of *Lazarus,* upon *Jeruſalem,* and upon the Croſs. But he is never read to have laughed in all his life. Hereof alſo is each mans own nativi-ty and death a ſignification and figure: which two extremities (I mean, our beginning and ending) being reſerved by God in his own hands to diſ-poſe; are appointed unto us in ſorrow, grief, and weeping, as we ſee and feel. But the middle-part thereof (which is our life) being left by God in our own hands, we paſs it over with vain delights,

Lib. 1. Part 2. *Againſt the love of the World.*   609

delights, never thinking whence we came, nor whither we go.

25. A wiſe Traveller paſſing by his Inne, albeit he ſee pleaſant meats ſet before him to banquet at his pleaſure; yet he forbeareth and reſtraineth his appetite upon conſideration of the price, and of the journey he hath to make; and taketh nothing but ſo much as he knoweth well how to diſcharge the next morning at his departure. But a fool layeth hands on every delicate bit that is preſented to his ſight, and playeth the Prince for a night or two; but the next morning, when it cometh to the reckoning, he wiſheth that he had lived onely with bread and drink, rather than to be ſo troubled as he is for the payment. The cuſtom of Gods Church is to faſt the Even of every Feaſt, and then to make merry the next day following, which is the Feſtival it ſelf. And this repreſenteth the abſtinent life of good men in this World, thereby to be merry in the World to come. But the faſhion of the World is contrary; that is, to eat and drink merrily firſt at the Tavern, and after to let the Hoaſt bring in his Reckoning. They eat, drink, and laugh, and the Hoaſt he ſcoreth up all in the mean ſpace: and when the time cometh that they muſt pay, many a heart is ſad, that was pleaſant before.

26. This very ſelf-ſame thing holy Scripture affirmeth alſo of the pleaſures of this World: *Riſus dolore miſcebitur & extrema gaudii luctus occupat:* Laughter ſhall be mingled with ſorrow, and mourning ſhall enſue at the hinder end of mirth. The Devil, that playeth the Hoaſt in this World, and will ſerve you at an inch with what delight or pleaſure you deſire, writeth up all in his Book; and at the day of your departure (which is, at your death) he will bring in the whole Reckoning, and charge

*A ſimili-
tude.*

Prov. 14.

R r   you

you with it all, and then ſhall follow that which God promiſeth to Worldlings, by the Prophet *Amos* :

Amos 1.
Tob. 2.

Your mirth ſhall be turned into mourning and lamentation. Yea, and more than this, if you be not able to diſcharge the reckoning, you may chance to hear that other dreadful ſentence of *Chriſt* in the Apoca-

Apoc. 18.

lyps : *Quantum in deliciis fuit, tantum date illi tormentum :* Look how much he hath taken of his delights, ſo much torment do you lay upon him.

The concluſion of the firſt point.

27. Wherefore to conclude this Point, and therewithal this firſt Part of the Parable, touching vanities; truly may we ſay with the Prophet *David*, of

Pſal. 39.

a worldly minded man: *Univerſa vanitas omnis homo vivens :* The life of ſuch men containeth all kind of vanity. That is to ſay, both vanity in ambition, vanity in riches, vanity in pleaſures, vanity in all things which they moſt eſteem. And therefore I may well end with the words of Almighty God

Eſay 56.

by the Prophet *Eſay* : *Væ vobis, qui trahitis iniquitatem in funiculis vanitatis :* Wo be unto you which do draw wickedneſs in the ropes of vanity. Theſe ropes are thoſe vanities of vain-glory, promotion, dignity, nobility, beauty, riches, delights, and other ſuchlike before-touched, which always draw with them ſome iniquity and ſin. For which cauſe holy *Da-*

The ropes of vanity.
Pſal. 3.

vid ſaith unto his Lord, *Thou hateſt (O Lord) obſervers of ſuperfluous vanities.* And the Scripture reporting the cauſe why God deſtroyed utterly the Family and Linage of *Baaſa* King of Iſrael, ſaith it

I Reg. 17.

was, *For that they had provoked God in their vanities.* And laſtly, for this cauſe the holy Ghoſt pronoun-

Pſal. 39.

ceth generally of all men, *Beatus vir qui non reſpexit in vanitates, & inſanias falſas :* Bleſſed is that man which hath not reſpected vanities, and the falſe madneſs of this World.

SECT.

Nicholas Cross, *A Sermon Preach'd before her Sacred Majesty the Queen, in her Chapel at Windsor, on the Twentyfirst Day of April, Anno 1686* (1741), pp. 123–50

In 1850 the Gloucestershire parson Francis Witts inspected 'some curiosities' found during building work at a country home he was visiting – a hidden trove of Catholic liturgical vessels, 'with a number of Roman Catholic devotional books and a set of single sermons, chiefly of the date 1685 to 1688 preached at the chapels of James II and his Queen' and thought to have been 'secreted' away at the Revolution by a Catholic domestic chaplain.[1] What Witts was being shown was, in fact, part of the residue of the court patronage of Catholic preaching (as well as of the press) during James's reign. Both Witts's memo and the present volume remind also us that the Queen, the pious Maria Beatrice, or Mary of Modena (1658–1718), was, along with James, active in promoting the Catholic cause.

This particular homily, on the subject of 'the Joys of Heaven', was delivered by one of the Queen's chaplains, the Franciscan Nicholas Cross (1614/15–98). Cross (in religion: Nicolaus a Santa Clara) was born in Derbyshire and joined the Franciscans, probably in Douai. He was ordained in 1640 and proceeded to become a procurator for the English Province and, in 1662, Minister Provincial. In 1670 he published his paraphrase of Psalm 50, *Cynosura, or, a Saving Star that Leads to Eternity* (London, J. Redmayne, for Thomas Rooke [or Rooks]), reissued 1679, and around the same time became chaplain to the convert Duchess of York, from whom he obtained funds for the English Poor Clares in Bruges. Cross was once more Minister Provincial in 1672 and, for the third time, in 1680. Under James II he was preacher and chaplain at court under the patronage of Mary of Modena, in whose presence he preached this sermon in 1686. Late in 1688 he left with the royal family for St Germains but may have returned to England after the Revolution, when he was elected Provincial in 1689, retiring in 1691 to Douai, where he published his *Pious Reflections and Devout Prayers on Several Points of Faith and Morality* (1695), dedicated to Mary of Modena. He died in Douai in 1698.

The first version of Cross's sermon was printed in London by Nathaniel Thompson, without publisher or place of publication given, but with the Queen's mandate, in the year of its delivery. Its republication in 1741 indicates, not, of course, that the triumphalist atmosphere of James II's reign still prevailed but that the pious themes Cross had evoked continued to evoke a response.

1.   David Verey (ed.), *The Diary of a Cotswold Parson, Reverend F. E. Witts, 1783–1854* (Stroud, Glocs., Alan Sutton, 1993), p. 176.

A

SERMON

Preach'd before her Sacred MAJESTY the

QUEEN,

IN

Her Chapel at *WINDSOR*, on the
Twentyfirst Day of APRIL, *Anno* 1686.

By the Reverend FATHER

NICHOLAS CROSS, of the Holy ORDER
of St. *FRANCIS*, and Chaplain in Ordinary
to Her MAJESTY.

As Publish'd by Her MAJESTY'S *Command.*

Printed in the YEAR MDCCXLI.

SERMON XVIII.

Preach'd before her Sacred M A J E S T Y the

Q U E E N,

Of the *JOYS* of *HEAVEN.*

P S A L M lxxxiii. 5.

Beati qui habitant in domo tua, Domine.

Blessed are those, O Lord, who dwell in thy house.

 H E *Egyptians*, most Sacred Majesty, willing to decypher, and pencil out *Nature*, whom they look'd upon, as the Source and Fountain, whence all Favours were derived to Men, represented her in a *human* Shape; having a *Breast* that continually gush'd forth a precious and sovereign Liquor: Her *Right-hand* was busy in removing Dangers from her Favourites, whilst the *other* was laden with Rewards to recompense those, who adored her.

Vol. II.　　　　R 2　　　　THESE

SERMON XVIII. *Of the*

THESE Inventions of *Antiquity* do lively set forth the Portraicture of our *eternal Father*, who, from an unexhausted *Spring* of Charity, inebriates with ineffable Sweetnefs thofe, who love him; *Inebriabuntur ab ubertate domus tuæ, & torrente voluptatis tuæ potabis eos,* fays the *Pfalmift*; *They fhall be inebriated from the plenty of thy houfe, and of the torrent of his pleafure he will make them drink.* So that God may juftly be term'd to have a *Breaft* which conveys a moft delicious Stream, whofe Sweetnefs cannot be exprefs'd, and only comprehended by thofe, who have happily experienced it! His *Right-hand* is always ready to fhield his Servants from Dangers in this Life, whilft the other is ready, in the next, to veft them with a State of Glory, as far furpaffing human Eloquence to unfold, as our Sufferings to merit: *Quia non funt condignæ paffiones hujus temporis, ad futuram gloriam, quæ revelabitur in nobis*; becaufe, *The Tribulations in this Life, are no ways proportionable to that future Blifs, which fhall be revealed unto us*; When the Curtains of our Mortality fhall be drawn, and that we have ended the laft Act of this Life by a happy Period.

THIS

JOYS *of* HEAVEN.　　

THIS Text gives me occasion to speak of the Joys of Paradise; and tho' they exceed *what either Eye hath seen, Ear hath heard, or the Understanding of Man can comprehend:* However, *First*, I will venture to give you a rough Draught of them; And in the Sequel chalk out to you the Means, by which they may be obtain'd. But before I begin, I beg the Concurrence of your Prayers, to purchase the Gift of the *Holy Ghost*, by the Intercession of the *Blessed Virgin*.

MOST Sacred Virgin, *who art the Conduit conveying Life and Grace from the Bosom of thy Son, to wretched Creatures, and whose happy Soul is advanced to the highest pitch of Perfection, of which any pure Creature can be capable; assist me, if you please, so to describe a* State of Glory, *as that my* Audience *may be enflamed with a Zeal for its Acquisition; and we will salute thee saying,* AVE MARIA, &c.

I T is an *Axiom* in *Philosophy*, that all things created have allotted to them, as proper to their Being and Consistence, a Center, or Resting-place, whereunto they naturally tend, wherein they are fully satisfied, and unto which they are united by so strict a Sympathy, as, without Violence they

126   S E R M O N XVIII. *Of the*

they cannot be feparated. We fee the *ele-mentary* Bodies have their Center, where they are in Quiet and Repofe. *Plants* grow to a certain Greatnefs, proper to their Species: The natural Appetite of *Brutes* encounters that, which gluts their Avidity; all other things find here their utmoft Perfection. Man therefore being the moft noble Creature of this inferior World, adorn'd with the lively Image of his Creator, and conftituted Lord and Mafter of the Univerfe, cannot want fome Term, or Object, to which he is born by an impe-tuous Inftinct of Nature, and which once acquired, all Motions and Pretentions would ceafe : Yet 'tis moft certain that he alone, during this Life, cannot attain and reach unto his Center: For his Underftanding elevates his Thoughts above the Heavens, and all the Power of Nature; his Will frames infinitely more Defires, than the World hath Perfections ; by which we are taught, *That for* Man *to be happy, he muft enjoy a fovereign Good* ; For all the Beauties, Empires, Riches, and Pleafures of the World, cannot give a full Satisfaction to the Will; it ftill longs and breathes after an univerfal Being, which cannot be found in things created. Wherefore we muft con-clude, *There is a Goodnefs infinite, an Ef-fence*

Joys *of* Heaven.

fence moſt ſimple, which containing all Good, is ſovereignly happy in himſelf: And this is the due and right Object of our Wills and Deſires. The Royal Prophet inſinuates as much, when he ſays, *Satiabor cum appa-ruerit gloria tua:* That *nothing can ſatiate the boundleſs Soul of Man, but the ſight of God in eternal Bliſs. Fiſhes* live not but in the Water, *Birds* in the Air, *Plants* with their Roots fix'd in the Earth; all other things in the Place proper to their Being: So the *Mind of Man* cannot be free from Anguiſh, whilſt ſeparated from God; He is the *Center of our Hearts:* In whom, as St. *Paul* ſays, *We live, move, and are.* Excellently well St. *Auſtin* expreſſes this, ſaying, *O Domine, aliquando introducis me in neſcio quam dulcedinem, quæ ſi perficiatur in me, neſcio quid erit, ſed ſcio quod vita iſta non erit: O Lord, thou doſt ſometimes lead me into unknown Delights, which if compleated in me, I know not what it will be; but ſure I am, it cannot be this Life.* For he clearly diſcern'd, that the Condition of our Mortality, wherein we here lie groveling, is no ways capable of thoſe raviſhing Delights prepared to fill the Extent of our God-thirſting-Souls. He goes on ſaying, *Feciſti nos Domine, ad te, & inquietum eſt cor noſtrum,*

donec

128   SERMON XVIII. *Of the*

donec requiescat in te: O Lord, thou hast made us for Thee, and our Hearts are restless until they rest in Thee.

CAST your Thoughts on whatsoever your Fancy and Imagination can frame, and you will find this a Truth undeniable. If you consider *sensual Delights*; behold a *Solomon*, the greatest of Wits, a Prince, young, rich, powerful, and swelling in a full Plenty of all things; who made it his Study, to delight himself, in whatever might be agreeable to his Senses: Yet infine, he publish'd his little Satisfaction, crying, *Vanitas vanitatum, & omnia vanitas:* He avows his Folly, and all his Experience had but taught him, there must needs be some transcendent Object, to correspond with his unsatisfied Desires

AGAIN, if you go more rationally to work, and weigh the Operations of our spiritual Substance, these likewise we shall find here deficient, though not in the Object, yet in the manner of enjoying it: Of this, we have a *Precedent* in the Person of St. *Paul*, who was rapt up to the *third Heavens*, admitted unto Secrets unfit to unfold to Man, privileged with the Dignity of an Apostle, and acquitted himself of that Charge, the most gloriously that ever Man did; was become so Spiritual as to
find

Joys *of* Heaven.

find folid Contentment amidft Chains, Prifons, and all forts of Perfecution: Yet notwithftanding all this he iffues forth this affectuous Note, *Cupio diffolvi, & effe cum Chrifto; I defire to be diffolved and be with Chrift;* which evidences, there was yet fomething wanting to accomplifh his *Defires.*

SINCE then 'tis clear, *there is another Life, wherein muft be terminated the Motion of our ever active Souls;* let us, if you pleafe, a little glance upon it, and folace our felves, in the Difcourfe of what will be one Day, I hope, the Subject of our Fruition; though at prefent, but of our fweet Expectation. And here, methinks, I am juft like a Veffel lanch'd into the main Ocean, without Helm or Compafs, which tells me, I may wander, but whither, and to what Port, uncertain: So I, about to fhadow forth a State of Glory, am diftracted into as many Thoughts as there are *Idea's* of things, which caufe pure Delight; fain would I fix on fomething, but alas! each Glimpfe of Glory ftrikes me dumb, and makes me cry out, with that great Father of the Church St. *Auftin, Amari poteft, æftimari non poteft: It may be loved, not prized,* nor confequently exprefs'd.

YOU fee then, my *dear Auditors*, into what a Labyrinth I am caft, and how unable to perform my defigned Task. How-

SERMON XVIII. *Of the*

ever, I will venture to fpeak one thing, and this *one thing* is all ; 'tis the Sum and Epitome of what ever may be faid thereof; to wit ; *That we fhall one day be made happy, by that fame Felicity, wherewith he himfelf,* who is fovereign Lord of all things, *is bleffed and made happy.* For his Beatitude is, to enjoy himfelf, and contemplate his own Beauty and Perfections : And this fame Beatitude will be communicated to us poor Worms through his Liberality ; *Similes ei erimus, & videbimus eum ficuti eft,* 1 John cap. iii. *We fhall be like to him, and fee him as he is :* Then, that *divine Effence,* which hath given Life and Being to all Creatures, from whence they derive what ever they have of Beauty and Perfection, will be laid open to our Embraces. Then, that *divine Effence,* which hath ravifh'd into Admiration, by the Splendor of his Glory, the *Seraphims,* and all the *Bleffed Spirits,* for above thefe five thoufand Years, will be given up to our Poffeffion, to gaze thereon and feed our glorify'd Senfes for all Eternity. Then will happen, what I faid to you in the Beginning, *Satiabor cum apparuerit gloria tua. Then all Motions and Pretenfions will ceafe.* Then this Will of ours, which leads us here inceffantly from one Pleafure to antoher, ftill as unwearied as unfatisfied, will

have

JOYS *of* HEAVEN.

have nothing more to will, or defire. For the Soul, freed from Encumbrances of the Body, and Allurements of Flefh, will plunge her felf into the Abyfs of the *Divinity*; and will there be neceffitated to love; for it is impoffible not to love this fovereign Object propofed unto us by a clear Vifion: And as Iron red hot is divefted of its own Form, to put on that of Fire; fo the Soul, enflamed with this Love and beatifick Fruition, will by a Way wholly ineffable, even melt from her felf, and diffolve into God; where all her Affections will be *in a manner* deified, and loft *as it were* in the *divine Effence.*

THEN this Underftanding of ours, which toils it felf in the Search of *Nature's Secrets*, will be at reft; reading in the *divine Nature, divine* and *human Myfteries*, and all the Wonders that have been wrought by the Omnipotence, Wifdom and Goodnefs of God; for, elevated by the Light of Glory, we fhall fee all things, which are *formally* in God, that is, all his Perfections; his *Wifdom, Goodnefs, Power, Eternity, Immenfity*, and his other *Attributes. Videbimus eum ficuti eft,* fays St. *John; We fhall fee him as he is*; which would not be fo, if any of thofe lay hid from us. And whereas all the Perfections in God, is but

one

132   S E R M O N XVIII. *Of the*

one pure, and moſt ſimple Perfection, hence
it is, that his *divine Eſſence* cannot become
our perfect Object, without a clear Diſplay of
all his Perfections. We ſhall ſee in the *Word*,
the *Beauty*, and Order of the Univerſe, all
the *Species*, and Kinds of natural Things.
For the *beatifick Viſion* will not be inferior
to the natural Knowledge of Angels, and
as they naturally know all things, ſo ſhall
the Bleſſed; it being a Condition requiſite
to their Underſtanding.

WE ſhall ſee all the *ſupernatural Myſteries*, which have been here matter of our
Belief; for then, paſſing from the Ob-
ſcurity of *Faith*, unto the Splendor of a
Viſion, we ſhall behold the *Lamb*, unclaſp-
ing *his myſterious Book*: We ſhall contemplate the *ſublime Myſtery* of the *Bleſſed
Trinity*, how the *Father* produces his *Son Co-
eternal* and *Conſubſtantial* to himſelf; how
the *Father*, and the *Son*, loving one another,
breathe forth the *Holy Ghoſt*: How Three
are One, and make up a *Trinity* in *Unity*.
Then ſhall we perfectly underſtand how
Chriſt is intirely contain'd after *Conſecra-
tion* under the *Species* of *Bread* and *Wine*,
and how the Lord of. Heaven and Earth is
confined to ſo ſmall a Compaſs, as to be
graſped by our unworthy Hands.

I

Joys *of* Heaven.

I cannot omit a curious Difpute amongft *Divines*, touching the Operations of the *Soul*, by which Beatitude is convey'd unto her, and made perfect. St. *Thomas* gives it to the Operation of the *Underftanding*, as comprizing the *Effence of Beatitude*, and looks upon the *Will*, but as an Accident, and Propriety infeparable from *Beatitude:* His reafon is, *That the Underftanding appears to him as the moft noble Faculty of the Soul, and confequently in its Operation confifts the Effence of Beatitude, which is the clear Vifion of God.*

SCOTUS, The fubtile Doctor, and our Countryman, attributes all unto the *Will*; which tranfports the Bleffed with ineffable Joys, and renders them fatisfy'd throughout the vaft Spaces of *Eternity*; his reafon is, *The* Will *is free, can make her Choice, grant, or refufe, which is not compatible with the Underftanding, and confequently, he efteems* Love *to be a thing more excellent than* Vifion.

But notwithftanding thefe Arguments, I embrace the Opinion of our more *ancient Divines*, who jointly require both *Vifion* and *Love*; and that *Man's higheft Perfection confifts in the Operation of thefe two Faculties united together.* For to fay the Truth, there is little Satisfaction to behold what we *love* not, be the Object
never

134   S E R M O N   XVIII.   *Of the*

never fo accomplifh'd; nay, could *Lucifer* fee God, and yet be barr'd from loving him, he would be miferable; for his *Will*, not permitted to love an Object, which appears to him infinitely amiable, would certainly be tortured in the higheft degree.

AGAIN, we enjoy God, by *contemplating* his infinite Perfections, and *relifhing* his immenfe Goodnefs and Sweetnefs; the *Firft* proceeds from *Vifion*, the *other* from *Love*; fo that thefe together are the *Effence*, and Accomplifhments of our fupream Happinefs.

To *conclude*, *Beatitude* gives unto God the greateft Glory; now, he is not lefs glorify'd in being eternally loved, than by being eternally feen; as a Prince is not lefs glorious by the Affection of his People, than by the Defire they have to behold him. Hence it is, that God's greateft Glory, being to be feen, and loved; 'tis evident, that our *Beatitude* confifts in the joint Operations of our Underftanding, and *Will*.

METHINKS, it were not amifs, *my dear Auditors*, to examine our felves, how we have imploy'd thefe noble Faculties of the Soul, in order to that End, for which they were ordain'd: And whether we have made our *final End*, and utmoft Perfection, the frequent Subject of our *Thoughts* and *Defires*.

                                For

J O Y S *of* H E A V E N.

For certainly the *Meditation* of heavenly
things, produces admirable Irradiations in
the Underſtanding, by which we may the
better diſcern our Concerns, in what relates to
God and our Salvation : *Meditation* is an
Entertainment with God, which is the Life
of Angels, a Life imparting to us the greateſt
ſhare of Paradiſe, that as poſſibly can be attain'd to in this World : So that truly it may
be juſtly term'd the *Beatitude of this Life :*
For it is moſt efficacious, to obtain a Grant
of our Petitions, as being perform'd with a
greater Fervency, and Elevation of Spirit ;
and hath likewiſe a wonderful Power, to
enrich the Soul with all kind of *Virtues*,
being the very Source and Root of all Holineſs and Devotion. Upon theſe Conſidera-
tions, many ſpiritual Maſters have aſſerted,
that not only Religious, but *all Perſons are
obliged to practice Meditation*, at leaſt in
ſome little meaſure. For they look upon it,
as a neceſſary means to avoid Sin, and to
preſerve our ſelves in the Fear and Love of
God ; which is hard to be done, without a
ſerious Reflection upon the Concerns of our
Salvation. Now by mental Prayer, above
all other Devotions, this important Affair of
our Salvation is moſt lively imprinted in us:
And though I do not approve the Opinion
of thoſe, who hold it *obligatory to all*, nevertheleſs

vertheless you may gather from hence, how injurious you have been unto your selves, if you have let your *Underſtanding* and *Will* be taken up in the purſuit of petty and triffling Pleaſures, in ſenſual Things; and for thoſe childiſh Baits of Fleſh and Blood, forfeit the ſweet Antepaſt of Heaven, convey'd unto us in a ſerious Meditation. Ah! Did you conſider the Advantages of mental Prayer, you would doubtleſs ſet a part one Hour at leaſt every Day, to rumi‑ nate upon your *final End*, and utmoſt Per‑ fection; which Conſideration cannot but ſtir in us ardent Deſires after that bleſſed State; and ſweeten all the Acerbities of this Life, by that *bleſſed Hope*, as St. *Peter* terms it.

CERTAIN it is, in the tranſitory Paſſage of this Life, we experience the moſt ſolid Contentment and Satisfaction, to conſiſt in the ſweet Meditations of divine Myſteries: For alas! Without thoſe Hopes, which Faith gives us, no Creature is more wretch'd than Man; for we are baniſh'd *as it were*, into a Land of Miſery; enſlaved by Sin, where we truckle under unruly Paſſions, that hurry us into many Diſaſters and Cala‑ mities; at laſt, we finiſh a deplorable Life, by Death, in whoſe Face is ſeated nothing but Dread and Horrour; After this, Cor‑ ruption,

JOYS *of* HEAVEN.

ruption, Stench, and Infection are the laft
Farewel and Monument of us; fo that
without Faith, actuated by mental Prayer,
we are center'd within thefe Miferies, unable to carry our Sight beyond the low Condition of a Brute. Whereas, on the contrary, *Faith* teaches, *We are born to a fu-*
pernatural and bleffed End; which we are
to purchafe by Acts of Religion. Next, *that*
our Souls are immortal, by which refem-
bling the Angels, we are excluded from Pu-
trefaction, and approach the nearer unto
God. Laftly, *That he hath created all things*
of nothing; in which Belief, we acknowledge his Omnipotence, and from thence
cherifh our Hopes, that, if he could ex-
tract us out of nothing, with more facility
we believe he can, after Death, re-join
our dif-united Parts.

WHAT a Comfort then, to confider, that
this State of the Bleffed is Eternal; witnefs
the Royal Prophet, *Longitudine dierum ad-*
implebo eum, That *he will replenifh us with*
length of Days; that is, with Eternity,
as all the *Fathers* expound it. For an Apprehenfion to be deprived of what we enjoy,
doth often blaft our Contentment even in
the Bud. But thefe joy-blafting Fears have
no place in the Elect: As they can covet
nothing more than what they have, fo fhall

VOL. II.   T   they

S E R M O N XVIII. *Of the*

they poffefs it, as long as they defire : and as their Defires are fed with an Object, infinite, immutable, and fovereignly bleft ; fo their Joys fhall be immenfe, without end, unchangeable, and in all Points accomplifh'd. In the Poffeffion of this divine Being, its attractive Features both delight, and ravifh ; and in fuch a manner, as ftill enkindle new Flames and new Defires : For after Millions of Ages have wax'd old, in this our Fruition we fhall feel the fame Fervour, Complaifance and ravifhing Tranfports, as at the firft inftant of our Happinefs.

Now, as it is eternal in it felf, fo is it inamiffible to us, *Gaudium veftrum nemo tollet à vobis* ; John xvi. *No envious or repining hand fhall wreft it from you*; for thofe bleffed Copartners, and Coheirs to that rich Inheritance, are fully fatisfied each with his Portion ; he that has a leffer Share of Grace and Glory, maligns not him that is more amply enrich'd, becaufe he hath enough to make him happy : Befides, their *Beatitude* confifting in a Conformity to the divine Will, the Difpenfation of his heavenly Largeffes, is Part of their Felicity; fo that each appropriates to himfelf the Good of his Neighbour, and joys as much in it, as in his own ; and whatever accidental Glory excelling, is found in one, occafions

JOYS *of* HEAVEN. 139

occafions matter of *Thankfgiving*, and *Be-nediƈtions* to the other.

FELICITAS *eſt habere omne quod cupis, & nihil habere eorum quæ odiſti*. *St.* Auſtin *defines Felicity to be a Colleƈtion of all that you love, and an Excluſion from all that you hate.* St. *Gregory* ſtiles it, *Satietas deliciarum*, ſuch a *Surcharge of all Delights*, ſuch a delicious Stream, that if one Drop thereof ſhould fall into Hell, it would mitigate and aſſwage all the Torments of the Damned. Hence I wonder not, if that unfortunate rich Man, mention'd in the Scripture, did ſo howl, and cry, but for one Drop of that heavenly Stream, ſince it had been ſufficient to allay all his Heat, and charm his Miſery into Felicity.

HAVING now, *my dear Auditors*, as I hope at leaſt, in ſome little meaſure warm'd your Affeƈtions, *in order to this bleſſed State*, I am perſuaded it will draw your Attention unto the *Means how it is to be obtain'd*, which ſhall be my *Second Point*, and ſo I ſhall end.

OUR Bleſſed Saviour, in the fifth Chapter of St. *Matthew*, declares who may lay a Claim to this great Inheritance, ſaying, *Beati qui perſecutionem patiuntur propter juſtitiam, quoniam ipſorum eſt regnum cælo-*

T 2   *rum;*

140   S E R M O N   XVIII. *Of the*

*rum; Bleſſed are thoſe who ſuffer perſecu-
tion for juſtice ſake, for theirs is the
kingdom of heaven.* Theſe are the *Letters-
Patents,* and *grand Deeds,* by which you
may enter into Poſſeſſion. But alas! *My
dear Auditors,* I muſt here change my
Stile, and draw your Thoughts from that
ſweet Repoſe, wherein perhaps I have
lodged them, to fill you with Tempeſts and
Whirl-winds; and tell you, *If you will
have a Crown, you muſt fight for it.* Holy
Job weighing Man's Condition here, defines
it thus; *Militia eſt vita hominis ſuper
terram; The life of man is a warfare
upon earth. Within,* unruly Paſſions diſturb us; *Without,* the Envy and Malice of
others : So that from our very Infancy, to
the Tomb, the Noiſe and Terror of Combats attend us. This ſharp Decree was
paſſed immediately after our firſt Parents
Tranſgreſſion, and God declared it to him,
that he ſhould not eat his Bread, but at
the rate of ſweaty Brows. And tho' God
diſpenſed with this his ſevere Sentence in
the *Old Law,* promiſing unto the exact Obſervers of it, long Life, abundance of
Wealth, a plentiful Poſterity, and the like;
yet this was done, as he will leave no Virtue
un-rewarded, becauſe Heaven's Gates were
then ſhut up. But when *Chriſt* had clear'd
        the

the Paffage unto our *eternal Felicity*, and clapt the *Thorns* (which were the Fruit of our Sins) upon his own Head, then Sufferings recover'd fo high a Being, and grew to that Value, *As the heavier God lays his Hand upon us, the more his Love appears*; and of this what greater Evidence, than that the Kingdom of Heaven, is an infallible Confequence to fuch, as *fuffer Perfecution for Juftice fake*.

DIVINES affert *three Beings*, which are capable to enjoy a fovereign Good; to wit, *God*, *Angels* and *Man*: *God* reaches his *Beatitude*, without any Motion; becaufe it is natural, and effentially feated in him: But *Creatures*, who by their Natures are inferior to *Beatitude*, ought not to arrive unto it, without fome previous Endeavours for its Acquifition. The *Angels*, who are of a fpiritual Subftance, made this great Purchafe by one fingle meritorious Operation. But *Man*, who is fet at a greater diftance from *Beatitude*, clog'd with the Mafs of his Body, ufually fpeaking, by reafon of Infants baptized (who, without any Action of their own, are admitted unto Glory) is obliged to many reiterated Acts of Virtue ere he come to the Acquifition: Wherefore, the term of this Life is given him, as the time of his
Tryal;

Tryal ; God likewife allots to him, many
fupernatural Aids, which proportion his
Good-works unto the Greatnefs of *Beatitude:*
And thus by Degrees, by many Hardfhips,
by many pious Exercifes, he raifes himfelf
unto his fupream Felicity : And furely, none
can repine at this, efpecially if we reflect
how unweariedly, and with what Zeal,
we labour in the purchafe of fading and
tranfitory Things.

How then, to perform this Task, decreed by Heaven, and to bring it to a
happy Iffue, I know no *Medium* more fuitable to our frail Condition, *than to plant
within us, an interior Abnegation of our
felves,* by which we give a Repulfe to our
natural, corrupted Inclinations ; For when
once we come to diveft ourfelves of our
felves, that is of *Self-love,* then all the Terrors of Mortification and Adverfity find no
Effect; then, nothing but generous and heroick Acts are Products of fuch a Soul ; for
folid Virtue, like a Rofe amidft Thorns,
fprings not forth, but in the Soil of Afflictions ; and when once a Soul comes to be
feized with this holy Averfion againft herfelf,
fhe minds not the Difficulties fhe is to wade
through, to make good her Fidelity to God;
fhe cafts herfelf upon the points of Hal-
berts, and other Inftruments of Severity,
                                              without

JOYS *of* HEAVEN.   143

without the leaft flinching or whining at
their Sharpnefs. She takes in, with the fame
relifh, the Gall of Misfortunes and Defo-
lations, as fhe does the Hony of Profpe-
rities and Comforts. No ftormy Seafon
hinders her Journey, and that which
difturbs weak, and effeminate Spirits, is to
her matter of Joy, becaufe having her
Thoughts always fix'd upon *Beatitude*, fhe
looks upon Afflictions, as the *Medium* to
lead her to it. So that all things, which pafs
under the Name of Adverfity, is not fo,
but to the Wicked, who make ill ufe of
them, in prizing the Creature more than
the Creator. Hence it is, that the general
Spirit of *Saints* have made them ambitious
after Sufferings; and to look upon them as
the choiceft Favours of Heaven; for they
had learnt by happy Experience, that, if
Almighty God was pleafed, fometimes, to
reach unto them the *Cup* of his *Paffion*,
it was but by Snatches, and as it were a
Sup; whilft, with the other Hand he gave
them large Draughts of Confolation : To
verify this *Text*, relating to my *Second*
Point, *Beati qui perfecutionem patiuntur :
Bleffed are thofe who fuffer perfecution*, &c.

IT is noted in the *facred Text*, that God
laid open the Perfon of *Job* to all the
Affaults

144   S E R M O N XVIII. *Of the*

Affaults of *Sathan*, yet with this referve, he fhould not touch upon his Life; not that Death would have eclipfed his Glory, but becaufe God would not be deprived of fuch a Champion, to whofe Conflicts, he, and his bleffed Angels were intent, with much Satisfaction ; and therefore he would not lofe the Pleafure to fee this ftout *Skirmifh* fought out to the laft, betwixt him and his Adverfary.

NAY, *Seneca*, out of the Principle of human *Wifdom*, drew this excellent Saying, *There is no Object*, fays he; *fo pleafing in the Eyes of the Gods, as to fee a ftout Man, with a fettled Countenance, unmoved, to ftruggle with adverfe Fortune :* And truly the Delay our Bleffed *Saviour* made, in lending Succour to his *Difciples*, when endanger'd by a Storm at Sea, fufficiently hints unto us the Pleafure God takes to fee the Juft row againft the Stream, to wreftle and ftruggle with the Afflictions of this World.

Now, that God is pleafed with thefe painful and fatisfactory Acquittances, which we often give him, writ in our Sweat and Blood, and which *Chrift* our Lord receives and makes a prefent of to his eternal Father, together with his own, from
whence

JOYS *of* HEAVEN. 14?

whence ours derive their Value: 'Tis not, I fay, upon the fcore, that he is delighted to fee us tormented, either in Mind or Body; but meerly, in that by them his *Juftice* is exalted, and the *Palms* of our Victory made more refplendent.

IT may be objected, as oft it is by our *Adverfaries*, that God is the *Searcher of Hearts*, he knows what we will do, and therefore he needs not thefe exterior *Teftimonies*; next, that *Chrift*'s *Merits* are of infinite Value, and confequently, ours altogether fuperfluous. To which *I anfwer*, to the *Firft*, That as to God's external Glory, confifting in the vifible Homages, render'd him by his Creatures; this would be wanting, unlefs he gave occafion to manifeft to the World, he hath Dependents, who value no Suffering in proportion to the Duty they owe him; befides, when we fhall arrive at a State of *Blifs*, and reflect we have done fomething, in fome little meafure, by the Concurrence of our *Free-will*, to merit *Beatitude*, queftionlefs it will be a great addition to our Contentment.

As to the other *Objection*, I acknowledge the Merits of *Chrift* of an infinite Value, and abundantly fufficient; yet this will not excufe me from offering what I can in Satisfaction; for the Glory of all our Actions belongs unto God: Now as it is an Act of Injuftice to defraud any one of his

VOL. II, U Eftate,

146   S E R M O N XVIII. *Of the*

Eſtate, no leſs is it againſt Equity, to de-
prive God of what is his Due ; if the Tree
be mine, I have right to the Fruit it bears ;
if the Land be mine, the Crop likewiſe is
at my Diſpoſal: So in like manner, all that
we have, all that we do, or ſhall do that is
Good, is the Work of God, and a *Preſent*,
wherewith he enriches us, that we may be
able to give ſomething to him : Wherefore
as all is his, our Duty binds us to conſecrate all our *interior* and *exterior Actions*
to promote his *Honour*. That Life then,
which contributes nothing to his Glory, is
pérverſe and wicked ; and ſince it is rational, Sin ſhould be puniſh'd, we ought to
ſubmit unto this *grand Decree*, expoſe our
ſelves to be rack'd, or tortur'd by what
Puniſhment the *divine Majeſty* ſhall think
fit, either in Soul or Body ; nor can we
ever repine, if we remember, *Beati, qui
perſecutionem patiuntur*, &c.

     O U R Bleſſed *Saviour* was not content to
give bare *Documents* to his *Diſciples*, but he
confirm'd his *Doctrine* by his own *Example :*
To this End, he advances undauntedly to
meet his perfidious *Apoſtle*, attended on by
a Squadron of Soldiers, bent on his Deſtruction : For this Cauſe he yields his delicate
Limbs to the ſtroaks of *mercileſs Executi-
oners*, his unſpotted Reputation to the *black-
eſt Calumnies* ; infine, like an *innocent Lamb*,
dies upon the *Croſs*, laden with Confuſion,
ſacrificing

JOYS *of* HEAVEN.

facrificing his Life to their Rage. And why all this? *Quia oportebat Chriſtum pati, & ita intrare in gloriam ſuam.* It is his own *Decree,* and tho' he is the *Law-giver,* yet he will not be difpenfed in it; it is his own *Doctrine,* that this Evangelical *Pearl* fhall not be purchafed, but at the rate of *Perfecution.*

THOSE *Bleſſed Apoſtles,* who had the Honour to receive thefe Prefcripts from *Chriſt's* own Mouth; and many of them to be Witneffes how he feal'd them with his *Blood,* all manifefted by the Sequel of their Lives, and Deaths, that they were true *Diſciples* of fo glorious a Mafter; you fhall not find one, who was not like a perpetual Motion, unweariedly fpending himfelf in the Labours of preaching, difputing, drawing Men from their Errors, and inceffantly doing acts of Charity; in recompence, they were reviled, imprifon'd, laden with Chains, torn in pieces by Inftruments of Cruelty, and at laft taken away by a moft ignominious Death.

FROM their Times, in the Courfe, and Revolution of fo many Ages, until this prefent, you fhall find that the Servants of Almighty God were ftrangely opprefs'd, and made as it were the Mockery of the World: Some fhrowding themfelves in Caves, others roving up and down in Solitude. *Quibus dignus non erit Mundus;* Hebr. cap. xi. *Of whom the world was not worthy;*

U 2 fome

148 SERMON XVIII. *Of the*

fome caft into Dungeons, others dragg'd unto
Execution, and amidft all thefe Calamities,
they had only this Confolation, *Beati*, *qui
perfecutionem patiuntur*, &c. *Bleffed are
they*, *who fuffer perfecution*, &c.

AFTER then the *Authority* of our *Bleffed
Saviour*, and fo many glorious *Examples*,
it were to grope in the Sun Beams, not to
fee by what means this great Inheritance
is to be purchafed. *Non coronabitur nifi
qui legitimè certaverit* ; Tim. cap. ii. *Without combats no crowns*, and without Perfecution no Heaven. *Et violenti rapiunt illud* ;
Matt. xi. And *the violent fhall bear it away* ;
that is, who ufe Violence, not fo much
Active as *Paffive*, by forcing their Natures
to ftoop to Oppreffion, and to the fervile
Acts, which *Poverty*, *Want*, *Contempt* and
Difgraces do throw upon them.

IT is a Pofition of *Ariftotle*, that *'tis a
more noble Act of Fortitude, pati quam agere* ;
To endure than to act. For to fee a mighty
Prince with a powerful Army bear all
before him, and lay the World *proftrate* to
his Conquefts, is fomething I confefs ; but
thefe Perfons find here their Reward, their
Temples are circled with Crowns, they
have the Applaufe and Acclamations of the
People, they have a full Sway and Dominion over thofe they have conquer'd : But
to fee a Courage, amidft the Storms of
Perfecution, unfhaken, like a Rock in
the

Joys *of* Heaven.

the Ocean, whose hard Flanks play with the Waves; and to affront, with a patient Suffering, the Rage of Tyrants; this is a Spectacle, that ravishes the very *Angels*, and makes them emulate our Glory; this is an Action, not to be crown'd on Earth; all under Heaven is too small a Reward; *Quoniam ipsorum est regnum cælorum;* Because *theirs is the Kingdom of Heaven.*

To conclude you see, *my dear Auditors,* there is nothing conveys an Odour so pleasing unto Heaven, as that of a Soul, persecuted upon the Score of God's Cause. The Oblation of a *Holocaust* imports the Reduction of it to *Ashes*; that of an afflicted Person, resigned in the Extremity of worldy Afflictions, is a Transmutation into the *Holy Ghost*, who destroys not the matter of Sufferings, but allays them, by the Infusion of a supernatural Virtue, that is divine Hope. St. *Hierom*, calls a Soul crush'd with Persecution, *a Sacrifice*; nay, it is a *Sacrifice* of what is most dear unto us, to wit, the Friendship of Men : For *Christ* foretold his Servants they should be hated by the World; so that in suffering for his Name, we forfeit what is natural, and most delighful to us. But whilst we are in this consuming Task, we must remember, that as the Husbandman expects not the Fruit of his Labour, until the Seed he casts into the ground be corrupted, and thence a plentiful Generation springs forth;

so

150 SERMON XVIII. *Of the,* &c.

so we muſt continue periſhing, to the laſt, that ſo we may riſe, under a new Form, never more to be cruſh'd by the *Flail*, or *Grinding-Mill* of Perſecutors; but to flouriſh in *eternal Quiet*, as the juſt Recompence of an afflicted Spirit.

O all ye bleſſed Spirits, be glad and rejoice, for your Reward is great in Heaven; your Tears are now dry'd up, your Sighs and Groans are ſtopt, and all your weary Steps at an end; *Triſtitia veſtra vertitur in gaudium*; all your Sorrows are drown'd in a Deluge of Joys. What a Comfort now to look upon your Chains, turn'd into a moſt grateful Liberty? What Gladneſs to behold your horrid Dungeons converted into a magnificent Structure, irradiated with the ever-riſing Sun of Juſtice; your Lands and Goods here raviſh'd from you, changed into the fruitful Plains of *Sion* clad with an eternal Spring? You now happily experience, there is not a turn of the Hand, glance of the Eye, or leaſt motion of the Heart, employ'd for God's ſake, which is not confider'd in that great Reward, in that excelling Recompence, and that juſt Retribution of all good Things. May we happily follow your Steps, and ſo manage thoſe exciting Graces imparted to us, by your liberal Mediation, as one Day to be inliſted into that Reward you now enjoy, and ſhall for all Eternity. This we beg by your Interceſſion of Him, who is God for ever. *Amen.*

A

John Persall, *A Sermon Preach'd before the King and Queen,*
In their Majesties Chapel at Windsor, on Trinity-Sunday,
May 30, 1686 (London [T. Meighan], 1741), pp. 257–78

Another court sermon dating from the brisk and brief revival of English Catholic public activity sponsored by James and Maria Beatrice was
the Jesuit John Persall's homily for the feast of Trinity Sunday, *A Sermon*
Preach'd before the King and Queen. Persall's sermon was published by royal
order by Henry Hills in London in 1686 and the present imprint dates
from 1741.

John Persall (or Purcell, alias Harcourt), born in Staffordshire in 1633,
studied at St Omer between 1648 and 1653 and became a Jesuit in 1653 at
Watten in Flanders, being ordained priest in *c.* 1666. He lectured in Philosophy at Liège from *c.* 1668 and was Professor of Theology there between
1672 and 1679. In 1683 he was on the English Mission, in Hampshire, and
was subsequently appointed Preacher-in-Ordinary to James II. He delivered two court sermons, the first in October 1685 and the present one on
30 May 1686. Persall lived in the Jesuit College in the Savoy, which was
inaugurated in May 1687. With the Revolution, he left for the Continent
but may subsequently have gone to Ireland in James II's entourage. He
was made rector of the Liège college in 1694, and Jesuit Vice-Provincial in
England in 1696 and was at work in the Jesuit mission in London in 1699,
dying in 1701.

A

SERMON

Preach'd before the

KING and QUEEN,

In their MAJESTIES Chapel at

W I N D S O R,

On TRINITY-SUNDAY, *May* 30, 1686.

By the Reverend FATHER

J O H N   P E R S A L L,

Of the Society of *JESUS*, Profeſſor of DIVINITY.

As Publiſh'd by His MAJESTY's *Command.*

Printed in the YEAR MDCCXLI.

SERMON XXII.

Preach'd before their

MAJESTIES,

On *TRINITY-SUNDAY*,
May 30, 1686.

MATTH. xxviii. 19.

In Nomine Patris, & Filii, & Spiritûs Sancti.

*In the Name of the Father, and of the Son,
and of the Holy Ghost.*

 HE infcrutable Myftery of
the moft Bleffed Trinity,
propofed to our Veneration
in this Day's Solemnity, is
fo fublime, that no created
Intellect can reach it, the
moft high-flying Wits fall infinitely fhort
of it; fo profound and deep, that the moft
penetrating Judgments cannot fathom it;

VOL. II. L l fo

258

SERMON XXII.

fo infinite in all its Excellencies and Perfections, that neither Human nor Angelical
Capacity can comprehend it. The great
St. *Auguſtin* thought it once worth his Labour to employ his noble Thoughts in Diſcovery of theſe admirable Secrets, that are
couch'd in this ſacred Myſtery; he walked by
the Sea-ſhore, contemplating the divine
Proceſſions and Relations, a true Trinity of
Perſons in a perfect Unity of Subſtance,
the Father, Son, and Holy Ghoſt, three
really diſtinct Perſons, yet ſo, that the Father is in the Son, the Son is in the Father,
the Holy Ghoſt in the Father and the Son,
all three in each by a ſtrict Indentity of one
Subſtance. The Father is not the Son, the
Son is not the Holy Ghoſt, the Holy Ghoſt
is neither Father nor Son ; and yet the Father, Son, and Holy Ghoſt are one and the
ſame thing: *Idem omnino.* In the middle of

Lat. 4. c. 2. theſe Thoughts, St. *Auguſtin's* Eyes chan-
ced to glance upon a Child juſt by the Sea-
ſide, very buſy in lading out the Sea into a
little Pit he had made there; and asking
him what he meant to do, the Child anſwer'd, *To empty the Sea into this Pit: But
doſt thou not ſee* (ſays the Saint) *that thy Pit
is too little to hold all thoſe Waters? I can
more eaſily do this* (replies the Child) *than you
compaſs*

compafs what you are about. Thus Almighty
God did teach this great Servant of his, how
little Proportion all human Induftry has in
order to the underftanding this ineffable and
incomprehenfible Myftery ; far lefs than the
Child's little Pit, in order to contain an
Ocean of Waters: Yet for all this St. *Augu-*
ftin ceafed not from contemplating this great
Myftery, of which he wrote fifteen learned
Books, befides divers Sermons; but he
changed his way of fpeculating, he ftudies
no more to underftand it ; and therefore to
How can this be ? he ever anfwers, *Nefcio,*
I know not ; I am a Chriftian, I believe it.
I adore, I reverence, refpect, and love it,
but to underftand it, comprehend it, exprefs it as it is, I am not able. He contem-
plated it as the prime Object of his Faith,
Adoration, and Affection. In like manner
we, in imitation of this great Doctor, neither fearching too curioufly into that which
Faith teaches to be infcrutable; nor yet paffing over in filence what the Church on this
Day propofes to our Thoughts, as a Myftery, which is to be the Subject of our eternal Happinefs, will confider it, Firft, as
the Object of our Faith; Secondly, as the
Object of our Love ; Thirdly, as the Object
of our Imitation. In the Firft Point we fhall

SERMON XXII.

260

fee what we are to believe, and from the Hardnefs of it learn a Principle, which will ground us in true Faith and Religion. In my Second, we fhall learn where to fettle our Affections: In my Third, how to make our Souls (what they were created) perfect Images of the Trinity, by fquaring our Actions according to this divine Pattern: Three Parts of one and the fame Difcourfe ; fo that the Second proceeds from the Firft, Love from Faith ; the Third from the Firft and Second, Imitation from Faith and Love. Now that all may fucceed to the greater Glory of this Great Trinity, let us have re-courfe to the Interceffion of the Immaculate Virgin-Mother, Daughter to the eternal Father, Mother to the Eternal Son, Spoufe to the Holy Spirit, perfect Temple of the whole Trinity, faluting her with the Arch-angel, Ave Maria.

I know not by what better means we may arrive to frame a true, right, and pro-fitable Idea of this Myftery than by contem-plating its Image, the Soul of Man, where you will find that as often as any thing ex-cellent and amiable is objected to her, fhe prefently fpeaks it, faying, This is fine, this is admirable, this deferves to be beloved
indeed ;

On TRINITY-SUNDAY.

indeed; from whence connaturally proceeds
a certain breathing, an Affection, or Defire
of enjoying that fo amiable Object. In like
manner, Almighty God with an infinite
Clarity comprehending his own infinitely
amiable Effence, and in it all created
Truths that are poffible, fpeaks what he
knows, expreffing himfelf as he is infinite
in all Perfections; then he breathes forth a
certain divine Love proceeding from his
fpeaking and the Word fpoken; this fpeaking or producing the Word, conftitutes the
firft Perfon, God the Father; the Word
fpoken is the Second Perfon, God the Son;
the third Perfon is the Love, which both
the Firft and Second jointly breathe forth,
God the Holy Ghoft or Spirit. The fecond
is the Son, becaufe as it is the Property of a
Father to propagate his Nature, and give it
a fecond Being in his Son; fo the eternal
Father fpeaking, propagates his own divine
Nature, giving it, as it were, a fecond
Being in that confubftantial Image; whereas the Holy Ghoft, being Love, gives not any
Being to its Object, but only embraces
what it finds. Now becaufe nothing can be
in God, or affect God, but what is God,
each Perfon muft needs be God. Again;
becaufe the very Notion of God excludes a
Multiplicity,

SERMON XXII.

Multiplicity, as including all Perfection imaginable, and confequently, leaving none to be poffeffed by an other, only by Participation, the Property of a Creature; it follows, that all three Perfons are but one and the fame God; now how can this be, three Perfons, one only God, is above our reach; here it is we are to obey the Apoftle, making Reafon ftoop to Faith. But what, fays the Atheift or Heathen, muft I then become Irrational before I can be a Chriftian? Muft I renounce that very Faculty which diftinguifhes me from a Brute? Muft I admit things that evidently contradict the firft Principles of Reafon, and thwart the very Light of Nature? Three Perfons one God, the Father and the Son the felf fame thing, and yet two Perfons really diftinct? Nay then, adieu all Difcourfe, adieu all Knowledge, if we renounce the very Grounds of Knowledge and Difcourfe. This Objection lies under the very fame Inconveniences it objects againft the Myfteries of our Faith; 'tis irrational, it contradicts the firft Principles of Reafon, and thwarts the very Light of Nature; whereas our Faith, tho' fupernatural, tho' above Reafon, yet confirms true Reafon; for Almighty God only exacts of us to be-
                                          lieve

On Trinity-Sunday. 263

lieve when we have reafon to believe; then we muft make Reafon ftoop to Faith, when we have reafon fo to do. We are to underftand then, that there is in us a twofold Reafon; one direct, coming from the Objects we difcourfe on; the other reflex, reflecting upon Reafon, and confidering how far it can go; this often forces us to fubmit our direct Reafon even to human Authority. So an ignorant Peafant looking upon the Stars in a clear Night, according to direct Reafon rifing from his Senfes, judges them not an Inch Diameter, and that ten or twenty of them join'd together would fcarce equal a Full Moon; but he hears all Mathematicians and learned Men agree, that each Star far exceeds the Moon, nay, and the whole Globe of the Earth; he fubmits his direct Reafon to this Authority, and by reflex Reafon difcourfes thus: *I, who am an ignorant Man, may well be deceived; therefore thefe learned Men all agreeing, I muft in prudence yield.* So he fubmits his direct Reafon even to human Authority, and is taught fo to do by reflex Reafon, and the very Light of Nature. This is more evident in the Myfteries of our Faith: Direct Reafon tells us, a Trinity in a perfect Unity is impoffible; but reflex

Reafon

SERMON XXII.

264

Reason corrects this Errour, discoursing thus: *My Understanding is but Finite and Limited; Almighty God is Infinite, and would not be God, if he were not in himself more than my weak and feeble Capacity can conceive: If then I have a moral Certainty, that my great God has reveal'd himself to be Three and One; if his Holy Church, which put into my Hands the Scripture it self, assuring me, that it is the Word of God, interprets these Words,* These three are one, St. John's *first Epist. c.* v. v. 7. *and these other,* I and my Father are one, St. John's *Gospel, c.* x. v. 39. *If, I say, this Church interprets these Words in a real strict Sense, which otherwise might bear a more easy Interpretation in a metaphorical or figurative sense, I must and will believe it, tho' it cost me the last Drop of my Blood, what seeming Impossibilities soever Sense and direct Reason objects against it; and this I am taught by reflex Reason, and the Light of Nature it self; this is a Duty I owe to my great God, to acknowledge that I ought to believe more than I can understand.* From this Discourse I hope it appears clear enough, how rational the Mysteries of our Faith are, and how irrational it is to discredit them upon this account, that we cannot understand them. This is a

Principle

Principle, which ought to be the Ground of
our Belief, *viz. That God can reveal more
than we can underſtand*; and that many
things to our Weakneſs ſeem impoſſible,
which to our great God are very feaſible;
this the Light of Nature teaches us, and it
muſt carry us through all the profound,
hard Myſteries of our Faith. To deny a
thing upon this account, that it contradicts
Senſe and direct Reaſon, is irrational, injurious to Almighty God, and deſtructive to
Chriſtianity. It is irrational; for Reaſon
teaches us, that our Senſes and direct Reaſon are often miſtaken: How often does
the Mathematician and natural Philoſopher
at firſt think *that* a Demonſtration, which
afterwards he finds, either by his own Study, or another's Diſcovery, to be a Paralo-
giſm? 'Tis injurious to God, becauſe it
limits his Omnipotence to our Weakneſs;
'tis deſtructive to Chriſtianity, becauſe it
deſtroys the two chief Myſteries of Chriſtianity, the Trinity and Incarnation, both
which ſeemingly contradict direct Reaſon.
I do not believe Chriſt to be a natural Door,
tho' I hear him ſay, *I am a Door*, *John c.*
x. *v.* 9. nor a natural Vine, tho' I hear
him ſay, *I am the true Vine*, *John c.* xv.
v. 1. but God forbid I ſhould deny either

Vol. II.   M m   upon

SERMON XXII.

266

upon this account, that I cannot underftand how it can poffibly be done; but I
deny it, becaufe the Church teaches me that
I muft underftand thefe Words in a Metaphorical Senfe. There have been Herefies
from the Apoftles times downwards to our
Age, and many have died obftinate in their
Herefy; but I verily believe, that both
their Herefy and Obftinacy proceeded from
a want of this Principle, *That God can reveal more than we can underftand.* Let us
then pay this Duty to our great God, an
humble Acknowledgment of our Weaknefs
and his Power, that he can reveal more,
infinitely more, than we are able to conceive.
And fo much for my firft Part, of the Trinity as it is the Object of our Faith; Let us
now launch forth into a Sea of Love, and
confider this great Myftery as the thrice
happy Object of our Affections.

THE Almighty Architect created Man
according to his perfect Image, with intent
to make him happy for an Eternity in the
perfect Enjoyment of his God; and therefore has imprinted in his Soul fo violent an
Appetite and Defire of that bleffed Fruition,
that let a thoufand Worlds join their Stocks
together, let Men and Angels, and all that is
created, confpire to regale him, his capaci-
ous

ous Heart will never be perfectly satiated, never at rest and quiet, but in the divine Embraces of an Omnipotent, Immense, Eternal Trinity, the Fountain of all Beauty and Amability. O you young Gallants of the World, who spend your Time, Fortunes, Life and all, in the pursuit of a fading Beauty, a Rose surrounded with so many pricking Thorns of Cares and Sollicitude, a Flower so soon wither'd with Time, so often blasted with Sickness, so easily cropped by Death; stop this your unadvised Career, and know, that you are far out of your Way, if you pretend to look for Happiness in the Enjoyment of mortal Beauty. 'Tis true, your Souls were created to love and enjoy a Beauty, but a true and infinite one, for an Eternity; not a false Representation thereof for a Moment; 'tis the Blindness of your Understandings, and Pravity of your Wills (the sad Effects of Original Sin) that make you thus mistake the Object of your Happiness, and apply your natural or innate Appetite to Creatures, which in reality seeks only the Creator, One in Substance, and Three in Persons.

LET us then raise our Thoughts as high as Faith can carry them, to the Contemplation of this all-beatifying Object,

which

SERMON XXII.

268

which will be our eternal Blifs, if we make
not our felves fo miferable as eternally to
perifh. Firft then, Each-Perfon is Omnipotent, Eternal, Immenfe, All-knowing,
infinite in Wifdom, Goodnefs, and all Perfections; from the Complex of which ari-
fes fo great an Amability and Beauty, that
no rational Creature can behold it and not
prefently fall in love with it, fo far, that
whilft the happy Soul enjoys this Vifion,
no created Beauty, tho' never fo exact and
charming, can make any Impreffion in her,
but only as fhe fees it clearly reprefented in
the divine Idea's, and fuper-eminently contain'd in the Object fhe above all admires
and loves. Nay, even in this Night of
Mortality, fome Souls, by the help of divine Grace and Light of Faith, arrive to fo
high a pitch of divine Love, that nothing
here below, neither Pleafure nor Torment,
can move them. So St. *Vincent* in a Bed of
Rofes contemns the Allurements of Pleafures; and St. *Laurence* in a Bed of Flames,
upon a Gridiron, the Cruelty of Tyranny.
How many have fled to the remoteft De-
ferts? How many have fhut themfelves up
in Monafteries, betwixt four Walls of a
little Cell, not to be diverted from the delicious Contemplation of their great God?
Now

Now all this Amability is common to all
Three Perfons, with this Difference, that
in the Father it is originally as in a Fountain, received from no other Perfon ; in the
Son it is received by Communication from
the Father ; in the Holy Ghoft, from the
Father and the Son. Which very Communication is infinitely amiable, had we Eyes
to behold it. The chief Property of the Father is to fpeak ; which he does not to the
Ear, but to the Heart and Eye of the Soul,
delivering his great Word with fo divine a
Grace, that the moft delicious Voice that
ever was heard, the moft agreeable Manner
that ever a pure Creature fpoke with, is but
a meer Stuttering and Stammering, if compared to it. But the chief Perfection of
Speaking is taken from the Word fpoken ;
if that be clear, expreffive, fincere, and
eloquent, both it, and he who fpeaks it,
become in a high degree amiable. The eternal Word reprefents its Object to your
View, infinitely clearer than that could reprefent it felf tho' never fo intimately prefent ; fo expreffive it is, that being but one
only Word, it expreffes all Truth, all
Creatures, whether actual, or but barely
poffible ; all the delicious Objects of our
Senfes, whatever can be feen or heard, all
the

SERMON XXII.

the Truths our Underſtanding is able to conceive, all the Delights our Will can deſire :
'Tis moſt ſincere and true, expreſſing all
juſt as 'tis repreſented in the divine Knowledge, as it is in itſelf; 'tis eloquent above
Expreſſion, exhibiting to our View all the
Tropes and Figures, all the Art and Skill
of ſpeaking, that is poſſible.

Now from the eternal Father thus ſpeaking, and from the eternal Word thus expreſſing, muſt needs proceed an infinitely
amiable Love. What can be more amiable
than Love it ſelf? Love, I ſay, a divine,
and infinitely perfect Love of an infinitely
beautiful God. *Quàm bonus & ſuavis eſt,
Domine, Spiritus tuus!* How good, how
ſweet is thy divine Spirit ! How good, dif-
fuſing it ſelf by Grace and Charity in pious
Souls ; how ſweet, giving them even in
this Life by anticipation a Taſte of thoſe Joys,
which will beatify them for all Eternity in
the next. The Perfection of Love is taken
from the Lover, the Beloved, and the natural Intenſeneſs of the Love ; the nobler
the Lover is, alſo the more deſerving the
Beloved is, the perfecter is the Love. The
Lover here are the three Perſons of the Blef-
ſed Trinity, the Beloved are the ſame three
Perſons meeting and embracing each other

in

in the perfect Unity of one God. The Father loves the Son ; the Son loves the Father ; the Father and the Son love the Holy Ghoſt, the Holy Ghoſt reciprocally loves the Father and the Son, and moreover is the very Love whereby they love each other, all infinite in all Perfections. Dearly beloved Chriſtians, no Tongue or Pen can ever expreſs the Amability of the three Divine Perſons ; it may perhaps by a pious Soul in Prayer be felt, and as it were taſted ; expreſſed in Words it cannot be. Do you deſire to experience, even in this Life, a feeling and taſte of it ? Remember what the great *Moſes* was bid to do, when he approach'd the burning Buſh, *Gen c.* iii. *v.* 3. *Draw not nigh hither, put of thy ſhoes* ; we muſt not approach to contemplate this great Myſtery, till we have caſt off all the Dirt and Duſt of terrene Deſires ; our Converſation muſt be no more on Earth, but in Heaven ; Almighty God never regales ſenſual Souls with ſpiritual Delights ; but ſuch as neither find, nor ſo much as ſeek after the vain Paſtimes of this World. This makes your great Saints proclaim War againſt Fleſh and Blood, always annoying, vexing, and mortifying their Bodies, becauſe they experience, that the more they withdraw themſelves from
Earth,

272　　　　S E R M O N XXII.

Earth, the more Almighty God permits
them to tafte of Heaven. 'Tis a real Truth
(though few will believe it) that none lead
a pleafanter Life in this World, than thofe
who give themfelves wholly to Almighty
God; for his divine Majefty will never be
overcome in Love. The three Perfons of
the Bleffed Trinity will love fuch a Soul,
come to it, and regale it, according to our
Saviour's Promife, St. *John c.* xiv. *v.* 23. *If*
any Man love me he will keep my Words, and
my Father will love him, and we will come
unto him, and make our abode with him:
The eternal Father will perfect that Image
he created to his Likenefs; the Son will illu-
minate it with the Rays of new fupernatural Lights; the Holy Ghoft will fweetly
inflame it with divine Love. But remember the Condition, we muft keep his Commandments: and in order to this, let us
look upon the facred Trinity as a Pattern to
fquare our Actions by, which is my third
Point.

You will, perhaps, wonder, how fo
profound and incomprehenfible a Myftery
can ever ferve us as a Pattern for our poor
and weak Actions. Is it poffible for a miferable Creature to imitate thefe ineffable
Operations of the divine Perfons? But remember

member, that our Soul, tho' now by Original Sin plunged in Flesh and Blood, is created to the perfect Image of her God ; *God made man to his own image Gen.* i. 27. What wonder then if we endeavour to reform the Picture, by comparing it with the *Prototypon?* Besides, does not our Saviour himself assign the Perfection of his eternal Father for a Pattern to frame ours by ? *Be you perfect* (says he) *as your Father which is in Heaven is perfect* ; *Matth. c.* v. *v.* 48. Come then, let us once more cast an Eye towards this great Mystery, and see whether we cannot find something for our Imitation. We learn'd to believe in the first Part, to love in the Second ; let us learn to rectify our exterior Actions in the Third. The first thing, which occurs for our Imitation, is the Unity of all three Persons in one Substance : We cannot identify our Natures really distinct, but we may unite them by Charity and Love. Hence Christ, just before his Passion, prays to his eternal Father, in St. *John c.* xvii. *v.* 20, 21. not only for his Apostles, but for all that were to believe by their Word, *That they might be one as his Father in him, and he in his Father are One.* We must remember, we are all Members of the same Body, under the same Head *Christ,* and consequently each

VOL. II.　　N n　　　　one

S E R M O N   XXII.

one is to be in one another, fo as to make his Intereſt our own; we ought to condole as much for the Adverſity of another, and rejoice for his Proſperity, as if it were our own; we muſt redreſs the Neceſſity of another, as much as if it were our own; we muſt as earneſtly concur to one another's Preferment, as to our own, and rejoice as much for it. Then Almighty God will look upon us as making one with his Servants; and what our Tepidity does not deſerve, he'll bountifully confer upon us, for their ſakes, with whom Charity has united us : For tho' you are endow'd with never ſo great Gifts and Virtues, *ſi charitatem non habuero*, if Charity be wanting, if you make not one with all the faithful Believers, all is nothing. Away then with all Piques, all Miſunderſtandings, all envious Practices; let us all become one Soul by a perfect Love. Our great God Incarnate has ſo united himſelf to us, that he takes as done to himſelf whatſoever is done to another, and when he comes to judge, will reward charitable Actions done to our Neighbour, as done to himſelf; and revenge all Injuries, as offer'd to himſelf. He will invite the Elect to an eternal Happineſs, not as having done charitable Actions to their Neighbours, but to himſelf; and condemn to eternal Torments
the

the Reprobate, as injurious to himfelf: He will not fay, come you Bleffed, becaufe you gave an Alms to fuch a poor Man; but, becaufe you gave it to me: Nor, go you Curfed, becaufe you refufed to redrefs the Neceffity of fuch a poor Body; but of me. If then Chrift makes himfelf one with his Servants, he who permits himfelf to be feparated by Envy and Malice from his Fellow-fervants, doth in effect feparate himfelf from Chrift.

In the fecond place, we muft imitate each Perfon in their Properties: The Father fpeaketh according to his Knowledge, conforming his Speech to his Thoughts, and expreffes all in one only Word: This muft teach us Sincerity, to fpeak what we think, and no more than we know. The eternal Father is the Father of Truth; the Devil, his deadly Enemy, the Father of Lies: Chufe what Pattern you'll follow. Befides, we muft learn to avoid Multiplicity and Idlenefs of Speech: The eternal Father expreffes all in one Word, and that neceffary; let us ufe our felves to fpeak little, for happy is he who exceeds not in Speech, and many Words always involve an Offence of God.

From the Son let us learn to exprefs things as they are in reality, not as our in-

ordinate

276   S E R M O N   XXII.

ordinate Paſſions would have them. The
eternal Word proceeds *per Intellectum*, by
the Underſtanding ; not *per Voluntatem*, by
the Will : But our Words often proceed not
from our Underſtanding, from a certain Knowledge of the thing, but from our Will ; ſo if
any Abſurdity be done, we preſently lay it at
their Doors we have a Pique againſt (ſo in
the primitive Church the Heathens aſcribed
all Miſchiefs and Miſchances to the Chriſtians, as we read in *Tertullian* and others)
Thoſe damn'd, what you pleaſe, did it. From
whence comes this Word ? From a knowledge of the Fact ? No ; but from the Malice of our Will. This is prepoſterous ; our
Words muſt proceed, as the eternal Word
does, from the Underſtanding, from a perfect Knowledge of what we ſpeak.

    F<small>ROM</small> the Holy Ghoſt we muſt learn
what and how to love. The prime and
final Object of our Love muſt be Almighty
God, other things we are to love only in relation to him ; he is the Fountain of all Good,
and therefore we muſt remember, when we
meet with any thing amiable, that it is but
a Rivulet flowing from that great Fountain,
and to be found in greater Perfection there.
The Holy Spirit proceeds from the Father
ſpeaking, and the Word expreſſing the divine *Being* infinitely amiable. Let all our
Love

On Trinity-Sunday.

Love proceed fo, not from a falfe Delufion
of our Senfes, making us fix on Creatures
tho' very meanly amiable, and that with
an Amability meerly participated and derived
from the Fountain of Amability. As often
as we feel our Hearts moved to a Tendernefs
and Kindnefs, let us confider from what it
proceeds; is it from a Word fpeaking the
Creature amiable without mentioning the
Creator ? O then it comes from a falfe,
from a lying Word; 'tis illegitimate, it muft
not inherit your Heart, you muft caft it out,
'tis a bafe fervile Affection, *ejice ancillam*; but
the true Legitimate Poffeffor of your Heart
muft be a divine Love, proceeding from a
Word expreffing the divine Fountain of all
Perfection.

But I muft draw towards an end not to
abufe your Patience; we have then learn'd
in my firft Part, to believe what we cannot
underftand, feeing that God would not be
God, could he not reveal of himfelf more
than we can comprehend. My fecond Part
has led us to the Fountain of all Amability,
and pointed unto us the true Center of our
Hearts. In my third Part we have learn'd
to imitate all three Perfons in tending to a
perfect Unity by Charity; and each Perfon in
their Properties; the Father, in being fincere,
fpeaking what we know, and in as few Words
as we can; the Son, in feeing that our Words
proceed from Knowledge not from Affection;

from

SERMON XXII.

278

from Reafon, not from Paffion: The Holy
Ghoft, in loving God only as our End, and all
things elfe meerly in relation to him. There
only now remains, that with the Tears of
Penance, Acts of perfect Contrition, we
wafh away whatever deform'd the facred
Image of the Trinity in our Souls, and beg
Strength, Light and Grace to keep it entire
for the future. *O Omnipotent Father, whofe*
Power is without Limits, give us ftrength to
believe what we cannot underftand, to love
what our Senfes cannot reach, to keep thy Image
in our Souls entire againft the World, Flefh
and Devil, who endeavours to dif-figure it.
O Eternal Word! Increated Wifdom, illu-
minate our Souls with thy divine Rays, that
our interior and exterior Words may fpeak
according to Faith and Reafon, prefer Eter-
nity before Time, Heaven before Earth, the
Creator before the Creature. O Holy Spi-
rit, diffufe thy Grace and Charity in our
Souls, that we may all in a perfect Union be
One, as the Father, Son, and Holy Ghoft are
One ; that appearing in the laft dreadful Day
of Doom, we may appear not feparated, but
united with the Elect, and be received into e-
ternal Happinefs, as carrying clearly imprinted
in our Souls the characteriftical Note of a Chri-
ftian, grateful to Heaven, terrible to Hell,
beneficial to Earth, the Sign of the Holy Crofs,
In the Name of the Father, Son, and Holy
Ghoft, *Amen.*

A

[William Crathorne (ed.)], *Mr Gother's Spiritual Works: In Sixteen Tomes. Tome I. Instructions on the Epistles and Gospels of the Sundays from Advent to Trinity Sunday, (Lent excepted). Part I. There Are Added General Indexes and Tables to each Tome. Faithfully Corrected* (London, 1718), pp. 234–77

The present text is from the first volume of the first edition of *Mr Gother's Spiritual Works: In Sixteen Tomes* compiled by William Crathorne (1670–1740), the Douai professor and missioner in Hammersmith whom the Vicar Apostolic Bonaventure Giffard (1642–1734) commissioned to edit Gother's works of edification. Other editions of *Mr Gother's Spiritual Works* were published in eighteen volumes in London in [1726] and in sixteen volumes in Newcastle-upon-Tyne in [1792]. The volumes included such items as *Instructions for the Afflicted and Sick*; *Instructions for Masters, Traders, Labourers, Servants, Apprentices, Youths etc.*; and *A Practical Catechism, Divided into Fifty-Two Lessons, for Each Sunday in the Year.*

Gother's *Spiritual Works* were originally delivered as allocutions, given twice every Sunday and feast-day and on every day each Lent, during the quiet years of his domestic chaplaincy, between 1688 – when he took up his position as resident priest to George and Anastasia Holme at Warkworth, Northamptonshire – and his death in 1704 (see vol. 1, *A Papist Misrepresented*, pp. 1–35). Tracts of instruction designed for internal didactic purposes within the Catholic community, the *Spiritual Works* are indeed markedly different in tone and content from the seventeen combative controversial works Gother produced in James II's reign. Their emphases are on morality, good neighbourliness, charity, a peaceful demeanour and an overall address to the Catholic laity living in the everyday world of work in which they have their dutiful 'callings', such as those of parents, employees, employers and priests. In their very practicality, Gother's pastoral writings also represent a radical abandonment of the other-worldly mystical approach characteristic of the Benedictine devotionalist Augustine Baker (1575–1641).[1] At the same time – and anticipating the standpoint of Richard Challoner – Gother, in the undemonstrative sobriety of his writing, and with his roots in the medieval English tradition of spiritual literature, has seemed quintessentially English in his Catholic piety, indeed devising a mildly 'ecumenical' spirituality ideally suited to the context in which Georgian Catholics lived.[2]

Certainly, he avoided excess, whether of credulity over miracles or of excessive mariolatry, but stressed instead the sacraments, moderate self-denial, and Scripture (especially St Paul). While he drew on the Fathers, on the medieval devotional school including Thomas a Kempis (1379–1471) and on some of the writers of the Catholic Reformation of the sixteenth and seventeenth centuries, he was not too far removed from the mainstream of English Protestant spiritual writing in its golden age of the seventeenth and eighteen centuries – and he was as fearful as any concerned Protestant at his country's apparent drift into atheism, irreligion and profanity.

1.   Vincent Guazzelli, 'John Gother: priest', *The Clergy Review*, New Series, 26 (1946), pp. 583–590.

2.   Sister Marion Norman, 'John Gother and the English Way of Spirituality', *Recusant History*, 1972, pp. 306–14.

Mr. *GOTHER's*

Spiritual Works:

In Sixteen Tomes.

TOME I.

Instructions on the Epistles and Gospels of the *Sundays*, from *Advent* to *Trinity-Sunday*, (*Lent* excepted.)

PART I.

There are added,
General *Indexes* and *Tables* to each TOME.

Faithfully Corrected.

LONDON:
Printed in the Year 1718.

Inſtructions

FOR THE

WHOLE YEAR.

PART I.

TOME I.

FOR

SUNDAYS,

BEING

Practical Thoughts on the *Epiſtles* and *Goſpels* of all the *Sundays* and *Moveable Feaſts*, from *Advent* to *Whitſunday*, excepting thoſe of *Lent*.

Faithfully Corrected.

Printed in the Year 1718.

234   II. *Sunday after Eafter.*

And if, reflecting now upon the whole, we confider wherein it is we follow the Example of our Lord in peaceably Suffering, according to the Copy he has fet us, truly, 'tis hard to find it : for how do we imitate him, whilft he voluntarily chofe to fuffer, and we take all the care we can to avoid it ? How are we his Followers, whilft we take a way quite contrary to his Example, ufing all poffible Endea-vours to decline whatever is capable of mortifying us ; and whenever we are furpriz'd with it againft our Wills, we then render it ufelefs and unchriftian, by Paffion or Impatience ? O bleffed Redeemer, how far is this from the true Character of thy Difciple ? Thou haft fuffer'd, to teach us to fuffer; and if thy Example has no effect on me, but I am ftill follicitous to gratify my own Inclinations, rather than be directed by thy Rule, how can I pretend to be thy Follower ? And if reigning with thee, be promis'd upon condition of Suffering, is it not plain, by avoiding Suffering, I fet Heaven at a greater dif-tance from me ?

II. *Sun-*

II. *Sunday after Easter.*
G O S P E L.

John C. 10. V. 11. ends V. 16.

I Am the Good Shepherd. The Good Shepherd gives his Life for his Sheep. Chriſt fill'd up this Character in a very particular manner, giving his Life for the Salvation of Man, in his Prayers, in his Labours, in his Journeys, in his Preaching, in his Miracles, in all he did, in all he ſuffer'd, and at the End, offering it a Sacrifice on the Croſs for their Redemption. A Paſtor cannot be Good, but by continual Endeavours for coming up to this Character. His daily Buſineſs muſt be to give his Life for his Sheep. He muſt give his Labour for them, in taking Pains for their Inſtruction, and being ever ready to Comfort and Aſſiſt them in all their Spiritual Neceſſities. He muſt give his Thoughts for them, in a perpetual Sollicitude for their good. He muſt give his Prayers for them, in daily petitioning in their behalf, and in rendering God Propitious to them. He muſt give his Peace for them, by drawing upon himſelf the Diſlikes, Calumnies and Inſults of Men, by thoſe Unwelcome Truths, which his Duty obliges him to ſpeak. He muſt give

L 6   his

236   II. *Sunday after Easter.*

his Friends for them, by letting no Considerations prevail for his conniving at
such things, which cannot be tolerated,
without prejudice to Innocence or Justice, and cannot be reprov'd but with his
Loss.   He must give away many Satif-
factions for them, in considering not only, what is lawful, but likewise what is expedient; that so he may not give Offence
tohe Weak, nor Encouragement to the
Vicious. *Many things may be in themselves
Indifferent, and yet are not so to him; because an ill use is likely to be made of them
by some of the Flock, for justifying themselves in such things, which are unjustifiable.
Hence, how many Inclinations must be renounce, that so his Life may not countenance, but be a standing Censure of their
Disorders, who are under his Care, and
which he is oblig'd, by his Post, to study all
ways to redress? If therefore he observes a
general Failing in the Flock, in the Love of
Vanity and Pride; and that by the expen-
sive Support of these Evils, Children, Families, and Poor are robb'd: Must not his Life
Preach up the Humility and Poverty of the
Gospel, in such a Dress, that Pride and Affectation may take no shelter under his Example? And if Circumstances are such, as
will not allow the Habit of his Profession,
must not he, at least, come as near it as he
can, and not let the Iniquity of the Times,
be made a Plea for a Vain and Extravagant
Hu-*

II. *Sunday after Easter.* 237

Humour? If the *Vice* of his *Flock* be Intemperance in *Drink*, and *Mis-spending* both *Time* and *Money* in *Idle Company*, to the neglect both of *Soul*, and *Family Duties*; ought not his *Example* to be the Condemnation of their *Crimes*, by *scrupulously* declining such *Company*, and *Idle Meetings*, and never *setting Foot* within those *Places* of *Sin*; that so the *Excesses* of the *Flock* may have no *Countenance* from his *Indiscreet*, though *otherwise Innocent Divertisement*? If the *Sin* of the *Flock* be in *Extravagant Gaming*, in *neglect* of *Order*, or *Family Discipline*, or *Covetousness*; ought not he to *shew* his *Abhorrence* of their *Evil Ways*, by never joining with their *Prodigality*, nor even *standing* to be a *Witness* of it; by being *exact* in the *Order* of his *Life*, and keeping good *Hours*; and avoiding every thing, that betrays a *love* of *Interest* and *Money*, or has the *look* of a *greedy* or *grasping Humour*?

In this manner he ought to *Preach against* the *Disorders* of his *Flock*, and *Condemn all* their *Irregularities* by his *Example*; thus he is to be Lux Mundi, a *Light shewing* the *Way* of *God's Commandments*. And if this cannot be, but by *Violence* to *Inclination*, it is the *Task* he has undertaken, and without it he cannot *satisfy* the *Duties* of his *Charge*. He cannot *deserve* the *Character* of *Good*, but by giving his *Life* for his *Sheep*, and in this manner is he daily to give it for them.

For

238   II. *Sunday after Easter.*

For if Nature and Corruption so far prevail, that his Sollicitude is more for his own Quiet and Interest, than the Good of his Flock; if by his Example he encourages those Evils in them, which he ought to reform, he is not to be esteem'd a Shepherd, but a Hireling; and 'tis well if he be not found to have taken part with the Wolves, in helping to devour those, whom he undertook to preserve.

This Character then of Christ being the Good Shepherd, is particularly design'd for the Direction of Pastors: but there's another in this Gospel, which is for the Instruction both of Pastors and People; that is, where Christ says, *I know my Sheep, and my Sheep know me.* All that are in the Fold of Christ, in whatever Degree, cannot be truly his Sheep, except they know Christ, as they are known by him. The Reason is, because they are to follow him; and how shall they do this, if they do not know him? He has taught them by his Example what they are to do: And hence S. *Augustin* says, The Son of God became Incarnate, not only to Redeem us by Suffering, but also, that being made Man, he might be an Example to us of all Virtues. By his Example he has taught us the Love of our Neighbour: *Love one another, even*

II. *Sunday after Easter.* 239

as I have loved you. He has taught us Meeknefs; *Learn of me, becaufe I am Meek, and Humble of Heart.* He has taught us to forgive Injuries; *Bear with one another, and forgive one another, if any one has a Complaint againft another: as our Lord has forgiven you, fo do you alfo forgive.* He has taught us to fuffer reproaches; *The Difciple is not above his Mafter; if they have called the Mafter of the Family* Beelzebub, *how much more thofe of his Houfhold?* He has taught us to fuffer Perfecution; *The Servant is not greater than his Mafter; if they have perfecuted me, they will perfecute you alfo. If they hate you, know, that they have firft hated me.*

Now Chrift having given himfelf for a Rule, how fhall they follow it, if they know not him? There is a neceffity, then of knowing of Chrift; and there can be no hopes, either of a Virtuous Life, or of the Fruit of it, which is Eternal Happinefs, but what is built upon this Knowledge; whence S. *John* fays, *This is Life Everlafting, to know thee the only God, and whom thou haft fent, Jefus Chrift.* Where this Knowledge is not, Men muft neceffarily walk, as St. *Paul* faid to the *Ephefians,* in the Vanity of their own Senfe, having their Underftanding clouded with Darknefs: For

240 **II.** *Sunday after Easter.*

For this Darkness is what every one
brings with him into the World ; and
it cannot be remov'd but by Christ,
who is the Light, that enlightens every
one that comes into the World. What
then must Christians do ? If they think
of following Christ, they must learn to
know Christ, and him Crucified, because they cannot abide in Christ, except they walk as he walk'd. If the
Pastors know him, they will, like him,
give their Lives for their Sheep. If
the Flock know him, they will make
his Example their Rule, and their Practice will be in all Charity, Patience,
Meekness and Humility, because this
is the Way he has shew'd them.

What then is all other Knowledge,
without this ? What is the Learning of
Pastors, if they know not Christ ? By
other Sciences they may gain Applause
with Men; but 'tis by the Study of
Christ only, they can save their own
Souls, and guide their Flock in the Ways
of Salvation. What are all other Arts
and Accomplishments of the Flock ?
They may be Ornamental or Gainful,
as to this World ; but what help are
they for gaining that which is Eternal ?

Does not then the Christian World
forget its Christianity, when all the
Expense in the Education of Youth, is
to

II. *Sunday after Easter.*   241

to teach them to be Vain, to be in Love with themselves, and to court the Admiration of others; when the great Concern is in Modes and Carriage, and the leaft part of their Care is to learn Chrift; nay, when they fo far follow the World, as to forget Chrift, and his Spirit, and let a Univerfal Pride be Authoriz'd amongft them? Do not they forget their Chriftianity, whilft Fraud, Injuftice, Oppreffion, Malice, Diffenfions, Animofities, Revenge &c, are in fuch Repute, that there's more danger of becoming a Reproach amongft them, by ftrictly following the Gofpel, than by forfaking it? Is this to be a Chriftian? 'Tis but too plain therefore, O Jefus, that amongft thofe, who profefs thy Name, they are but few, that know thee. A great Zeal is pretended for Religion; but where is the Zeal for walking by thy Example, and manifefting thy Gofpel by the Practice of our Lives? Teach us therefore, we befeech thee, to be more fincere in what we profefs, enlarge our Knowledge of thee; give us a docil Heart, that we may in all things hear thy Voice, and not be Followers of the World, while we make Profeffion of following thee; for thus only can we be thy Sheep, and thou our Paftor.

III. *Sun-*

242   III. *Sunday after Easter.*

❦❦❦❦❦❦❦❦❦❦❦❦

III. *Sunday after Easter.*
EPISTLE.

1 *Pet.* C. 2. V. 11. ends V. 18.

BRethren, I exhort you, as *Strangers and Travellers,* to abstain from carnal Desires, which war against the Soul. The Direction and Method of a Christian Life, is fully compriz'd in these two Words, of *Strangers* and *Travellers,* in both which the Apostle informs us, that we are not of this World, that we belong to another; that as long as we are in this World, we ought to consider it as a Strange Country, and that, as Travellers, we are only going thro' it. As therefore Strangers are not allow'd to purchase in a Foreign Country, nor settle an Inheritance there; as Travellers stop not on their Journey, but only to inform themselves of the nearest and safest way home: they march diligently whilst 'tis day, and for Rest and Nourishment, they only take, what is necessary to enable them to perform their Journey: If they are revil'd or affronted on their Way, they go on still, make a Jest of it, and let no sort of anger or ill will seize their

Spi-

III. *Sunday after Easter.* 243

Spirits, nor think in the leaft of any revenge : if they fee what delights them,
whether as to Houfes, Sports, Company, Entertainments, &c; thefe raife fome
pleafing Thoughts indeed : and though
they may ftop to caft a paffing Eye, yet
they go on ftill, not daring to take part
in thefe Diverfions, left thus hindred,
they fhould not reach their Home.
Thus their main concern is ever to
advance, and to deny themfelves every
thing, that may either ftop or clog
them in the way. If it rains or blows,
they go on with patience through it,
hoping it will foon give over : if the
ways are uneafy, heavy, or deep, they
march on ftill, hoping before long, the
ways will mend.

Oh ! that we could thus go through
this World, and ever efteem ourfelves
no otherwife than Strangers or Travellers : how would this put us upon
paffing by whatever is dangerous or
hurtful to us, and never let us ftop
fo eafily at what delights, without reflecting, how far fuch Amufements may
hinder us from ever feeing our Journey's end ? How fhould we pafs by many Inconveniencies without concern :
and be careful never to burthen ourfelves with fo much bufinefs of the
Inn, as to forget, that we have farther

ftill

244 III. *Sunday after Easter.*

still to go? Heaven is our Country, and as we are Christians, 'tis thither we pretend. Art thou now going on, Dear Christian? Or art thou at a stand? Or goest thou backward? If Business hinder thee, remember, the great Business of one, that's on the way, is to be going on: there are many things thou wouldst willingly be doing on a Journey, but only thou canst not stay: The Business, that hinders thee from going to Heaven, is not thine, and must either be laid aside, or the concern of it must be lessen'd. If Troubles hinder thee, learn to manage them right, and they'll help thee forward. If it be Sloth that hinders, spur on the Beast. But if it be thy Pleasures and Passions; these must necessarily be avoided and reform'd. I *exhort you to abstain from Carnal Desires, which war against the Soul.* Every thing is Carnal, that keeps thee from God. .Whatever it be, that is not thy Duty, or in order to it, is only to feed some Passion; and thou wilt soon discover, 'tis the corruption of thy Heart, which withdrawing thee from God, puts thee upon seeking other satisfactions out of him. And all these generally war against the Soul; for the Soul being design'd for an Inheritance above, and the Possession of an
eternal

III. *Sunday after Easter.*   245

eternal Good, all things created are much beneath that End, and all Affections to them muft greatly prejudice the Soul ; the ftronger thefe are, the more they weaken the Defires of Heaven ; they ftop the Chriftian on his way, make him in love with his Inn, and caufe an unwillingnefs to leave it ; and is not this injurious to his great Concern ; whilft, as the Love of the World grows in him, fo in proportion is diminifh'd the Love of God ? The Heart of Man is very ftraight ; Affeftions of no kind can rife there to any degree, but it muft neceffarily be to the lefs'ning of fome others : and 'tis thus the wicked, and even unwary Chriftians, in their Pilgrimage below, come by degrees to forget they are Strangers and Travellers here.

Another Caution the Apoftle gives to as many as are on this Journey ; that is, to Edify all by good Example and holy Converfation. For this is a Duty common to every Chriftian, to be fo watchful in all their Aftions, as to do nothing that may offend or fcandalize their Neighbour : It being impoffible there fhould be true Charity, where one prefers his own particular Satisfaftion before the Salvation of others : Salvation, I fay, for tho' there be no Fault

in

246   III. *Sunday after Easter.*

in me, when some, thro' a Disposition
notoriously unjust, are scandaliz'd at
Actions truly good and beneficial to my
Soul ; yet there can be no Excuse for
those, who yielding to the violence of
their own Desires, live in the continual
practice of great Disorders, and such
Liberties, which give sufficient grounds
of Offence to others, and make Strangers
blaspheme that Church, whose Members they are, as guilty of encouraging
those Vices which they see practis'd by
such as belong to it.   In this number
must be included all those, who cul-
pably live in the ill habit of Cursing,
Swearing, Lying, Drinking, Covetousness or Cheating : such as use immodest
Discourses or Actions, such as give
themselves to Passion, Revenge, or
Backbiting, who through carelesness
neglect their Families, through prodigality or vain expenses expose them to
ruin, and through a Life of idleness,
betray a want of application to the
Means of Bliss : In fine, all those, whose
Lives run counter to their Profession,
who answer not the Obligations of their
State or Charge, whether Ecclesiastick,
or Civil : all these, with infinite others,
if not reform'd, will find no place for
excuse ; but must be condemn'd as
Enemies to themselves, in thus evidently

III. *Sunday after Easter.* 247

ly hazarding their eternal Welfare ; to their Neighbours, in giving them Scandal and ill Example ; and to their Church, in giving just occasion to Strangers to revile and blaspheme it. If these could but frame a true Idea of their own State, and see, how many Souls are defil'd with Sin, how many lie buried in Hell, drawn into this state of Misery through their ill Example : if they could see how many have been discourag'd from seeking the Truth, and quite put out of the way, by the Scandal of their Liberties : if they could hear, how many Blasphemies are cast out against God's Church, occasion'd by their loose and unexemplar Lives : this prospect would either oblige them to reform their Ways, by entring into the rigours of Penance, or if obstinate in their Sin, cast them into despair : For truly, it is accompanied with so many dreadful consequences, if consider'd in all its branches, into which it unhappily spreads itself, that it must needs terrify a Christian, to think, how many Souls he must give an account of besides his own ; and when he comes to reflect, the part he has acted in this Life, has been that of Devils, in suggesting and propagating Sin, and betraying Souls to Hell, it

must

248   III. *Sunday after Easter.*

muſt be a very powerful Grace to preſerve him from making this concluſion;
That his crime having a reſemblance
with the Devils, muſt certainly be as
unpardonable as theirs.   Look, O God
of Mercy, on theſe unhappy Chriſtians,
and by the effect of thy Grace, reclaim
them from their evil ways; preſerve
them from all deſpair; and turn their
Feet into the ways of thy Commandments.   Pardon us all our Sins, and forgive all thoſe, who have been miſled
by our ill Example.   Direct our Lives
in the Paths of Moderation and Prudence, that we may edify every Neighbour, and thus contribute to the removing that Scandal, which other's
Vices and Indiſcretion have drawn upon us.

III. *Sunday after Easter.*

G O S P E L.

John C. 16. V. 16. ends V. 22.

A Little *while, and now you ſhall not
ſee me; and again, a little while,
and you ſhall ſee me.* Chriſt Exercis'd
his Apoſtles with this change of his Ab-
ſence and Preſence.   He abſented himſelf from them by his Death; he again
was

III. *Sunday after Easter.* 249

was prefent with them by his Refur-rection : He abfented himfelf from them by Afcending into Heaven ; he again was prefent, by taking them, af-ter their Deaths, into the participation of his Glory. This fame is the Exer-cife he gives to all his Elect ; fome-times feeming to leave them, and then comforting them again with his Pre-fence ; and by this Conduct, through divers Changes, he prepares them for a more conftant Difpofition of Soul, and leads them to a State Unchange-able. He lets neither their Storms nor Calms be here without interruption, but with a wonderful variety mixes both Extremes. This St. *Chryfoftom* ob-ferves particularly in St. *Jofeph*, who, by a fingular Privilege of Grace, being chofen Spoufe to the Mother of Chrift, was not however privileged from thefe Trials : For obferving the Bleffed Vir-gin to be with Child, his Spirit was overwhelm'd with great Difquiets ; but prefently an Angel is fent, who removes all his Fears. Then feeing Jefus born, his Soul is enlarg'd with unfpeakable Joy ; but this Joy is foon follow'd with a fur-prizing Terrour, when he fees the whole City in Commotion, and a Jea-lous King feeking the Life of the Child. This Terrour is again fweetn'd

M with

250   III. *Sunday after Easter.*

with unexpected Comforts, when an unusual Star brings the Wife Men from the East, to Adore, and make their Offerings to their New-born King : But this Comfort is check'd with new Dangers ; *Herod* designs to destroy the Child, and they must retire into a Foreign Land.

If this was the Method of God with this Holy Patriarch, and Jesus is no sooner Born into the World, but he has his Share in it ; must not all Faithful Souls here prepare themselves against all surprize, if they experience no Comforts lasting, and that their most desirable Peace is interrupted with frequent Disquiets ? Their Business ought rather to be, in learning to submit to this Order of Providence, and to make that Improvement under it, as is design'd by him, whose Wisdom cannot be question'd in the Appointment.

There is no Disposition more necessary for a Christian, than that of a true disesteem of himself, and of all things in this World : And nothing can lead more directly to this, than the Experience of his own Inconstancy, and of all other things about him. 'Tis good, he should be convinc'd, that all things pass, and that his most settled Judgments are uncertain. How often does he

III. *Sunday after Easter.* 251

he think, when he is under the weight of Evils, that he shall never more have Comfort? And yet he finds Relief again, either by being deliver'd from his Oppression, or in the patient support of that, which before he believed to be intolerable. How often does he imagine, in time of interiour Peace, that he shall never more be mov'd : *Dixi in abundantia mea ; non movebor in æternum ;* and the Weakness, that follows upon this Presumption, does it not more fully convince him of his Inconstancy, than if he had been never forced from his ground ?

By these Vicissitudes then, and Changes, he comes at length to frame this settled Judgment of himself ; That he is without force, without vigour ; that he has nothing of his own to trust to ; and therefore is in a necessary dependance on the Divine Grace, to secure him against the Consequences of his own Weakness and Uncertainty. By the Experience of this Inconstancy, he learns to desire with more earnestness that Unchangeable Rest, which, in the other Life, shall be the Recompence of the Just, and to seek Establishment in the Divine Grace, whereby he may come to that Happy State.

M 2   The

252   III. *Sunday after Easter.*

The Chriſtian then muſt ſet this
down for a ſtanding Principle ; That
Uniformity is not to be expected in
this Life, either as to Body or Soul.
This Principle, when under Trouble,
is to be his Defence againſt Anxiety
and Deſpair ; the ſame, in time of
Peace, is to ballance his Mind againſt
Exceſs of Confidence and Preſump-
tion. For ſince Chriſt here in expreſs
Terms foretold his Apoſtles, that they
ſhould weep and mourn, while the
World rejoyc'd ; all the true Servants
of Chriſt may hence know, what Portion to expect ; and in this place of
Baniſhment, rather to look for Trouble than Peace. This is unavoidable,
as to their Spiritual State ; becauſe this
Life being appointed them, not to live
to themſelves, and the World, but to
learn to die to both, by a laborious diſ-
engagement from all Carnal and Corrupt Affections, which is the Death
of the Old Man, repreſented by the
Death of Chriſt ; hence the whole time
of Chriſtians here, comes to be a Life
of Mourning and Tears, becauſe there
is no forſaking that without Grief,
which is retain'd with Satisfaction, and
has Pleaſure in the Enjoyment ; there
is no dying to the World without
Trouble and Violence, ſince 'tis by
                                    this

III. *Sunday after Easter.* 253

this Violence they muſt die to the
World; And is it not hence plain,
that while the World rejoyces, they
muſt be in mourning; ſince, while
thoſe of the World are waiting upon their Inclinations, ſtudying all
ways to gratify both themſelves and
the World, and turning all the Bleſſings of God to this vile End, theſe
are labouring to mortify the ſame Inclinations, by denying them what with
moſt earneſtneſs they deſire?

Again, as to their Temporal Affairs,
they cannot fail of frequent occaſions
of Mourning; becauſe, on the one ſide,
God deſigning to perfect them in what
they propoſe, permits them not to have
long reſt or ſatisfaction in Creatures;
and therefore, on the motive of his
Goodneſs towards them, ſometimes deprives them of one Object of their Affections, ſometimes of another; and o-
ther ways thwarts them with many Difficulties, that by theſe Trials they may
come to know themſelves, and obſerving
thus both their Wants and Weakneſſes,
may ſee which way to direct their Labours and Prayers, and ſo gain a
more perfect command of themſelves.
Then, on the other ſide, the World
ſeldom fails of giving them ma-

M 3 ny

254 **III.** *Sunday after Easter.*

ny uneasy Exercises, First, By the course of its profess'd Impiety and Injustice, which they cannot see without Grief. Secondly, By raising Jealousies, Calumnies, and Scandals, in their Disfavour; and often managing these with so much dexterity, as to draw even the Good into an Interest against them. Thirdly, By making the Ways of Virtue so difficult, that they cannot possibly espouse the Cause of Justice, Innocence, and Truth, but by making all those their Enemies, who love nothing but Flattery and Dissimulation, and cannot bear either Opposition or Reproof, though in the most unwarrantable Ways, without being exasperated against those that undertake it; whence all, that know them, are under the necessity of betraying the Cause of Virtue, by a base Connivance, or of losing their Favour, by being Advocates for it. Thus the Portion of the Good, either from one side or other, comes to have a great mixture of Bitterness in it, and the Words of Christ are generally verified in them : *Amen, Amen,* I say to you, you shall mourn and weep, but the World shall rejoyce.

But however, though these Difficulties should continue even till Death, there is still this Comfort, that all
these

III. *Sunday after Eafter.*   255

thefe Evils, as Chrift has promis'd,
fhall in the other Life be chang'd into
endlefs Joys; and can it be then reafonable to make a difficulty in fubmit-
ting to them? For what are the Evils
of this Life, in comparifon of Eternity? They are not fo much as a Minute
in proportion to our Life, and who
would not imbrace fo fhort a Suffering,
when 'tis for avoiding that, which is
Eternal, and to be recompens'd with
Joy, that is Infinite? We are all, one
way or other, in continual Sollicitude
and Labour; and what is it generally
for, but fuch things, whofe quiet Enjoyment is many times fhorter, than
the trouble of getting them; and when
otherwife, 'tis for that which muft foon
end? Since therefore we are here to
Suffer, is it not the beft Management,
fo to order it, that it may be the Purchafe of Everlafting Happinefs? Thus,
O God, may we learn to be Wife.
Give us Grace peaceably to fubmit to
all thy Appointments; may neither
Quiet make us Prefume, nor Troubles
deject us; but may all be ballanc'd
with fuch Moderation of Spirit, as to
improve both in Calms and Storms.

IV. *Sunday after Easter.*
EPISTLE.

St. *James* C. 1. V. 17. ends V. 21.

*B*E *slow to Anger.* The Apostle having shewn, that every good and
perfect Gift is from above, coming down
from the Father of Lights, prescribes
afterwards some means proper to dif-
pose our Souls, that those Gifts may
not be lost on us, but that they may
abundantly bring forth Fruit in due
Season : and amongst some others, is
that set down now mention'd ; That
we should be *slow to Anger* : and the
reason he gives, is, Because *the Anger of
Man works not the Justice of God.* In
which Words he, in short, but fully
describes the mischievous effects of this
Passion : letting us know, that when
this has once seized the Heart, it renders
it unfit for complying with the Laws of
God, and discharging those great Duties he exacts from us. For the most
immediate effect it has upon us, is to
cast a blind upon, or at least, disturb
our Reason ; so that at that time, it is
not capable of discerning or judging any
thing aright : and when the Eye, that
                                    should

IV. *Sunday after Eafter.* 257

fhould direct us, is thus clouded, is it
not to be expected, that whatever elfe
depends on its Conduct, fhould be out
of order? How can a Man fhoot at a
Mark, when he has a Cloud of Duft or
Smoke before him? It can be nothing
but rafhnefs to undertake it. This is
our Cafe; for Paffion is both Duft and
Smoke to our Reafon; and while all
our other Faculties are of their Nature
blind, and Reafon, that is to guide
them, is become blind too; all we do
then, can be little better than the Blind
leading the Blind; and this is not
walking on in the way of Duty or Precept, but running into the Ditch.

And when Reafon is once thus indif-
pofed, that it is not capable of difcer-
ning, it is likewife uncapable of governing too: and what then becomes of all
thofe violent Paffions, that are under
its Charge? they all break loofe; then
Fears and *Jealoufies*, *Sufpicions*, *ill Will*,
Hatred, *Malice*, *Revenge*, with all the
reft, make their Attempts, and like a
Mob in a diforder'd Government, pretend to counfel, direct, and rule; and
that, amongft them, which moft favours Conftitution or Convenience, and
counterfeits Reafon beft, ever gets the
Reins: So that at that time a Man is
not under the government of Reafon,

M 5   but

258   IV. *Sunday after Eafter.*

but of Fear, Hatred, or fome other Paffion : and what poffibility of a Chriftian's acting then according to Duty, when he is not in a condition of acting according to Reafon? Hence the effects of Anger become prejudicial to all States.

Firft, To Chriftians, as to their Devotions ; they being very much indifpos'd for Prayers, Meditation, Reading, or going to the Sacraments, as long as their Minds are difturb'd with this Paffion : for thefe Duties requiring a great Serenity and Calm of Spirit, can never be perform'd well in a Storm: for tho' they may ufe fome weak endeavours, in order to raife their Thoughts to God ; yet the aggrievance, whatever it be, fo naturally and violently returns, that it foon takes up the Heart, to the exclufion of all that is good ; and then, inftead of Prayer, there's nothing but a gathering of dark Clouds, ready to break forth into Storms and Thunder. They are alike then unfit for all good Works, as of *Charity*, &c : for the Mind being gall'd, every thing then frets it, and they cannot be willing or eafy in admitting any good Propofals.

Secondly, 'Tis prejudicial to them in the ordering the Affairs of the Soul : for

IV. *Sunday after Easter.* 259

for tho' the Anger be such, which seems most justifiable, as occasion'd from the displeasure of their own Sins, Infirmities or Relapses; yet when once it comes to cause an Anxiety, Disquiet, Melancholy or Fretfulness within them, they are then unfit for framing any true Judgment of themselves, or determining what Method is most expedient for them; 'tis then they are in danger of being deluded by an indiscreet Zeal, into some rash or violent undertaking; or if it happens upon a Melancholy or Frightful Temper, to sink into all manner of Dejection, be ready to give all over for lost, and conclude, that Praying, and all the Endeavours of Amendment, are to no purpose: thus they are in danger of running out of the way, on one side or the other. And therefore are strictly oblig'd to adhere to some prudent and experienc'd Director, thus to escape the danger of being misled by themselves; being at that time so expos'd to Mistakes, that however positive they may seem in their own Thoughts, they may yet generally suspect themselves, and even conclude they are in the wrong: it being not then their Reason that directs, but Passion or Fear, both which are very unsafe Guides, such as a Wise Man

M 6   ought

260   IV. *Sunday after Easter.*

ought not to trust a very inconsiderable Affair to, much less his Soul.

Thirdly, It has its ill Effects in treating of Matters of Religion: For when a Person undertakes to be Advocate for Truth, and either by the peevish Prejudice, Obstinacy, or false Charges of an Adversary, is by degrees warm'd into a Passion, he then certainly injures the Cause he undertakes to defend; there being nothing that renders a Man more averse to Truth, than to hear it press'd with Violence and Anger; these being sufficient even to change a well inclin'd Person into a profess'd Enemy; there being very few, who seem willing to be inform'd, but have too much Pride to own themselves overcome; and therefore this rough method seems nothing less than a Temptation to draw Men into the Sin against the Holy Ghost, by provoking them to oppugn the known Truth. Meekness is a necessary Qualification of an Apostle, 'tis one of the Gifts of the Holy Ghost; those who undertake the Cause of Truth without this, fight not with the Arms of Christ or his Holy Spirit; and cannot expect a Blessing from above; since tho' our Redeemer, sending his Apostles abroad with the mildness of Sheep, promis'd to be with them; yet
they

IV. *Sunday after Easter.* 261

they can claim nothing of this, who laying by the Sheep, are turn'd into Wolves.

Fourthly, 'Tis pernicious to all Parents, Masters and Superiours in regard of such as are under their Charge : for tho' these have a right to reprehend and correct, when a just Occasion requires it, and the omission of this is a great Fault, often attended with very ill Consequences ; yet certainly St. *Teresa's* Advice, of *Never reprehending any one in Anger*, ought to be the Rule of their Practice, if they desire to see any Fruits of their Correction : for they that reprove others in a Passion, do it generally to satisfy themselves, and in compliance with their own Impatience ; and generally betray so great a Weakness, in the doing it with so much of unkindness, ill will, and even exceeding the bounds of Truth and Justice, that 'tis ever likely to produce much greater effects of Passion, Stubbornness and Contempt, than any Thoughts of Amendment. Furious or Passionate Correction is therefore carefully to be avoided by those, who have others under their Care ; if, like good Christians, they desire to benefit those recommended to them ; and cure the Evils, to which they are subject.

But

262   IV. *Sunday after Easter.*

But if avoiding this Excess, they fall into another degree of this Passion, which is, of being ever uneasy, out of humour, ready to fret and quarrel upon every trivial occasion, this is a less noisy Evil, but not less pernicious than the former ; and, I fear, has as many degrees of Madness in it. It makes Parents and Masters unfit for all those purposes to which their State calls them ; and causes so great uneasiness in all under their care, that truly there can be no Comfort in a Family, where this Canker is ever gnawing at the Breast of the Superiours, which is not only a disturbance to them, but likewise to all that belong to them : upon which consideration the guilt of many Sins must necessarily be charg'd on it. And I am apt to think, amongst the many occasions given to young People of being Disobedient, of taking ill Courses, of unhappily disposing of themselves both to their disadvantage and discredit, is the uneasiness they find at home under the Government of Humoursom, Peevish and Jealous Parents : from which the desire of being deliver'd, puts them upon very rash and unjustifiable Methods. I fear it causes not less Mischief betwixt Man and Wife.

Now

IV. Sunday after Easter. 26.

Now all manner of Paffion being of fo pernicious a Temper, the Apoftle had great reafon to command us, to be flow to Anger, as not working the Juftice of God, and it ought to be our daily Care, to remedy whatever degree of it we obferve in ourfelves. It is the occafion of many Evils, and becaufe hard to be mafter'd, requires a watchful Eye and laborious Hand. The Enemy and a corrupt Nature is ever fuggefting Arguments to make it appear reafonable : but upon reflection, we have too great reafon to fufpect it: fince the reafons we have, are too much in favour of our Inclination and Impatience.

IV. *Sunday after Easter.*

G O S P E L.

John C. 16. V. 5. ends V. 15.

I Go to him that fent me, and none of you ask me, Whither doft thou go ? The Apoftles were fo much feiz'd with the News of Chrift's departure from them, and of the Perfecution they were to fuffer, that they thought not of enquiring whither he was going, nor how they were to prepare to follow him.

But

264   IV. *Sunday after Easter.*

But Chriſt knowing the weakneſs of
Man, and diſtinguiſhing betwixt that
want of Attention, which is occaſion'd
by Indifferency and Coldneſs, and that,
which is the effect of ſome ſurprize
caſting a preſent damp on the Spirits;
does not preſs the Apoſtles on this
Point, but giving them a paſſing Reproof to remind them of their Weakneſs, comforts them in the following
Words ; I ſay to you the Truth ; 'tis
convenient for you that I go : for if I
go not, the Comforter will not come to
you.

It is impoſſible ſo to live, amidſt the
various Occurrences of this World, but
that ſometimes Chriſtians will be under
the ſame Oppreſſion with the Apoſtles
at this time, and Sadneſs will fill their
Hearts. The many Ties we have in
this World of Nature and Affection,
the Dependance we have on Friends,
the great Intereſt we have for our Subſiſtance, the Concern we have in the
Publick, the Sollicitude we are bound
to have for the well-being of our Corporal and Spiritual State, all afford
Matter for this Diſturbance ; becauſe
there is not one of theſe things, to
which we are thus link'd by Affection
or Intereſt, but what are all ſubject to
change, and ſuch change, as cannot but
make

IV. *Sunday after Easter.*   265

make some impreffion of Sadnefs upon the Mind.   This is the effect of a Weaknefs infeparable from our Condition in this mortal State, which being made fenfible, cannot but feel, when 'tis touch'd to the Quick in any fenfible Part ; but however, if this goes no farther, than it did in the Apoftles, by way of furprize, tho' it be a hindrance for the time to the greateft Duties, in putting a ftop to all, yet it is a Weaknefs, that carries its Excufe with it, and deferves rather Compaffion, than any fharp Reproof.   This may ferve for a Caution to all tender Souls, not to difquiet themfelves with the apprehenfion of having grievoufly offended, when they have been thus furpriz'd with Grief ; as likewife to thofe, under whofe Care they are, to endeavour to heal fuch Wounds, rather with Lenitives, that Comfort, than Corrofives, which exafperate the Sore ; left, otherwife, they encreafe the Trouble, tho' they change the Subject, in making them more unreafonably anxious for their imagin'd Offence, than they were for their Misfortune ; which, tho' having now a better Face, is yet as prejudicial to the Soul, and more difficult to be cur'd.

But

26*8* IV. *Sunday after Eaſter.*

But the Caſe is very different, if ſuch ſurprizing Grief be either careleſly or affectedly indulg'd ; for then, what was an excuſable Weakneſs in the Beginning, becomes Criminal in the Progreſs ; for there is nothing, except profeſs'd Vice, more deſtructive of all that is good ; it being one of the moſt ſubtle Contrivances of the Enemy, by which he overthrows Virtue, without the appearance of Vice : It being by this way he ſo weakens the Spirits, as firſt to render the Soul uncapable of all brave Attempts, ſuch as are neceſſary in the Soldiers of Chriſt ; then takes off all reliſh of Spiritual Duties, perſuades them they are all uſeleſs, and to no purpoſe ; thus, by degrees, he leſſens both Faith and Hope, oppreſſing the Mind with Darkneſs and Fears, and ſuggeſting ſuch Crowds of wild Imaginations, not ſparing even the Divinity itſelf, that it is now upon the brink of Deſpair, and nothing but a miraculous Grace can ſupport it againſt the force of theſe Terrours.

Where it does not ariſe to this height, 'tis however attended with ſo many ill Conſequences, either of a ſlothful Heavineſs, or a peeviſh Uneaſineſs, or of perplexing the Conſcience with endleſs Fears, that it ought to be every Chriſtian's

IV. *Sunday after Easter.*   267

tian's Care to defend himfelf againſt it ;
even ſo, as not to give way to any degree of Anxiety, Melancholy, or Dejection upon any Account whatever ; for
that there is a certain Indiſcretion in all
ſuch yielding ; and it can ſeldom be
done without the Guilt of Sin, by putting that to the hazard of an ungovern-
able Paſſion, which ought to be preſerv'd with greater Care.

But their Danger is not from Grief
only, but from whatever elſe ſo poſſeſſes
the Mind, as to put by all Concern of
obſerving the Way, in which they are,
and of the Place, to which they ought
to go. This was the overſight here reprov'd in the Apoſtles ; their Trouble
upon the Thoughts of loſing their
Maſter, was in itſelf Innocent, and
could deſerve no Cenſure ; but whilſt
it ſo takes up their Mind, as to exclude
all Enquiry of the Way, in which they
are to go, here it becomes reprovable,
and is no longer to be tolerated in them.
All Chriſtians have the ſame Way to
go, as the Apoſtles had ; and there being a daily Neceſſity of obſerving,
whether they go right, all that muſt be
ſet down as Faulty, which hinders them
from making this Enquiry. The Queſtion therefore they are every Day to
put to themſelves, is, Whether going

on

268   **IV.** *Sunday after Easter.*

on in the Way, in which they at prefent are, will bring them to their
Journey's End ? For if this be not a
part of their conftant Concern, their
Profeffion and Faith are vain, and their
Religion will avail them nothing.   It is
not enough to obferve, that they give
fome time to Prayer and Reading,
and that they make Refolutions of doing well ; for this may be no more,
than looking towards the End of their
Journey, accompanied with fome weak
Defires of coming at length to it ; but
as propofing a Journey, and preparing
for it, will never bring a Man to the
End, if, after fuch Propofals, he goes
out of the Way that leads to it : So it
is here ; for if Chriftians every Day
think of Heaven and pray to come to it,
and afterwards are but little follicitous of their Steps, but live on in fuch
a way as to have their Backs turn'd upon God and his Commandments, is
this likely ever to bring them to him ?

This is rather the Folly of him mention'd in the Gofpel, who beginning to
build a Tower, had not wherewith to
finifh it.   Chriftian, thou haft undertaken a Journey; art thou in a way of
finifhing it ? Will the Method of thy
prefent Life bring thee to Heaven ? If
Death fhould now feize thee, is thy
                                    Soul

IV. *Sunday after Easter.* 269

Soul in a difposition of being united to God? Is it thy daily Bufinefs to keep the Commandments? Doft thou walk according to the Spirit of Chrift, and his Gofpel, by ferioufly labouring to overcome the World, and to fubdue all thofe Paffions which carry thee from God? If this work be not yet done, where is the Stop? If thou haft often attempted it, but without Effect, is not this a fign of fomething being wanting in thee; that thou muft yet take more Pains, be ftill more in earneft, than hitherto; and that if thou goeft on at thy ufual rate, thy Work will never be done?

Here is the Examen, this the Enquiry thou art daily to make of thyfelf. If thou art wanting in it, it is an Argument of thy Thoughts being otherwife taken up; and be affur'd, whatever it be, that fo poffeffes thy Mind, as to exclude this neceffary Enquiry, it is all of Evil. If it be the immoderate Love of the World, or of thyfelf; if it be Senfuality, Intemperance, or other Vice, thefe are doubly Evil, both in themfelves, and in withdrawing thee from thy only neceffary Work. If it be fondnefs of Company, or Divertifements, if the eagernefs of Gain, if an exceffive Sollicitude for thy worldly

Affairs,

270　**IV.** *Sunday after Easter.*

Affairs, *&c*; tho' the principal Object of these be never so innocent, yet can that be esteem'd Innocent, which takes thy Heart from God, and excludes all that Sollicitude, by which thou shouldst look into thyself, and consider of the Ways, that lead to him ? What if these very Motives should prevail on thee to be unjust to thy Neighbour, couldst thou then esteem thyself guilt-less ? and art thou less Criminal, when by them thou art drawn into the greatest of all Injustices, which is that against thy own Soul and thy God ?

Deceive not therefore thyself, for tho' with all thy Care thou canst not be exempt from some Failings ; yet if thou com'st to that degree of Indiffe-rency or Neglect, as not to observe thy Ways, nor consider of the Place, to which thou art going, let the occasion of it be what it will, it is a criminal State, and such, as admits of no Ex-cuse. O God, if this be so, how un-happy are we, amidst the necessary Engagements, the grateful Sollicita-tions, and distracting Terrours of this Life ! We cannot but feel them, and yet to open our Hearts to them, can-not be without danger of excluding thee. Establish us, we beseech thee, amidst all these Difficulties ; and as
　　　　　　　　　　　　　　long

V. *Sunday after Eafter.* 271

long as we are on the Way, permit nothing to take from our Hearts the Sollicitude of going right.

✦✦✦✦✦✦✦ ✦✦✦✦✦✦✦✦

V. *Sunday after Eafter.*
E P I S T L E.

St. *James* C. 1. V. 22. ends V. 27.

*B*E *Doers of the Word, and not Hearers
only.* A good Chriftian then, in
the firft place, ought to be a Hearer of
the Word, that is, ought to be ever diligent, willing and ready to be inform'd
or put in mind of his Duty, whether
by Hearing or Reading, at all fit Opportunities : becaufe the Word of God
thus heard or read, is the daily Food
and Nourifhment of our Souls : 'tis what
we fo often pray for in the *Our Father,*
when we fay, *Give us this Day our daily
Bread:* this being a great part of the Bread
of Life, ever neceffary for the fupport
of our Spiritual Being : Great Numbers
there are, that ftand in need of it for
their Inftruction, as not having yet a
fufficient knowledge of their Chriftian
Duties, neceffary for Salvation : and as
great Numbers there are, who, knowing
their Duties, are in want ftill of being
often put in mind of them, that fo they
may

English Catholicism 1680–1830, Volume 2

272 *V. Sunday after Easter.*

may practise what they know : for
Reading and Hearing is not always to
have fomething new propos'd to us, but
to revive and quicken that Knowledge
we already have; 'tis to make us reflect
on what we know. For what with
converfing with the World, both as to
its Neceffities, Conveniencies and Vanities, and what with hearkning too
much to our own Inclinations, our
Minds are generally fo taken up with
worldly, vain, unprofitable, if not
finful Thoughts, that truly the Knowledge we have of God, and our Duty,
lies generally opprefs'd and fmother'd
under heaps of either weighty or empty
Trifles; and the Concern of thefe appears
fo very preffing and important, that all
Motives to good are too much hid from
our Eyes, grow by degrees fo weak
and cold, that, whatever it be in
fpeculation, 'tis certain in practice,
Earth is above Heaven in our Hearts,
and the Concern of Salvation gives place
to other Bufinefs : and thus in time,
the World, Vanity or Sin gains poffeffion of our Souls, if by frequent Hearing or Reading what is good, we are
not daily fpur'd forward to our Duty,
if thus we revive not the Maxims of the
Gofpel in our Hearts, and labour not
to keep that Ground, which is due to
God

V. *Sunday after Easter.* 273

God in our Souls. Upon which consideration we are oblig'd to apply ourselves often to these Exercises, as we
desire to have an interest in God : for
as the Scripture says, *He that is of God,*
hears the Words of God : So St. *Augustine*
declares ; There's no more certain sign
of Predestination, than willingly to
give ear to the Word of God. And
the reason may be ; Because, as those
who live in Slavery or Banishment,
are ever willing to hear of their own
Country ; and 'tis easy discovering of
what Nation or Province every Man is,
by the Satisfaction and Joy they express in hearing it spoken of : So truly
those Christians, who find comfort in
hearing of Heaven, and of the safest
way of going to it, may hence ground
some hopes, that 'tis the place they belong to : as those, who delight to hear
and read nothing, but of the World,
its Vanities and Follies, may likewise
hence guess at the temper of their
Souls, and what place they belong
to.

Hence it must be concluded a very
laudable, if not a necessary practice for
all Christians, who have any sort of
leasure, to give their Souls as daily an
allowance of this Spiritual Food, as
they do of nourishment to their Bodies ;

N by

274　　V. *Sunday after Eafter.*

by being conftant in reading fome good
Book every Day : as likewife for all
fuch, as have young People under their
Care, whether as Children, Scholars or
Servants, to accuftom them daily to
this Exercife ; but efpecially on *Sundays*
and *Holidays*, and in *Lent* &c, and
this in publick or common, if it may be:
that fo thofe violent Inclinations, which
carry them to Levities, Vanities, and
exceffive Divertifements, may be thus
corrected or moderated, by feafoning
their Minds with the frequent apprehenfion of more fubftantial Goods. And
where this is neglected, thro' their
Fault, who have the charge of them, I
cannot but think, they offend in a
matter of great Concern, and may one
Day find the guilt of it, in all its Confequences, to be more weighty and
terrible, than they generally apprehend.

Befides hearing the Word, we muft
be Doers alfo : for all Hearing and
Reading, being in order to the performing our Chriftian Duties, wherever
this is not done, all the reft are but barren and fruitlefs Exercifes, fuch as are
apt to delude Men into a Vanity of their
own Knowledge, and a good Opinion of
themfelves ; but can never recommend
them to Almighty God, who requires
not

V. Sunday after Easter.　2 7 ⅞

not only Leaves on the Trees in his Vineyard, but Fruit also : So that Knowledge without Practice, can be no Plea for the lefs'ning Faults, but comes in the End to be an encreafe of Damnation. The benefit then of frequent Reading, muft be by ferious Reflections on the Method and Conduct of our Lives, to examine, how far we practife what we know, and by conftant endeavours never ceafe, till, by degrees, we reform in ourfelves, what we obferve contrary to the Maxims of Chriftian Difcipline, of Juftice, and of Truth.

And for the more obvious Heads of this Examen, the Apoftle feems in the firft place, to put us upon enquiring, how we govern our Tongues : for that we are not to pretend either to the Truth of Religion in our Hearts, or Practice of it in our Lives, if this Member be not well regulated. In this point then we muft be Doers of the Word ; that is, have a careful watch on ourfelves, and fupprefs all thofe Evils, which chiefly manifeft themfelves by the Tongue ; as Anger, Hatred, Envy, Backbiting, rafh Judgments, Curfing, Swearing, Lying, and whatever provoking Expreffions are apt to give difturbance to others ; it being impoffible

N 2　　　　to

276   V. *Sunday after Easter.*

to conceive the Mischief, our Words many times cause in others, in extinguishing Charity, and exciting variety of disordered Passions. Then to correct that prodigious lightness or rashness, in advancing Falsities, Uncertainties or Doubts, for Truths; not to assert a thing at a venture, for fear of being thought Ignorant, which is often very prejudicial; but most especially if it be in a Matter relating to Conscience; such Decisions serving only to settle some in a false Peace, when disquiet of Mind would be much more to their Advantage; to put others on very indiscreet Undertakings; and are often follow'd with variety of Evils. These, with the many other Disorders of this Member, are to be corrected; since they generally proceed from a Corruption of the Heart; and where this is tolerated, there can be no truth of Piety or Religion.

Another Point recommended by the Apostle here, is to reflect, what our practice is, in regard of such as are in any Affliction or Distress: For this being a great Duty, we cannot pretend to be Doers of the Word, if we are wanting in it. To have no compassion for the Afflicted, to study to avoid them, to consider nothing of relieving them, to
be

V. *Sunday after Easter.* 277

be harsh, sharp and severe to them, is a sort of Cruelty not consistent with the Charity of the Gospel : and therefore however disagreeable to our Temper it may be, to converse with, hear and assist them, yet to overcome this uneasiness seems a necessary Mortification for all ; that they may find a like Charity, if it should come to be their turn to want it, and not to be confounded with the thoughts of their own hard-heartedness, when in their Spiritual Afflictions, and last Anguish of Death, they come to implore God's Mercy.

Thus to read and hear the Word of God, and practise it in our Lives, being our indispensable Duties ; we are seriously to apply ourselves to both : Help us, O God, in this our Obligation : let no Sloth be a hindrance ; let not the World and its Snares be a diversion to us : give a taste to our Souls, that we may relish and delight in what is good ; that so we may chearfully hear and resolutely perform whatever is thy Word to us.

V. *Sunday*

[Thomé de Jesus], *The Sufferings of our Lord Jesus Christ. Written Originally in Portuguese by F. Thomas of Jesus, of the Order of the Hermits of St Augustin. Newly and Faithfully Translated into English. In Three Volumes. Vol. III* (London, J. Marmaduke, 1753), pp. 166–94

The three-volume production *The Sufferings of our Lord Jesus Christ* is, like Caussin's work (below, pp. 171–97), an example of literature from the Counter-Reformation Continental devotional thesaurus being made available in translation for an English-language Catholic readership. The text examined here is from volume III of the 1753 London edition published by the Catholic bookseller, author and translator James Marmaduke (d. 1778). The work was also published in 1754 (Dublin) and twice in 1794, again in Dublin.

The meditation on the Passion laid out in these pages is based, sometimes somewhat loosely or imaginatively, on a symposium of readings of the gospel accounts, placing heavy emphasis on the alleged guilt (see, for example, the claims made in ll. 12–14, p. 161) and the general iniquity of the Jewish people. The style, especially in the exclamatory passages, is intensely emotive.

The original author, the Portuguese ascetic and writer Thomas Alvares de Andrade, was born in Lisbon in 1529 into a noble Castilian family. He became an Augustinian 'eremite', or friar, at the age of fifteen, studied Philosophy and Theology at the University of Coimbra and was known in religion as Thomé de Jesus: his aim as a religious writer was to restore the austere discipline of the Augustinian Order. He accompanied King Sebastian of Portugal (1554–78) on his ill-fated expedition to North Africa, was wounded at the Battle of Alcazar (1578) and imprisoned. While in prison he composed his meditations on the Passion of Jesus Christ, which appeared in Spanish, Italian, Latin and French translations, as well as in this English version. Thomé de Jesus was freed at the instance of the Portuguese ambassador and went on to devote himself to the ransom and care of Christian prisoners, dying in Morocco in 1582.

THE

SUFFERINGS

Of our LORD

JESUS CHRIST.

Written originally in *Portuguese* by

F. *THOMAS* of JESUS,

Of the Order of the Hermits of St. AUGUSTIN.

Newly and faithfully translated into English.

In THREE VOLUMES.

VOL. III.

LONDON:

Printed for J. MARMADUKE.

MDCCLIII.

THE

SUFFERINGS

Of our LORD

JESUS CHRIST,

In his death;

That is, from his condemnation, till he
expires upon the crofs.

XLI. SUFFERING of CHRIST.

The fentence of death pronounced againft. him.

*ILATE* was in hopes that no
heart would have been fo hard
as to have required the death of
Chrift, after feeing him in fo
piteous a condition. But he did not confider that it is the nature of thofe who are
actuated by mere malice, envy, and hatred,
not to defift from what they have once defired, and even never to defire it more ardently

XLI. *suffering of Chrift.* 167.

dently than when they fee themfelves near-
eft obtaining it. Thus *Pilate*, defigning,
by a fight fo worthy of compaffion, to ap-
peafe the fury of the *Jews*, provoked it
ftill more ; and they believed that after
having obtained of that weak judge the
fcourging of our Saviour, they could alfo
obtain his death.

It was therefore in vain for him to declare thrice that that man was innocent, and
that he found in him no caufe of condemnation : they all cried out with one voice ;
away with him, crucify him, crucify him.
This obftinacy appears furprizing, and it
is fo indeed. But if we reflect upon the
difpofition of our own nature, we fhall find
that we are taken from the fame corrupt
mafs, and that we have in ourfelves the
fame paffions which we deteft in the *Jews*.
For it often happens that he who thinks he
has entirely rooted out fuch a vice by penance, difcovers again in himfelf the fame
inclination, when the fame occafions offer,
and finds himfelf excited to his firft diforders with as much violence as if he had
never bewailed them.

Thofe who have lived long in the habit
of fin, know by their own experience, the
truth of what I fay. Tho' they often condemn themfelves, either by fome interior
motion given them by God, or by a pious
leffon, or an affecting fermon, or the advice of their friends, or the example of

3   good

good people, or their own reaſoning, and ſometimes by the views of honour and intereſt; the love of ſin, and the enchantment of a wicked habit gains over them by degrees ſo abſolute an empire, that they proceed to ſuch a length at laſt as to commit ſin without remorſe, and even ſo far as to think it lawful.

II. The malice of the *Jews* teaches us therefore what we are capable of, what the corruption of our nature is, how much we ought to fear ourſelves, and to have recourſe to the remedy which we procure from the example of Chriſt.

Pilate being unable to ſuffer any longer the cruelty and importunity of the *Jews*, ſaid to them: *take ye him, and crucify him; for my part I find no cauſe in him.* They anſwered: *we have a law, and according to the law he ought to die; becauſe he hath made himſelf the ſon of God* (John xix. 6.). Tho' *Pilate* was convinced on one hand of our Saviour's innocence; and on the other admired his ſilence, moderation, and patience amidſt ſuch cruel torments; yet he had not the power of taking him out of the hands of ſo many unjuſt accuſers. But when he heard the name of the ſon of God pronounced, he obſerved him more cloſely; he reflected upon his meekneſs and conſtancy; began to ſuſpect that there was ſomething perhaps more than human in that man, of whom he had heard ſo many
wonders;

XLI. *ſuffering of Chriſt.*   169

wonders; and to be afraid leſt he had ſinned againſt heaven, in condemning him to
be ſcourged. He therefore went back into
the judgment hall, in order to be more fully
informed concerning our Saviour.

Ah! how important it is to ſcrutinize the
motion of the ſoul, and to comprehend well
what it loves, what it fears, and what it
hopes for: for objeĉts ſcarce ever appear
ſuch as they are in themſelves; but ſuch as
they are repreſented by the diſpoſition of
thoſe who regard them. Hence it is that
an aĉtion, which being done with a pure
intention, would be a virtue, becomes a
ſin, when the intention is bad; that the
ſame work of piety which paſſes for hypo-
criſy in the mind of one man, is looked
upon by another as a good example; and
that the ſame honour which gives a pleaſure to the friends of him that is honoured,
is the cauſe of diſpleaſure to thoſe that envy
him. Thus the miracles of Chriſt, which
made him paſs for a magician among his
enemies, cauſed *Pilate* to fear leſt there
ſhould be ſomething divine in him.

III. He therefore interrogated him in
private; and aſked him from whence he
was, whether he came from heaven with
ſome divine power, or whether he was
born on earth as an ordinary man. Our
Saviour anſwering nothing to theſe queſti-
ons, *Pilate* who would have ſaved him, was
offended at his ſilence, and ſaid to him:

170 **XLI.** *suffering of Chrift.*

*speakeſt thou not to me? knoweſt thou not that
I have power to crucify thee, and that I have
power to releaſe thee?* As if he had meant:
Why wilt thou not diſcover thyſelf to me
who am not one of thy enemies?

It is true that *Pilate* could have done juſtice, but did not. Jeſus therefore anſwered
him: *thou wouldſt not have any power at all
againſt me, unleſs it were given thee from
above: therefore he who delivered me to thee,
hath the greater ſin.* If *Pilate* had had more
light, he would have comprehended by
that / anſwer, that there was ſomething
above man in the perſon of Chriſt, who
declared to him in ſo poſitive a manner,
that that affair not only depended on the
divine providence and eternal counſel; but
alſo that he clearly knew the degree of malice which was in every ſin. This was a
fine occaſion for *Pilate* of acquiring a
greater knowledge of the truth, if he had
ſaid to our Saviour: I am very far from
doing any thing againſt thee for the future;
and am ſincerely ſorry for what I have
already done, by expoſing thee to be
ſcourged.

But we muſt here obſerve, that Chriſt
deſigned not to ſay by that anſwer; that
becauſe it was from the divine will and per-
miſſion that he was condemned to death by
Pilate, the ſin of that judge was leſs than
that of the *Jews.* For the divine permiſ-
ſion neither increaſes nor diminiſhes the
ſin,

XLI. *ſuffering of Chriſt.* 171

ſin, the whole malice of which proceeds
from the will of him that ſins, tho' God
knows how to draw from that evil already
accompliſhed, a very great good for his
own glory and the ſalvation of his elect.
If *Pilate*'s malice was leſs than that of the
Jews, it is becauſe he did not abandon our
Saviour to them but in order to deliver
himſelf from their importunity ; whereas
they demanded his death out of the hatred
and envy wherewith they were animated
againſt him. The ſin was great on both
ſides ; but there was more weakneſs than
malice in *Pilate*, and in the *Jews* more malice than weakneſs.

IV. Theſe words of Chriſt : *thou wouldſt
not have any power at all againſt me, unleſs it
were given thee from above,* contain great
matter of conſolation for the juſt that are
in ſufferings : for being perſuaded by the
light of faith, that nothing happens to them
in this world, but what is the effect of the
loving conduct of God towards them, they
mind not the malice of men, or of devils,
that torment them : they regard only the
divine love which afflicts them for their
good ; receive with love his chaſtiſements
and trials ; and humble themſelves under
his omnipotent hand with an entire acqui-
eſcence.

Pilate, after that anſwer which he had
miſ-underſtood, ſeeing Chriſt, amidſt ſo
many pains, had his mind in heaven, and

referred

172 **XLI.** *suffering of Christ.*

referred all to the divine providence, judged
that if he was not the son of God, he was
innocent at least of the crimes that were
laid to his charge ; and consequently that
it was requisite to save his life. But when
the *Jews* perceived that *Pilate* heard them
with great indifferency, when they accused
Christ of calling himself the son of God,
they had recourse to their first accusation.
They cried out that he had designed to
make himself a king, and threatned that
judge with the emperor's anger. *If thou
dost release this man, thou art not* Cefar's
friend, said they to him.

Behold the stroke that dejected *Pilate*'s
courage : and it is still at this day the common rock on which all those split that are
slaves to the favour of princes. They cannot bear that one should so much as hint
to them the danger of a disgrace : and
God often permits them to be destroyed by
the same arm of flesh in which they trusted.
For *Pilate*, by abandoning justice, in order
to preferve *Cefar*'s favour, lost both at last.

V. Having therefore shewn Christ to the
Jews from a balcony, he said to them out
of mockery : *behold your king. But they
cried out* immediately : *away with him, away
with him, crucify him.* What, replies *Pilate,* continuing his rallery ; *shall I crucify
your king !* They answered ; *we have no king
but* Cefar. They still to this day experience the consequences of that judgment,
which

XLI. *fuffering of Chrift.*   173

which they then pronounced againft themfelves : for after having rejeɛted their true
king, they were difperfed over the whole
earth, odious, contemptible to the whole
world, and fubjeɛt to ftrange mafters.

Pilate feeing that he gained nothing upon them, and that the tumult of the people increafed, called for water, and wafhed
his hands, protefting that he had no fhare
in the effufion of that innocent blood, and
that he threw the whole crime thereof upon
them.. But thefe blind people anfwered all
with one voice : *his blood be upon us and upon our children.*

There are here two refleɛtions to be made
upon ourfelves : the firft, that for juftify-
ing ourfelves in the eyes of men, we often
bring as frivolous excufes as thofe of *Pilate,* who thinks, by wafhing his hands,
to exculpate himfelf from the unjuft fentence he pronounced againft Chrift : for
how many times have we thrown upon the
devil, the weaknefs of the flefh, or the
prefling occafion, the fin we committed by
the free motion of our own will. But God,
who knows the nature of our freedom, and
the helps he has given us, will judge quite
otherwife thereof.

The fecond refleɛtion is, that as the evil
appears lighter and of fmall confequence
to us, when we are drawn thereto by pleafure or paflion, fo much the greater will it
appear to us, when we muft expiate it by

H 3   penance.

penance. So true it is that we have no
enemies more dangerous, nor judges more
unjuſt, than ourſelves, in what regards the
accompliſhment of our deſires; ſince in
order to follow them, we often engage ourſelves in misfortunes, out of which all the
power of man is not able to bring us.
Thus the *Jews*, blinded by their hatred,
thought it a ſmall matter to take the blood
of the ſon of God upon themſelves and
upon their children. They bear it ſtill to
this day, by the blindneſs and obduracy
of their heart; and they will feel it hereafter in a much more terrible manner, by
eternal damnation.

Pilate having delivered *Barabbas* at the
deſire of the *Jews*, abandoned our Saviour to
their will; and a herald publiſhed, according to the cuſtom, that by the emperor's
orders, and in conformity to the *Roman*
laws, Jeſus of *Nazareth*, for having attempted to make himſelf king of the *Jews*,
was condemned to die on a croſs between
two thieves, appointed for their thefts to
the ſame puniſhment. The enemies of
our Saviour received that ſentence with joy,
and his friends were in a conſternation
thereat; whilſt that innocent lamb, in ſpite
of the repugnancy of nature, and all the
pain which ſo great an injuſtice occaſioned
him, offered his condemnation to the eternal father for the ſalvation of men, and
accepted

XLI. *suffering of Chrift.* 175

accepted alfo of death with a loving obe-dience.

That action was accompanied with as many different pains for Chrift, as it con-tained circumftances; becaufe he diftin-guifhed and felt them all. He was fenfible of the extreme ingratitude of that people, who had fubjected themfelves to a foreign yoke, and to a perpetual banifhment, by refufing to acknowledge him for their king; altho' he had come to fecure to them an eternal liberty. He was fenfible of the blindnefs of thofe who confented fo readily, that the very blood which he fhed for their falvation, fhould become the fource of their ruin, and of the ruin of their chil-dren. He was fenfible of the forrow of his friends, of his difciples, and of his holy mother, who beheld him fo unjuftly condemned to death; and he fuffered that condemnation, to fhew us thereby, that we were dearer to him than his own life.

We muft not here forget that we cannot confider with fufficient attention and ac-knowledgment, that this kind of death was not chofen by the judge, but required by the people: for the confufed outcries of a whole populace, who demanded the death of Chrift, reprefent the voice of our fins, which afcend to the tribunal of God, in order to demand of him the death of our Saviour, who took upon himfelf the fins of the world. This makes St. *Paul* fay,

H 4   that

176   *XLI. suffering of Christ.*

that thofe who fin demand again the death of the fon of God, or to make ufe of his own words, *they crucify him again*; becaufe they renew the caufe of his death. (*Heb.* vi. 6.)

Therefore our Lord was pleafed, fince he died for all men, that his death fhould be demanded by all the people, as in the name of all finners; that we might all acknowledge the fhare we have therein; might be afhamed of having provoked him fo unworthily; might return to him with love; and might confecrate all the ftrength of our body and foul to his fervice. As that death was to be the fource of our life, and the remiffion of our fins, Chrift was pleafed alfo that the kind of his death fhould be of our chufing; in order to affure us thereby, that if we have found him ready to die for us, in the manner as we have defired; he will alfo be ready to make us live with him, when we fhall defire it.

Behold the works of his infinite love, and the certain affurances that he will always grant us what we fhall beg of him for our falvation; for he who has vouchfafed to fuffer for the cure of our evils, a death which we have chofen, would never fend us either death, or the troubles of this life, if they did not contain the feed and merit of eternal life.

CONTEMPLATION

*On Chrift having the fentence of death pro-
nounced againft him.*

WHO can hear, without horror, that
cruel fentence of death pronounced
againft thee, O thou true life of our fouls!
O the only hope of finners. Can the human heart comprehend how men, feeing
thee thus covered with wounds, and reproaches, inftead of being touched with
compaffion, fhould require thy death, and cry
out all with one voice, *away with him, away
with him, crucify him.* Take him away then,
Pilate, take him from thofe favage beafts,
that cannot bear his prefence, and give him
to me; I will receive him in my arms, will
drefs his wounds, and will adore and ferve
him. Come to me, O my Saviour and my
love! Come to me that defire thee, feek
thee, and love thee, wholly disfigured as
thou art. Enter into my foul, live in it,
and grant that I may die for thee.

But pardon me, O my God! for I am
more wicked than that people. They are
unwilling to fee thee, becaufe they know
thee not, nor believe in thee; and I who believe in thee, adore thee, and acknowledge
thee for what thou art; how many times
have I turned away my eyes, when thou

H 5   pre-

178   *Contemplation on* XLI. *suffering.*

prefentedft thyfelf to me, to look upon what feparated me from thee? Remedy this diforder, O Lord! that I may never lofe fight of thee; that thou mayft always be the object of my looks, defires, and love. For if my interior eyes are continually fixed on thee, my foul will find in thee a moft celeftial food, and the remedy of all its evils. It is in thee, *O my refurrection and my life!* that every thing that is dead in me, fhall revive. It is in thee, O eternal mercy! that I fhall be delivered from all my miferies. It is in thee, O my fovereign beatitude! that I fhall be comforted in the duration of my banifhment.

II. O eternal fire always burning, and art never confumed; how admirable are the inventions of thy love! even thofe for whom thou dieft, chufe the kind of death by which they make thee die. My fins were then prefent to the eternal father, their cries were joined to the clamours of the *Jews*, and demanded juftice againft thee; becaufe thou hadft taken my debts upon thee, and I could not fatisfy for them but by thee. Thou didft fo fubject thyfelf to my will, and facrifice thyfelf to my neceffities, O immenfe charity! that thou haft left me the choice of my remedy. Thou haft fuffered the death of the crofs, becaufe we required it; and thou wouldft have fubmitted thyfelf to another kind of punifhment, if we had defired it.

If

Contemplation on XLI. *suffering.*   179

If thou hadſt that complacency for ſuch cruel deſires, how readily wilt thou hear me, when I ſhall beg of thee the grace of loving and ſerving thee! O treaſure of eternal goods! who giveſt thyſelf ſo liberally to me, and deſireſt ſo ardently that I ſhould poſſeſs thee as my own good; come to me, I receive thee this day for my only and ſovereign good. I abandon for thee, and return into thy hands all that is mine. In poſſeſſing thee alone, I am rich enough. Thou alone ſufficeſt me, O my God! and thou alone canſt ſatisfy all my deſires.

III. Thou haſt already more than ſatisfied for me, and art not content; but wilt accompliſh the work of my redemption, by the death of the croſs. Thou buyeſt me too dear, O my Saviour! thou haſt already acquired me by juſtice, look upon me as thy ſlave, and never free me from the obligation I lie under of being wholly thine. Since I am thine by juſtice, I will alſo be thine by love. I rather chuſe a corner in thy houſe, than all the abundance of the earth; but why do I ſay abundance? I ſee nothing therein but poverty, miſery, and affliction of ſpirit; and no happineſs but in being thine. O that I were engaged for ever in ſo ſweet a ſervitude! that nothing could ſeparate me from thee, O my God! Unhappy am I, if I depart from thee, and if I am wanting one ſingle moment in the obedience I owe thee.

Were

180 *Contemplation on* XLI. *ſuffering.*

Were it not more advantageous for me not to live, than to live without thee? thou art my creator, and I am thy creature. Thou art my Lord, and I am the ſlave thou haſt redeemed. Thou art my ſurety, and I am thy debtor. But my poverty is ſo great, that I can give thee nothing but myſelf. Receive, O Lord! this faithleſs ſervant, who returns to thee, and will never ſerve any other maſter but thee.

IV. Hear, O ſinful ſoul! the voice of the herald. He proclaims that Jeſus of *Nazareth* is condemned to die upon the croſs between two thieves, as a malefaƈtor and a mock king. Conſider with what ſorrow the ſacred humanity received that cruel ſentence. Lend an ear to the loud rejoicings of his enemies, whoſe deſires are ſatisfied. Behold the ardour wherewith they urge the execution of the ſentence; and in the midſt of that tumult, obſerve the ſilence, peace, and meekneſs of Jeſus, who hears all, ſees all, and ſuffers all without complaint, or giving any mark of impatience. O God of my ſoul! how can I ſee what I ſee, and hear what I hear? What! thou art treated as a mock king, O ſovereign maſter of heaven and earth! thou art regarded as a perfidious perſon, O thou faithful friend of our ſouls! Thou paſſeſt for the chief of thieves, O liberal ſource of all good things! and the author of life is judged worthy of death.

I am

Contemplation on XLI. *suffering.* 181

I am, O my God ! what thou art ac-
cufed of being ; and I have the bafenefs to
defire to live. Thou dieft, and I am ftill
breathing.

O inflexible obduracy of my heart ! how
can I refift that tendernefs ? Shall my mifery never yield to fo great a mercy ? and
fhall my coldnefs always ftand out againft
that immenfe charity ? The guilty lives,
and the innocent dies ; and the mafter lofes
his life, in order to preferve that of his
flave.

V. Difcover to me the bottom of thy
heart, O fweet Jefus ! let me fee what thy
fentiments were, when thou hearedft that
cruel fentence pronounced againft thee ?
Make my foul feel with what mildnefs,
peace, and charity thou didft abandon thyfelf to the power of thofe who required thy
death, and to whom it was alfo much
more neceffary than they imagined. O divine love, O pure love ! why doft thou
not confume me with thy flames ? Why
doft thou not fubject me entirely to him
who facrifices himfelf for me ?

I adore thee, O infinite love ! O immenfe liberality ! I adore thee, O heart of
Jefus ! principle of my life, fource of my
falvation, treafure of all the goods which
I poffefs and expect ! Give me light to
know thee, charity to love thee, fubmiffion
to obey thee ; a deteftation of my fins,
which caufe thee fo much forrow ; the hatred

182 *Contemplation on* XLI. *suffering.*

tred of myſelf, who am ſo contrary to
thee; and grace to have from henceforth
no other thought or deſire but of pleaſing
thee; ſince thou art my glory, my ſovereign good, and the center of my repoſe.

VI. But, alas, O Lord! what is *Pilate's*
weakneſs? Againſt his conſcience, againſt
his own knowledge, and againſt the advice
of his wife, who had been tormented in
the night on thy account; *he judged that
their petition ſhould be granted. And he
releaſed to them him, who upon the account of murther and ſedition, had been
committed to priſon, for whom they peti-
tioned; but delivered Jeſus up to their will!*
thus it is that in regard of thee, O my
God! no order is obſerved, their perverſe
will takes place of reaſon, and hatred that
of juſtice; and without being guilty thou
art delivered up to the diſcretion of thy
enemies.

There is no greater diſorder in the world,
than when all depends on the will of a
ſingle man, and when that will happens to
be irregular. Thine alone, O my God!
is capable of maintaining that abſolute empire without injuſtice; becauſe it is always
holy, wiſe, full of reaſon and equity. And
nevertheleſs what paſſes for the greateſt
diſorder in the univerſe, and for the cauſe
of a multitude of evils, is made uſe of
for deſtroying thee, and for depriving thee
of

Contemplation on XLI. *ſuffering.*   183

of a life, which is the moſt precious treaſure under the heavens.

What ought my confuſion here to be? and what can I ſay before thee, O Lord! in beholding that thou art delivered up for me to the unjuſt and cruel will of thy enemies, and that I refuſe to reſign myſelf to thine? In order to condemn thee to death, it is ſufficient that thy enemies require it; and to make me acquieſce to the troubles which befal me, it is not ſufficient that thou willeſt it. Thoſe *Jews* are blind and wicked, and thou giveſt thyſelf up to their will. Thy will is the rule of all righteouſneſs, and I make a difficulty of ſubmitting myſelf thereto. O blindneſs of mind, O hardneſs of heart!

For what canſt thou ordain concerning me, O Lord! but what is for thy glory and my good? Thou converteſt into eternal ſweetneſs the croſſes I here endure for thee, and all my labours into a repoſe which nothing can diſturb. The injuries that are done me ſerve only by thy mercy to augment my juſtice. My evils are changed into goods; my temptations and deſolations tend to a moſt ſweet commerce with thee; death itſelf is no longer any thing to me but a paſſage to a happy life: yet I complain, I fly from thee, and am not content with that admirable order which thou haſt eſtabliſhed with ſo much wiſdom and goodneſs, what advantage ſoever I find
therein.

184   *XLII. ſuffering of Chriſt.*

therein. O earthly heart! O extreme ingratitude!

Change, O my God! this moment this
diſpoſition of my heart, ſo pernicious to
me, and ſo unworthy of thee.   I reſign
myſelf entirely to thy will; and in order to
comfort myſelf in all the troubles that befal me, I deſire no other reaſon than to
know that thou haſt ordained it.   There
it is that I fix and crucify myſelf; that
thy will may be done, and not mine, now
and for ever, in life and death, in time and
eternity. *Amen.*

XLII. SUFFERING of CHRIST.

He carries his croſs.

AFTER ſentence of death was pronounced againſt our Saviour, the
Jews thought of nothing more than to have
it ſpeedily put in execution, that *Pilate*
might not have time to reflect thereon,
and to revoke it.   Thoſe children of darkneſs imitated the conduct of the devil,
their father: for as he knows by his own
experience, what it is to offend God, and
is perſuaded that men would fly from ſin
more than from death, if they knew the
uglineſs

XLII. *suffering of Chrift.*   185

uglinefs thereof; he conceals from them
the frightfulnefs of fin, fhewing them only
the falfe fweetnefs that is found therein;
and ftuns them by the tumult and confufion of worldly affairs, left they fhould
give attention to the miferies in which they
are engaged. Thus it is that the *Jews*, after having brought *Pilate* into their opinion, by their outcries and menaces, gave
him no leifure to difcover his fault, and
repent thereof.

They had already prepared the crofs,
and had brought it immediately to *Pilate*'s
houfe, that our Saviour might alfo have
the pain and confufion of carrying it upon his fhoulders to the place of punifhment. They placed foldiers in divers
places, to prevent the people from attempting his delivery; and forgot nothing
that might accelerate or fecure the execution of their defign, whilft Chrift accom-
plifhing the prediction of *Ifaiah*, fuffered
himfelf *to be led to the flaughter as a lamb,
without opening his mouth to complain.* (Ifai.
liii. 7.)

II. But that he might not be taken for
another, and might be known by all, they
ftripped him of that old purple cloak
wherewith they had covered him, and put
him on again his own garment. As it
was without feam, and not open before,
they were obliged to put it over his head;
which could not be done without difficulty,
becaufe

186   XLII. *suffering of Christ.*

becaufe it was entangled by the thorns ; the crown of which was roughly moved, the pain of its fharp points renewed, and the blood began to trickle down afrefh.

Chrift wifhed no lefs than the *Jews*, that he might be feen loaded with his crofs ; defiring as well as they that he might be known in that ftate ; that after having declared to us, that if we would be his difciples, we muft bear our crofs and follow him, none might be miftaken therein, nor excufe themfelves on account of their ignorance, after having feen our Saviour himfelf at mid-day in his own cloaths, in the fight of all the people, carry his crofs thorough the moft public ftreets of *Jerufalem*, from *Pilate*'s houfe to *Calvary*. He was not afhamed of thofe reproaches, becaufe his love rendered them precious to him ; and he was pleafed to fuffer before all, what he fuffered for all.

People reckon it an honour in the world to have a fucceffion of illuftrious anceftors : they recount the great employments they have had, the noble actions they have done, the blows they have received, and the wounds wherewith they have been diffigured, for the fervice of their prince or country ; becaufe they regard thofe blemifhes as proofs of their valour and fidelity ; and efteem them without comparifon, more glorious and advantageous than all h: b:u: y and advantages of the body.

Thus

XLII. *suffering of Christ.* 187

Thus Christ, who had declared to us in the gospel, that he will acknowledge none for his disciples but crucified men, has made such account of his own cross, that he would not take any other garment than his own to carry it in, for fear it should be thought that he was ashamed of it; and to shew us at the same time the way which leads to true glory.

III. When all things were ready, our Saviour came out of *Pilate*'s house, in the midst of a double rank of soldiers, that kept off the crowd; and at his coming out he found the cross which was appointed for him. This was the most infamous of all punishments: for being condemned thereto, it was necessary one should be a slave, or convicted of some most shameful crime; and he that was fastened thereto, was looked upon as the object of the public malediction. But the son of God, who was soon to consecrate the cross by carrying it on his shoulders, and sprinkling it with his blood, began then to render it venerable, and to acquire it that glory which it now has on earth, and will eternally have in heaven, which is since become the abode and true country of crucified men.

As Christ earnestly desired to unite at last under that standard all his elect, who were to attain unto glory only by the cross; he viewed it with joy, embraced it with tenderness,

tenderneſs, and was not frightned by its
bulk, altho' it was about fifteen feet long.
He did not excuſe himſelf on account of
his little ſtrength, already exhauſted by the
blood he had abundantly ſpilt.

He conſidered his croſs as a wel-beloved
ſpouſe, as the refuge of his friends, as the
ſtar which was to conduct his elect amidſt
the rocks of this world, as the trophy of
his glory, and the eternal monument of
his infinite love : he united himſelf to it,
and they both became, as one may ſay, one
and the ſame thing, not by the union of
fleſh as *Adam* and *Eve*, for producing children of wrath ; but by a moſt ſpiritual
union, for begetting children of grace.
He faſtened himſelf to it then, never to be
ſeparated from it but by death ; he honoured it, and ſanctified it in ſuch a manner, that it is become, by the dignity to
which our Saviour exalted it, the ſource of
our hopes, and the object of our veneration.

IV. It was in theſe ſentiments of eſteem
and love for the croſs, that he ſuffered it to
be laid upon his ſhoulders, and that he
thus walked before us, as the head and
model of the predeſtinate. And becauſe
there was no perſon, either in heaven, or
on earth, of a more exalted dignity, and
of greater merit, to whom he deſigned
more good, or that had done more for him,
than the moſt bleſſed virgin his mother, ſo
he

XLII. *fuffering of Chrift.*   189

he gave her the firft rank under that ftand-ard. She followed him thorough the ftreets of *Jerufalem*; and whilft he carried that heavy crofs upon his fhoulders, fhe carried one in her heart, more painful than all thofe which the juft have borne fince the creation of the world, in order to teach all men,

Firftly : that it is a favour and diftinc-tion to carry the crofs after Chrift.

Secondly : how remote he, who is with-out croffes, ought to think himfelf from thofe two models of perfection.

Thirdly : what the blindnefs of man is, who neither defires, nor even comprehends that happinefs. All thefe things deferve to be ftrictly examined and confidered at leifure ; becaufe they are as fo many plentiful veins, from whence the faithful foul draws thofe infinite treafures of light, confolation, love, fortitude, and conftancy, which our Savi-our has acquired us by his blood, and which are open to every one.

But all the glory which he communica-ted to the crofs, diminifhed not the pain nor ignominy which he fuffered in carrying it. He had a lively feeling of its weight both within and without ; and was ftill more oppreft by that of our fins, than by that of the crofs. For he was at the fame time charged with our neceffities, obliga-tions, and reconciliation, which he interi-orly treated about with his father.

He

190   XLII. *ſuffering of Chriſt.*

He walked in that condition towards mount *Calvary*, preceded by a herald, and two thieves that were to be crucified with him, ſurrounded with ſoldiers who continually ill-treated him ; and followed by the prieſts, the doctors of the law, the *Phariſees*, and the chief of the *Jews*, who led him themſelves, and never quitted him, till after ſeeing him expire.

VI. In the mean time Chriſt recollected the little ſtrength he had remaining, that he might be able to carry unto the place of puniſhment, the burthen wherewith he was loaded. He ſweat, he loſt breath, and all his wounds burſt open again, by the great endeavours he uſed. In fine, when he was gone out of the city, being no longer able, he yielded under the croſs, and fell with his face on the ground. The ſoldiers who conducted him, loaded him with ſtrokes, and ſaid a thouſand injurious things to him, to oblige him to get up again ; but the *Jews* ſeeing he had not ſtrength for it, and fearing he might happen to die before he was crucified, forced a man of *Cyrene*, called *Simon*, who was returning from the country, to help him to carry his croſs unto *Calvary*.

There are ſome pious perſons, who in meditating on this myſtery, envy *Simon* of *Cyrene* the happineſs of having carried our Saviour's croſs. I blame not this ſentiment; but I can ſay that they would render

der

XLII. *suffering of Christ.*   191.

der themselves much more agreeable to our Lord, by carrying their own cross with love, and a sincere desire of imitating him, than by wishing to have carried his. That *Simon* was but an imperfect figure of those who carry their cross after Christ; and if that charitable master vouchsafed afterwards to receive *Alexander* and *Rufus* into the number of his disciples, both *Simon*'s sons, to recompense their father for the trouble he had taken against his will; what will he not do for those that shall receive the cross with submission, embrace it with love, and carry it with perseverance?

VII. There were also some devout women, who touched with compassion in seeing him suffer, and with sorrow in seeing themselves deprived of his divine instructions, followed him quite bathed in tears. But having at last made their way to him, that they might hear his last words, he turned towards them, and said, for comforting them: *daughters of* Jerusalem, *weep not over me, but weep over yourselves, and over your children.*

He thereby foretold them the misfortunes, which so unjust and so cruel a death was to bring upon the *Jews: for behold the days shall come,* adds he, *in which it shall be said: happy they that are barren, and the wombs that bare not, and the breasts that have not given suck. Then shall they begin to say to the mountains, fall upon us: and to the hills,*
cover

192   XLII. *fuffering of Chrift.*

cover us. For if they do thefe things in the green wood, that is, in me who am the tree of life, who have preferved all the frefh-nefs of innocence and virtue, and who bear nothing but fruits of grace and im-mortality, *what will be done in the dry,* which is barren, without grace and beauty, and which fo much care and labour could not make to produce any fruit ? What fhall there happen to the *Jews,* who, far from profiting by the blood which I have fhed for their falvation, require the revenge thereof to fall upon them and upon their children ? (*Luke* xxiii. 28.)

Our Saviour then thought, with an ex-treme forrow, on all thofe who, obftinate in fin, neglect the remedy of his fufferings. And for that reafon he exhorts thofe wo-men, to weep rather over themfelves, and over their children, than over him ; that they might obtain by their tears, for the one and the others, the grace of profiting by his death.

Where is the man, who in fo forrowful a ftate, could have thought on other things befides his own forrows ? Notwithftanding our Saviour is more taken up with our evils than his own, and feems to forget his torments, in order to think on our remedy.

Thus it was, that on the very day of of his triumph, when he was going to *Je-rufalem,* amidft the applaufes of the whole
people,

XLII. *suffering of Chrift.*   193

people, he wept fo bitterly over that unhappy city, forefeeing the miferies which
the blindnefs of its inhabitants were to draw
upon it, who were ignorant of the time of
their vifitation, and of the grace which
was offered them. We were alfo prefent
to his mind; and our neceffities took up
his thoughts and love in fuch a manner,
that as he clearly faw the depth of our
wounds, fo his pains were nothing to him
in comparifon of our miferies.

VIII. This would be a proper place to
fpeak of the crofs, and of the happinefs of
thofe who bear it; but our Saviour's example inftructs us much better therein than
any words can do. I fhall therefore only
fay, that the greateft grace which God
grants to a chriftian in this life, is to give
him the relifh and wifdom of the crofs,
and to make him live and die upon the
crofs.

I know this truth is fublime, and that
it cannot be comprehended in its whole extent, without a particular affiftance of the
divine light; but the means of obtaining
that light, is to confider with a lively faith,
that Chrift made choice of that kind of
death; that he himfelf carried his crofs
upon his fhoulders, which was till then
unheard of; that he embraced it with love;
that yielding under its weight, he muftered
up what ftrength he had remaining, in order
to fupport it to the laft; that if he confented

194 XLII. *ſuffering of Chriſt.*

for another to relieve him, it was that he might breathe a moment, and not die before he was faſtened to it; that being ſolicited to come down from thence, he would expire upon it; and that he left it at laſt to his elect, as a precious inheritance.

Hence it is that crucified men, who are the moſt lively images of Jeſus dying on the croſs, are alſo the moſt agreeable to God. Which makes me ſay once more, that he who has not the ſentiment of this ſo pure a truth in his heart, who is not interiorly perſuaded that the greateſt benefit which a ſoul can receive from the hand of God, is to be judged worthy of the reproaches of the croſs; and that this favour is preferable to all the extraordinary gifts of the ſaints and contemplative perſons; that ſuch an one, I ſay, ought to look upon himſelf as blind, and to beg this admirable light continually of God. And if he is ſo happy as to obtain it, let him preſerve a humble acknowledgment thereof all his life, conſider it as an ineſtimable treaſure, and embrace the tribulation as the ſecureſt pledge of eternal bleſſings.

[Nicholas Caussin], *Entertainments for Lent, Written in French by the* R. F. N. *Causin, S. J. Translated into English by Sir Basil Brook* (Liverpool, John Sadler, 1755), pp. 3–25

A work in the well-established genre of 'contempt for the world' by the French Jesuit Nicholas Caussin, *Sagesse évangélique pour les sacrez entretiens du caresme* was published in translation by Sir Basil Brook in 1643, dedicated to Charles I's Queen, Henrietta Maria (1609–69). It was republished in 1649, dedicated again to the Queen, as *The Penitent or Entertainments for Lent*. The work reappeared as *Entertainments for Lent*, and then, with the same title, twice in 1661 (again dedicated to Henrietta Maria), and in 1672, 1682, and twice in 1687. In 1696 it regained the title *The Penitent or Entertainments for Lent*. Brook's translation remained popular in the eighteenth century, being issued in 1741 by Meighan in London; the work had a particular following in Lancashire and Ireland, being put out in Liverpool by Sadler in 1755 (the present copy), in 1768 in Dublin by Gorman, in Preston in 1768, Dublin again in 1778 and Wigan in 1785.

The original author was a popular devotional writer, born in Troyes in 1583. Caussin became confessor to Louis XIII (1601–43) but opposed the allegedly pro-Protestant foreign policy of the King's minister Cardinal Richelieu (1585–1642) and fell from favour in 1637. Caussin died in Paris in 1651.

The translator, Sir Basil Brook or Brooke, was born into a Shropshire gentry family in 1576. He came to control coal mines and iron and steel manufactories in Shropshire and Gloucestershire and owned estates in Oxfordshire and Gloucestershire, as well as a house near London. He was knighted in 1604.

Well-connected to the courts of James I and Charles I, Brook emerged as a prominent lay Catholic who in 1635 took the side of the regular orders against episcopal control. As the crisis leading to the civil wars deepened, in 1639 he acted as treasurer for English Catholic donations towards the King's forces engaged against the Scots. In 1641 he was summoned before Parliament but escaped; then in January 1642, Brook was arrested at York and put in the custody of the Commons serjeant, and in August was put into the King's Bench prison. In late 1643 he was involved in a plot to set

London and Parliament at odds and in January 1644 was again arrested. On the orders of the Commons he was imprisoned in the Tower, and in May 1645 again in the King's Bench gaol. In 1645, too, Brook's estates were sequestrated by the Shropshire County Committee and his enterprises taken into management by Parliament. In 1646, Brook, as a papist in arms, was exempted from amnesty under the peace treaty between the King, Parliament and the Scots, known as the Newcastle Propositions, and his estates remained under Parliament's control. Sir Basil Brook died in December 1646, leaving debts of £10,000.

Arranged in orderly Scripture readings set for the Masses of the season of Lent and followed by reflective 'Moralities' or morals to be drawn from those Scriptures, and then by prayerful 'Aspirations', *Entertainments for Lent* not surprisingly remained a favourite in an English Catholic community that approached the penitential season with the utmost seriousness.

ENTERTAINMENTS

FOR

L E N T,

Written in FRENCH by the

R. F. N. Causin, *S. J.*

Tranſlated into ENGLISH
By Sir *BASIL BROOK*

*The Delight of Sin is momentary, the Torment
eternal.*

LIVERPOOL:

Printed by JOHN SADLER, M.DCC.LV

TO THE
Moſt Excellent Majeſty
OF
HENRIETTA MARIA,
QUEEN
OF
GREAT-BRITAIN.

MADAM,

MONGST all the public joys for your Majeſty's happy return, I know not better how to expreſs my own particular, than by moſt humbly preſenting to your Majeſty my tranſlation of this excellent French book, in the ſolitude of a priſon, which was made more eaſy by ſome relation it had to your Majeſty's ſervice.

And I preſume the rather upon this dedication, becauſe all that good which is derived to us from France, whereof I conceive this may be a part, ſhould receive honour and increaſe of value from your Majeſty, that it

A 2   may

The Epiſtle Dedicatory.

may ſo diffuſe itſelf with more authority and profit a-
mongſt thoſe who may be capable to receive it   Your
Majeſty, having read the original, doth well know that
the principal ſcope of it is to teach the love of God and
contempt of this world, with many other principal virtues.

And for the practice of them all, this age could not
have hoped for ſo rare an example to inſtruct all the
great ladies of Chriſtendom, as it hath found in your
majeſty, as well by your admirable fortitude and perfect reſignation to God's holy will in all your Majeſty's
extream afflictions, dangers and preſſures at ſea and
land, as alſo by your Majeſty's many ſacred retirements,
in the moſt holy time of the year, to ſprinkle your pleaſures (voluntarily) with ſome of that gall which was
upon our Saviour's lips when he ſuffered his bitter
paſſion and death for our ſins.   Our great divines affirm,
that the preſent ſufferings of mount Calvary lead directly to the future glories of mount Tabor.

And therefore, ſince your Majeſty hath patiently
endured ſo many unjuſt and rigorous croſſes in the
mount Calvary of this world, we have reaſon to hope
that our bleſſed Saviour hath prepared for your Majeſty
a moſt glorious crown in the next, which will never
have end.   And this ſhall ever be the inceſſant, and
fervent Prayer of,

MADAM,

Your MAJESTY's poor and

Moſt humbly devoted beadſman,

BASIL BROOK.

ENTERTAINMENTS

FOR

L E N T.

For the first day, upon the consideration of Ashes.

Thou art dust, and to dust thou shalt return.
Gen. 3.

1. IT is an excellent way to begin Lent with the consideration of dust, whereby nature gives us beginning; and by the same death shall put an end to all our worldly vanities. There is no better way to abate and humble the proudest of all creatures, than to represent his beginning and end. The middle part of our life, like a kind of Proteus, takes upon it several shapes not understood by others; but the first and last parts of it deceive no man; for they do both begin and end in dust. It is a strange thing that man, know-

A 3
ing

6   *Entertainments for Lent.*

ing well what he hath been, and what he muſt be, is not confounded in himſelf, by obſerving the pride of his own life and the great diſorder of his paſſions. The end of all other creatures is leſs deform'd than that of man. Plants in their death retain ſome pleaſing ſmell of their bodies : the little roſe buries itſelf in her natural ſweetneſs and carnation colour. Many creatures at their death leave us their teeth, horns, feathers, ſkins ; of which we make great uſe : others, after death, are ſerved up in ſilver and golden diſhes, to feed the greateſt perſons of the world. Only man's dead carcaſe is good for nothing but to feed worms ; and yet he often retains the preſumptuous pride of a giant, by the exorbitance of his heart; and the cruel nature of a murderer, by the furious rage of his revenge. Surely that man muſt either be ſtupid by nature, or moſt wicked by his own election, who will not correct and amend himſelf, having ſtill before his eyes aſhes for his glaſs and death for his miſtreſs.

2. This conſideration of duſt is an excellent remedy to cure vice, and an aſſured rampart againſt temptation. St. Paulinus ſaith excellently well, that holy Job was free from all temptations when he was placed upon the ſmoke and duſt of his humility. He that lies
upon

Entertainments for Lent. 7

upon the ground can fall no lower; but may contemplate all above him, and meditate how to raife himfelf by the hand of God, which pulls down the proud and exalts the humble. Is a man tempted with pride? the confideration of afhes will humble him. Is a man burnt with wanton love? (which is a direct fire) fire cannot confume afhes. Is he perfecuted with covetoufnefs? afhes make the greateft leeches and bloodfuckers caft their gorges. Every thing gives way to this unvalued thing, becaufe God is pleafed to draw the inftruments of his power out of the objects of our infirmities.

3. If we knew how to ufe rightly the meditation of death, we fhould there find the ftreams of life. All the world together is of no eftimation to him that rightly knows the true value of a juft man's death. It would be neceffary that they who are taken with the curiofity of tulips, fhould fet in their gardens a plant call'd Naple, which carries a flower that perfectly refembles a death's head : and if the other tulips pleafe their fenfes, that will inftruct their reafon. Before our laft death we fhould die many other deaths, by forfaking all thofe creatures and affections which lead us to fin. We fhould refemble thofe creatures, facred to the

8   *Entertainments for Lent.*

the Ægyptians, call'd Cynocephales, that died piece-meal, and were buried long before their death : so should we bury all our concupiscences before we go to the grave, and strive to live so that when death comes he should find very little business with us.

ASPIRATION.

O Father of all essences, who givest beginning to all things and art without end, this day I take ashes upon my head, thereby professing, before thee, my being nothing ; and to do thee homage for that which I am, and for that I ought to be, by thy great bounties. Alass! O Lord, my poor soul is confounded to see so many sparkles of pride and covetousness arise from this caitiff dust, which I am ; so little do I yet learn how to live, and so late do I know how to die. O God of my life and death, I most humbly beseech thee so to govern the first in me, and so to sweeten the last for me, that, if I live, I may live only for thee; and if I must die, that I may enter into everlasting bliss, by dying in thy blessed love and favour.

The

Entertainments for Lent. 9

The Gospel *for* Ash-Wednesday, *St.* Matthew vi.

Of hypocritical fasting.

WHEN you fast, be not, as the hypocrites, sad: for they disfigure their faces, that they may appear unto men to fast. Amen, I say unto you, that they have received their reward.

But thou, when thou dost fast, anoint thy head, and wash thy face; that thou appear not to men to fast, but to thy father which is in secret: and thy father which seeth in secret will repay thee.

Heap not up to yourselves treasures on the earth; where the rust and moth do corrupt, and where thieves dig through and steal: but heap up to yourselves treasures in heaven, where neither rust nor moth doth corrupt, and where thieves do not dig through nor steal. For where thy treasure is, there is thy heart also.

MORALITIES.

1. THAT man goes to hell by the way of Paradise who fasts and afflicts his body to draw the praise of men. Sorrow and vanity together are not able to make one christian act. He deserves everlasting hunger

10   *Entertainments for Lent.*

ger who ftarves himfelf that he may fwell
and burft with vain-glory. He ftands for
a Spectacle for others, being the murderer
of himfelf ; and by fowing vanity, reaps
nothing but the wind. Our intentions muft
be wholly directed to God, and our examples for our neighbour. The father of all
virtues is not to be ferved with counterfeit
devotions; fuch lies are abominable in his
fight; and Tertullian faith, they are as
many adulteries.

2. It imports us much to begin Lent
well, entering thofe lifts in which fo many
Souls have run their courfe with fo great
ftrictnefs; having been glorious before God,
and honourable before men. The difficulty
of it is apprehended only by thofe who have
their underftandings obfcured by a violent
affection to kitchen-ftuff. It is no more
burdenfome to a couragious fpirit, than
feathers are to a bird. The chearfulnefs
which a man brings to a good action in the
beginning, does half the work. Let us
wafh our faces by confeffion; let us per-
fume our head, who is Jefus Chrift, by
alms deeds. Fafting is a moft delicious
feaft to the confcience, when it is accompanied with purenefs and charity; but it
breeds

Entertainments for Lent. 11

breeds great thirſt when it is not nouriſhed with devotion, and watered with mercy.

3. What great pain is taken to get treaſure; what care to preſerve it; what fear to loſe it, and what ſorrow when it is loſt! Alas, is there need of ſo great covetouſneſs in life to encounter with ſuch extream nakedneſs in death? We have not the ſouls of giants, nor the body of a whale. If God will have me poor, muſt I endeavour to reverſe the decrees of heaven and earth that I may become rich? To whom do we truſt the ſafety of our treaſures? to ruſt, to moths and thieves. Were it not better we ſhould in our infirmities depend only on God almighty, and comfort our poverty in him who is only rich; and ſo carry our ſouls to heaven, where Jeſus on the day of his aſcenſion did place our ſovereign good? Only ſerpents and covetous men deſire to ſleep amongſt treaſures, as ſaint Clement ſaith. But the greateſt riches of the world is poverty free from covetouſneſs.

ASPIRATIONS.

I Seek thee, O invincible God, within the abyſs of thy brightneſs, and I ſee thee thro' the veil of thy creatures. Wilt thou be always hidden from me? ſhall I never

ſee

12   *Entertainments for Lent.*

fee thy face, which with a glimpfe of thy fplendor canft make paradife? I work in fecret, but I know thou art able to reward me in the light. A man can lofe nothing by ferving thee, and yet nothing is valuable to thy fervice, for the pain itfelf is a fufficient recompence. Thou art the food of my faftings, and the cure of my infirmities. What have I to do with moles, to dig the earth, like them, and there to hide treafures? Is it not time to clofe the earth, when thou doft open heaven, and to carry my heart where thou art, fince all my riches are in thee? Doth not he deferve to be everlaftingly poor who cannot be content with a God fo rich as thou art?

The Gofpel *for the firft* Thurfday *in* Lent, *St.* Matthew xviii.

Of the centurion's words : O Lord I am not worthy.

AND when he was entered into Capernaum, there came unto him a centurion, befeeching him, and faying, Lord, my boy lieth at home fick of the palfy, and is fore tormented.

And Jefus faid to him, I will come and cure him.

And the centurion making anfwer, faid, Lord, I am not worthy that thou fhouldft enter under

my

Entertainments for Lent. 13

my roof : but only say the word, and my boy shall be healed. For I also am a man subject to authority, having under me soldiers : and I say to this, go, and he goeth : and to another, come, and he cometh : and to my servant, do this, and he doth it. And Jesus hearing this, marvelled, and said to them that followed him, Amen, I say to you, I have not found so great faith in Israel.

And I say unto you, that many shall come from the east and west, and shall sit down with Abraham, Isaac and Jacob, in the kingdom of heaven ; but the children of the kingdoms shall be cast out into the exterior darkness : there shall be weeping and gnashing of teeth. And Jesus said to the centurion, go, and as thou hast believed, be it done unto thee. And the boy was healed in the same hour.

MORALITIES.

1. OUR whole salvation consists in two principals ; the one is in our being sensible of God, and the other in our moving towards him : the first proceeds from faith, the other comes from charity and other virtues. O what a happy thing is it to follow the example of this good centurion, by having such elevated thoughts of the Divinity, and to know nothing of God but

B   what

14   *Entertainments for Lent.*

what he is. To behold our heavenly father, within this great family of the world, who effects all things by his single word, creates by his power, governs by his counsel, and orders by his goodness this great universality of all things. The most invisible creatures have ears to hear him. Fevers and tempests are part of that running camp which marcheth under his standard : they advance and retire themselves under the shadow of his command : he only hath power to give measures to the heavens, bounds to the sea; to join the east and west together in an instant, and to be in all places where his pleasure is understoood.

2. O how goodly a thing is it to go unto him, like this great captain ! to go, said I ? nay, rather to fly as he doth by the two wings of charity and humility. His charity made him have a tender care of his poor servant, and to esteem his health more dear than great men do the rarest pieces in their cabinets. He doth not trust his servants, but takes the charge upon himself; making himself, by the power of love, a servant to him who by birth was made subject to his command. What can be said of so many masters and mistresses, now adays, who live always slaves to their passions ? having

no

Entertainments for Lent.   15

no care at all of the falvation, health or neceffities of their fervants ; as if they were nothing elfe but the fcum of the world. They make great ufe of their labours and fervice, which is juft, but neglect their bodies, and kill their fouls, by the infection of their wicked examples. Mark the humility of this foldier, who doth not think his houfe worthy to be enlightned by one fole glympfe of our bleffed Saviour's prefence. By the words of faint Auguftine we may fay, he made himfelf worthy by believing and declaring himfelf fo unworthy : yea, worthy that our Saviour fhould enter not only into his houfe, but into his very foul. And upon the matter he could not have fpoken with fuch faith and humility, if he had not firft enclofed (in his heart) him whom he durft not receive into his houfe.

3. The Gentiles come near unto God, and the Jews go from him ; to teach us, that ordinarily the moft obliged perfons are moft ungrateful ; and difefteem their benefactors for no other reafon but becaufe they receive benefits daily from them. If you fpeak courteoufly to them, they anfwer churlifhly ; and in the fame proportion wherein you are good, you make them wicked ; therefore we muft be careful that
B 2   we

16   *Entertainments for Lent.*

we be not fo toward God.   Many are dif-
tafted with devotion, as the Ifraelites were
with manna :   all which is good, doth difpleafe them becaufe it is ordinary : and you
fhall find fome, who, like naughty ground,
caft up thorns where rofes were planted.
But we have great reafon to fear that nothing but hell-fire is capable to punifh thofe
who defpife the graces of God, and efteem
that which comes from him as of no value.

Aspirations.

O Almighty Lord, who doft govern all
things in the family of this world, and
doft bind all infenfible creatures, by the bare
found of thy voice, in a chain of everlafting
obedience !   Muft I only be ftill rebellious
againft thy will ?   Fevers and palfies have
their ears for thee, and yet my unruly fpirit is not obedient.   Alas, alas, this family
of my heart is ill governed : it hath violent
paffions ; my thoughts are wandering, and
my reafon is ill obeyed.   Shall it never be
like the houfe of this good centurion, where
every thing went by meafure becaufe he
meafured himfelf by thy commandments ?
O Lord, I will come refolutely, by a profound humility and an inward feeling of
myfelf, fince I am fo contemptible before
thine

thine Eyes. I will come with charity towards thefe of my houfhold, and toward all that fhall need me. O God of my heart, I befeech thee, let nothing from henceforth move in me, but only to advance my coming toward thee, who art the beginning of all motions, and the only repofe of all things which move.

The Gofpel *for the firft* Friday *in Lent, St.* Matthew v.

Wherein we are directed to pray for our enemies.

YOU have heard that it was faid, thou fhalt love thy neighbour, and hate thine enemy. But I fay to you love your enemies, do good to them that hate you ; and pray for them that perfecute and abufe you : that you may be the children of your father which is in heaven, who maketh the fun to rife upon good and bad, and raineth upon juft and unjuft. For if you love them that love you, what reward fhall you have ? Do not alfo the publicans this ? And if you falute your brethren only, what do you more ? Do not alfo the heathens this ? Be you perfect therefore, as alfo your heavenly father is perfect.

MORAL‑

18 *Entertainments for Lent.*

MORALITIES.

1. **A** Man that loves nothing but according to his natural inclination, loves only like a beaft, or an infidel. The beft fort of love is that which is commanded by God, and is derived from judgment, conducted by reafon and perfected by charity. Methinks it fhould be harder for a good chriftian to hate than love his enemy. Hate makes him our equal, whereas love placeth us quite above him. By hating a man's enemy, he breaks the laws of God; he fights againft the incarnation of Chrift, which was acted to unite all things in the bond of love : he gives the lie to the moft bleffed Eucharift, whofe nature is to make the hearts of all chriftians the fame : he lives, like another Cain in the world, always difquieted by feeking revenge, and it is very death to him to hear of another man's profperity : whereas, to love an enemy doth not bind us to love the injury he hath done us ; for we muft not confider him as a malefactor, but as a man of our own nature, as he is the image of God, and as he is a chriftian. God doth only command perfect things, not impoffible. That which is very hard to flefh and blood becomes eafy

by

Entertainments for Lent.   19

by the help of grace and reaſon. Our
bleſſed Saviour Jeſus Chriſt, being the father of all harmony, can, and doth, reconcile all contrarieties at his will and pleaſure.

2. If revenge ſeem ſweet, the gaining of
it is moſt bitter : But there is nothing in
the world more profitable than to pardon an
enemy by imitation of our Saviour. For it
is then that our conſcience can aſſure us to
be the children of God, and inheritors of
his glory. We muſt not fear to be deſpiſed
for eſteeming virtue ; for ſuch contempt
can only proceed from thoſe who know not
the true value of that glory which belongs
to the juſt. There is no better way to revenge, than to leave it to God, who always doth his own buſineſs. When David
wept for Saul, who was his enemy, his
clemency did inſenſibly make degrees, by
which he mounted up to the throne of
Judah. A good work which comes from
the ſpirit of vanity is like an empty mine,
good for nothing. God, who is inviſible,
would have our aſpects turned always toward him, and blind toward the world.
Alms given by the ſound of a trumpet make
a great noiſe on the earth, but reap little
fruit in heaven. The fly of vanity is a
miſchievous thing, which deſtroys all the
                                        perfumes

20 *Entertainments for Lent.*

perfumes of charity. What need we any
spectators of our good works ? every place
is full where God is ; and where his is not,
there only is folitude.

ASPIRATIONS.

O God of all holy affections, when fhall
I love all that thou lovest, and have
in horror all that difpleafeth thy divine majefty ? If I cannot love in fome perfon his
defects and fins, I will love in him thine
image, and in that I will acknowledge thy
mercies. If he be a piece of broken glafs ;
in that little piece, there will fhine fome
lines of a God-creator, and of a God-
redeemer. If thou haft chofen him to exercife my patience, why fhould I make him
the object of my revenge, fince he gives me
trouble to gain me a crown ? He is a hammer to polifh and make me bright ; I will
not hurt him, but reverence the arm that
ftrikes me. I refign all vengeance into thy
hands, fince it is a right referved for thy almighty power. And certainly the beft revenge I can take, is to gratify my enemy.
Give unto me (O moft merciful prince) the
grace to fuffer, and let the facrifice of my
fufferings mount up to thy propitiatory
throne.

The

Entertainments for Lent. 21

The Gofpel *for the firft* Saturday *in* Lent, *St.* Matthew vi.

Of the Apoftles danger at fea, and relief of our Saviour.

*A*ND, *when he had difmiffed them he went into the mountain to pray; and when it was late, the boat was in the midft of the fea, and himfelf alone on the land. And feeing them labour in rowing, for the wind was againft them, and about the fourth watch of the night, he cometh to them walking upon the fea; and he would have paffed by them: But they, feeing him walking upon the fea, thought it was a ghoft, and cried out, for all faw him, and were troubled. And immediately he talked with them, and faid to them, have confidence, it is I, fear ye not. And he went up to them into the fhip, and the wind ceafed, and they were far more aftonifhed within themfelves, for they underftood not concerning the loaves, for their heart was blinded.*

And, when they had paffed over, they came into the land of Genefareth, and fet to the fhore. And when they were gone out of the boat, incontinent, they knew him, and running through that whole country, they began to carry about in couches thofe that were ill at eafe, where they heard he was. And whitherfoever he en-
tered

22 *Entertainments for Lent*

tered into towns, or into villages, or cities, they laid the fick in the ftreets, and befought him that they might touch the hem of his Garment; and as many as touched him were made whole.

MORALITIES.

1. WHAT a painful thing is it to row when Jefus is not in the boat? all our travail is juft nothing, without God's favour : A little blaft of wind is worth more than an hundred ftrokes of oars. What troublefome bufineffes there are ? how many intricate families do labour much and yet advance nothing, becaufe God withdraws himfelf from their iniquities ? If he do not build, the workman deftroys what he is building : but all falls out right to thofe that embark themfelves with Jefus. They may pafs to the Indies in a bafket, when others fhall mifcarry in a good fhip well furnifhed.

2. But how comes it about that the fhip of the poor apoftles is beaten fo furioufly by the winds and tempeft? There are many fhips with filver beaks, with fine linen fails and filken tackles, upon which the fea feems to fmile. Do the waters referve their choler only to vent it upon that fhip which carries juft perfons ? This is the courfe of man's life : the brave and happy men of this

Entertainments for Lent.   23

this world enjoy their wifhes, but their fhip doth perifh in the harbour as it is fporting; whereas God, by his providence, gives tempefts to his elect, that he may work a miraculous calm by his almighty power. Dangers are witnefles of their floating, and combats are caufes of their merit. Never think any man happy in his wickednefs, for he is juft like a fifh that plays with the bait when the hook fticks faft in his throat. We muft wait and attend for help from heaven patiently, without being tired, even till the fourth, which is the laft watch of the night. All which proceeds from the hand of God comes ever in fit time; and that man is a great gainer by his patient attendance, who thereby gets nothing but perfeverance.

3. They know *Jefus* very ill that take him for a phantom or an illufion, and cry out for fear of his prefence, which fhould make them moft rejoice; fo do thofe fouls which are little acquainted with God, who live in blindnefs, and make much of their own darknefs. Let us learn to difcern God from the illufions of the world: the tempeft ceafeth when he doth approach, and the quietnefs of our heart is a fure mark of his prefence, which fills the foul with fplendor and makes it a delicious garden. He

makes

24 *Entertainments for Lent.*

makes all good wherefoever he comes, and
the fteps which his feet leave are the boun,
ties of his heart. To touch the hem of his
garment cures all that are fick ; to teach us,
that the forms which cover the bleffed fa-
crament are the fringes of his humanity
which cures our fins.

Aspirations.

O Lord, my foul is in night and darknefs,
and I feel that thou art far from me.
What billows of difquiet arife within my
heart? what idle thoughts, which have been
too much confidered ? Alas, moft redoubted
Lord and father of mercy, canft thou behold,
from firm land, this poor veffel which labours fo extreamly, being deprived of thy
moft amiable prefence ? I row ftrongly, but
can advance nothing, except thou come into my foul. Come, O my adored mafter,
walk upon this tempeftuous fea of my heart ;
afcend into this poor veffel ; fay unto me,
take courage, it is I. Think not that I
fhall take thee for an illufion, for I know
thee too well by thy powers and bounties to
be fo miftaken. The leaft thought of my
heart will quiet itfelf to adore thy fteps.
Thou fhalt reign within me ; thou fhalt
difperfe my cares ; thou fhalt recover my
decayed

decayed senses ; thou shalt lighten my understanding; thou shalt inflame my will ;
thou shalt cure all my infirmities : and, to
conclude, thou only shalt work in me, and
I will be wholly thine.

The Gospel *for the first* Sunday *in Lent,* *St.* Matthew iv.

Of our Saviour's being tempted in the desert.

*T*HE N *Jesus was led of the spirit into the
desert, to be tempted of the devil; and
when he had fasted forty days and forty nights,
afterwards he was hungry: and the tempter approached and said to him, If thou be the son of
God, command that these stones be made bread:
who answered and said, It is written, not by
bread alone doth man live, but by every word
that proceedeth from the mouth of God.*

*Then the devil took him up into the holy city,
and set him, upon the pinacle of the temple, and
said to him, If thou be the son of God cast thyself down ; for it is written, that he will give
his angels charge over thee, and in their hands
shall they hold thee up, lest perhaps thou knock
thy foot against a stone. Jesus said unto him
again, it is written, Thou shalt not tempt the
Lord thy God.*

C

Again

[William Crathorne (ed.)], *Mr Gother's Spiritual Works. Tome XIV. Prayers for Every Day in Lent. Part II. There Are Added General Indexes to each Tome. Faithfully Corrected* (London, [T. Meighan], 1718), Preface and pp. 1–29

Volume XIV of the 1718 Meighan eighteen-volume edition of Gother's *Spiritual Works* comprised *Prayers for Every Day in Lent*, part of a set, along with his *Prayers for Sundays and Festivals, from Advent to Trinity Sunday, Lent and Easter-Week Excepted* and his *Prayers for Sundays, Holidays and Other Festivals* running from Trinity to the end of the season of Pentecost, which closed the Church's year. Throughout this series Gother provided a comprehensive calendar of prayer, in the vernacular, to march in step with the entire liturgical cycle. That said, it is clear that the Lenten and Pascal observance, to which this whole volume was dedicated, occupied an espe-cially prominent place in Gother's thinking, for, as he wrote in the Preface, 'The design of this Collection [was] to be a help to those Christians who think it reasonable to distinguish these forty days by some particular exer-cises of piety.'

At the same time, *Prayers for Every Day in Lent* was able to operate, within an English Catholic community in which regular access to Sunday and festal Masses could not be relied upon, as a kind of substitute for nor-mal liturgical provisions. It was, Gother explained, 'in particular proposed for the benefit of such as have not opportunity of being present at the public prayers of the church, that, either retired in their closet, or meeting in their families, they may repeat the prayers of every day, and so not lose the benefit of this holy time.'

The actual arrangement of the material considered here was in fact conceived by its author in a broadly congregational rather than individual-ized frame, based on forms of prayer such as the collect and the litany and designed for family or group recital rather than solitary devotion in one's 'closet'. In turn, the devout dialogues seemed to envisage the presence of a conductor, to whose invocations respondents would make their collective prescribed replies. If a priest were present in a home, we must assume that Mass itself would be celebrated, rather than these prayers intoned, and it therefore seems likely that the prayer-leader of these recitations would have been a lay person, presumably or normally a head of household, whether man or woman.

However, the prayers, which in part borrowed from or adapted liturgical tropes such as the *Kyrie Eleison* and the *Agnus Dei*, did not aim to reproduce the liturgy, so there was no attempt, in the prayers set for Ash Wednesday, to duplicate that day's liturgical blessing and imposition of the ashes. Indeed, to attempt to carry out any such rite outside the setting of Mass would have been to supplant the liturgical action, and that cannot have been in Gother's mind. Being constrained not to incorporate into these devotions any reproduction of the authentic liturgical programme prescribed for the day in question, Gother was, however, free to focus on where his real concerns lay: with interior spirituality, state of mind and repentance rather than ritual performance. And if fasting were more important than ashes, Lenten fasting itself was of value only insofar as it was the accompaniment of a change of heart. Gother supplied such messages with the richest scriptural references at his command.

Mr. *GOTHER's*

Spiritual Works.

TOME XIV.

Prayers for every Day in *Lent.*

PART II.

There are added,
General *Indexes* and *Tables* to
each TOME.

Faithfully Corrected.

LONDON:
Printed in the Year 1718.

PRAYERS

FOR

EVERY DAY

IN

L E N T.

TOME II.

Faithfully Corrected.

Printed in the Year 1718.

THE

PREFACE.

*T*HE *Defign of this Collecti-on is to be a Help to thofe Chriftians, who think it rea-fonable to diftinguifh thefe Forty Days by fome particu-lar Exercifes of Piety. I cannot tell that all will be fo well inclin'd; but when I confider the Morality of the prefent be-lieving World, and compare it with Pri-mitive Chriftianity, I cannot difcover it to be fo much better now, that there fhould be Reafon for laying that by at pre-fent, as a needlefs Ceremony, which was then judg'd proper, if not neceffary, for Sinners making their Peace, and regain-ing Favour with God.*

The PREFACE.

I do not mean here the Ceremonial Part only, being very *senfible* how little a way that goes alone; but *as* it comprehends the whole *Defign* of the *firft Inftitution*, and that is what the *Scripture fo* much approves, Of Sinners humbling themfelves under the Senfe of their Iniquities, and feeking God in Fafting and Prayer. *This has too evident Atteftation of Heaven to be call'd in Queftion, where there is a Faith in God: And if it be Sin that makes this humbling Method neceffary, I would willingly know, whether our prefent Age be fo privileg'd with a general Sanctity above all that went before, as to have it now voted needlefs?*

For my Part, as far as my Obfervation goes, I fear there can be no Ground for this Plea; and that the Ways of Chriftians are fo generally corrupt, that the Remedies of Sin, and the Gofpel-Expedients for finding Mercy, were never more neceffary than at prefent. And if, in Practice, they feem fomething unfafhionable, 'tis not becaufe Chriftians are fo good as not to want fuch Helps, but becaufe they are fo evil as either not to

be

The PREFACE.

*be sensible of their Unhappiness, or to
have almost laid aside the Concern for re-
medying it.*

*If this be the State of Christians, (I
wish I were mistaken) then it cannot but
be judg'd a reasonable Charity to call upon them to turn their dissipated and wan-
dring Thoughts upon themselves, to lay
before them their own Misery, and provide them with some easy Means, by
which they may be led into the Ways of
Repentance and Mercy.*

*This is what I here propose in some
short Exercises for every Day in Lent,
in which the pious Soul may see how to
advance in the Way of the Gospel, and
Sinners are shewn their own Deformity,
and by what Means they are to recover a
better State. 'Tis likewise in particular
propos'd for the Benefit of such as have
not Opportunity of being present at the
Publick Prayers of the Church, that, either retir'd in their Closet, or meeting
in their Families, they may repeat the
Prayers of Every Day, and so not lose
the Benefit of this Holy Time. And
since the Holy Scripture has furnish'd the
greatest Part of the Matter for this Col-*

A 3 *lection,*

The PREFACE.

*lection, I hope it will shelter it against
all Exceptions.*

*Not that I expect, for this Reason,
that worldly Souls will approve the Con-
tents ; rather I look for the contrary: For
since the general Business of their Lives
is to follow the Bent of Nature, and indulge it in many sinful Liberties; how
shall they approve that Self-denial which
the Gospel demands? Since they admire
what the World applauds, must it not be
expected they shall make a Party against
that, which condemns the World, and
gives both its Wisdom and Greatness no
better Character than of Folly and Smoke?
Since nothing is agreeable to them, but
where they have a broad Way, how can
they like that, which undertakes to strai-
ten their Passage, and calls them into a
narrow Way? Hence to recommend the
Spirit of the Gospel is so far from being
a Fence, that it must rather expose one
to their Censures. But with this I am
content, nay, I shall rejoice, so I can but
do any thing for their Good, either in a-
wak'ning them from their Stupidity, or
giving them a Sense of their Unhappiness, or lessening that Confidence they*
seem

The PREFACE.

ſeem to have, even while they are going out of the Way.

To prepare 'em for this (thoſe I mean who amidſt many Extravagancies retain ſtill Hopes of Heaven, and purpoſe to do well) I here conjure 'em to take ſome Time to be ſerious. I wiſh they would follow that admirable and ſaving Advice given in the Spiritual Retreat; *ſet a-part One Day in a Month, wherein to withdraw from their uſual Diſſipations, examine the general Method of their Lives, and make the trueſt Judgment they can of their inward State. The Buſineſs of Eternity is very well worth this Trouble; and if it were done with the Help of ſome pious and experienc'd Di-rector, I queſtion not, they would ſoon find a comfortable Recompence of their Labour in a new Light of Judgment, and a better Diſpoſition of Will ſo far, that the Reproach of their own Ways would ſoon oblige them to Reſolutions of ſeeking better.*

This, I ſay, I queſtion not; becauſe I know how very different things are found, upon a ſerious Examen, from what they appear'd upon a paſſing only, or heedleſs

Glance:

The PREFACE.

Glance : And that, *befides this Advantage, how much may be depended on the Bleſſing of God, who fails not in his particular Aſſiſtance to thoſe, who are but ſerious and ſincere in ſeeking him?*

Among the firſt of their Enquiries, *I would recommend to them the impartial Examination of two Principles, to ſee how far they can be, with Safety, depended on.*

The former is, Whether Cuſtom may be ſafely follow'd ; eſpecially where there are Perſons of ſome Reputation joining in it ? *If this be ſuf-ficient Warrant, I deſire it may be con-ſider'd, whether a Way will not be hence open'd into many Sins, ſo as to live in them with Peace of Conſcience ? I mean, into all thoſe which have* Cuſtom *to plead for them; into how much of Pride, Prodigality, Frauds, Injuſtice, Simony, Uſury, Backbiting, Neglect of Heaven, Love of the World, and Self-love, with many others, which have ſo much pre-vail'd amongſt the Followers of the Goſpel, that if a Judgment be made of them from common Practice, according to this Principle, they muſt all be reputed inno-cent ?*

The PREFACE.

cent? *And what is the Result of this, but that there needs no more than following this* Maxim *for walking on in the broad Way, without any Remorse of Conscience to interrupt the Course?* What Consult *of* Ten Infernal Spirits *could set up a more destructive Principle!*

The other is, Whether, upon hearing what the Gospel teaches, it be safe for Christians to pronounce this general Sentence? It is not a Command, but only by way of Advice or Counsel, and therefore we are not bound to observe it. *In this I desire it may be consider'd, Whether they are not very full of Presumption, who dare pronounce thus, and at the same Time have no Knowledge of what is deliver'd in the* Gospel *by way of* Command, *and what by way of* Advice *only?* Secondly, *Whether having no Knowledge in the Case, they may not be easily mistaken?* Thirdly, *Whether it can be safe to depend on such a Principle where a Mistake is so obvious, and the Concern is no less than of a Command of God?* Whether Inclination *and* Corruption *may not likely have an Influence very often in*

A 5 *apply-*

The PREFACE.

applying this Principle; and hence make void the whole Spirit of the Gospel, under the Notion of being no more than Advice ?

These, with other like Particulars, I desire may be consider'd ; for to me, I must confess, the Rule seems so very unsafe, that I think there needs no more for levelling a Christian Life with a Heathen. 'Tis but supposing such a Corruption of the Judgment as is ordinary to Mankind, and it will soon expound any Command it does not relish into a Counsel, and so vote it needless.

If this can be suppos'd the Consequence of this Rule, then how unsafe must the State of those Christians be, who have no other Principle but this, on which their inward Peace and all their Hope is built ? Who in Practice depart from many things taught in the Gospel, having nothing but their own Arbitrary Exposition to warrant the Dispensation; and if they find Custom favouring their Gloss, then rest on the Decision, as if there were now no Place left to question the Safety of their Method ?

And is there Safety in this ? O God ! I wish those would seriously consider it,

who

The PREFACE.

who here trust their Salvation. For to me I cannot but own it, Defectio tenuit me, *I am seiz'd with Terrour when I see Christians, in the Affairs of Salvation, trusting to a broken Reed; when I see them with Confidence following such blind and deceitful Guides; when I see them depending on such dangerous Principles as they cannot get approv'd by any that are serious, and seem no better than plausible Snares, fit for those who are design'd for Destruction. Thus desperate does their Case seem to me; and hence they cannot wonder if I call upon them, if I desire them to consider their Way, and to take Advice with those who are proper Judges in the Affair, that so they may not run on confident out of their Way, 'till Death comes to make too late a Discovery of their Errours. This is my Advice, and I hope they will discern so much Charity in it, as to think it worth their considering. For my Part, I am not for narrowing the Way, but I would willingly convince them that the Way is narrow; there is no other but that which Christ has taught; and they can have no Assurance that they walk in this, except they know*

it.

The PREFACE.

it. I pray God direct them to so much Seriousness, at least while they pretend to Heaven, as to enquire, whether they are in the Way that leads to it? Fasting and Prayer are the surest Means for obtaining this Knowledge, and I hope the following Collection may be some Help to it. If there be sufficient Reason to conclude they are already in the Way, I am not for giving them any Disturbance, but will encourage them to go on as they are; but if they find themselves very wide of it, I hope they will make a good Use of the Discovery. And for making short Work, which certainly will be the more welcome Proposal, let them but with one serious Glance look at the general Method of their Lives, *and then tell me, whether from their Conscience they believe that they* live and are led by the Spirit of Chrift : *For if they* are not, *their Case is already declared by St.* Paul, *who says,* That the Children of God are led by the Spirit of God; and that if any Man has not the Spirit of Chrift, he is none of his. *Rom:* 8. 9, 14. *Let this turn the Ballance; and I leave it to their own Conscience to pronounce upon it.*

PRAY-

PRAYERS

FOR

Every Day

IN

LENT.

Aſh-wedneſday.

 Ntring now, with this Day, up-
on the holy Time of Lent, let
us beg the Aſſiſtance of Almighty God, that we may obſerve this ſolemn Faſt in ſuch
a manner, as to anſwer all
thoſe great Purpoſes, for which it was ordain'd,

Let

2   *Aſh-wedneſday.*

Let us Pray.

O God, who haſt taught us in thy Holy Word, how acceptable a True Faſt is to thee, and how beneficial to Sinners : Grant, we beſeech thee, that we, who are here aſſembled, may be directed and ſtrengthen'd by thy Grace ſo to keep this Faſt, as to obtain all thoſe Good Effects, which thy Mercy has ſhew'd to others, who have ſought thee this Way.

We are ſenſible, O God, how loud our Sins cry for Juſtice againſt us : We know how much we ſtand in Need of thy Mercy : We confeſs likewiſe, it is the Effect of thy great Mercy to us, that thou haſt not cut us off in the midſt of our Sins, but haſt ſpared us, and given us this Time, wherein we may make our Peace with thee.

Hear therefore our Prayer, and grant, we beſeech thee, that we may not neglect this Mercy ; that we may not loſe this Opportunity ; that we may not let paſs this Acceptable Time, as we have already too often done ; but obſerve it in ſuch a manner, as to turn away thy Anger, which is juſtly provok'd againſt us, and obtain from thee a full Pardon of all our Sins.

Help

Aſh-wedneſday.   **3**

Help us, O God of Mercy.

R. And teach us to walk in the Ways of true Penance.

Let not Self-love prevail in us.

R. Let us not ſtudy to pleaſe, but to puniſh, our ſelves.

We have departed from thee by the Multitude of our Sins.

R. Let us now return in the Ways, by which Repenting Sinners have returned to their God.

Lead us, O God, we beſeech Thee, in ſuch Ways.

R. And let the Spirit of true Penance direct us theſe Forty Days.

Lord, have Mercy on us.

Chriſt, have Mercy on us.

Lord, have Mercy on us.

God, the Father of Heaven,⎫
God, the Son, Redeemer of the World,   ⎬ Have Mercy on us.
God, the Holy Ghoſt,   ⎪
Holy Trinity, One God,   ⎭

O God, to whom *Moſes* was well pleaſing, by faſting Forty Days in the *Mount.*

R. Give us Grace to Faſt in the ſame holy Spirit.

O God, who didſt deliver *Hezechias* and his People, humbling themſelves before thee in Faſting, Sackcloth and Aſhes.

R. Give us Grace to faſt in the ſame holy Spirit.

4   *Ash-wednesday.*

O God, who didst spare the *Ninivites*, doing Penance in Fasting, Sackcloth and Ashes.   R. *Give us Grace to Fast in the same holy Spirit.*

O God, who didst shew Mercy to *Judith*, seeking Thee in Fasting, Sackcloth and Ashes.   R. *Give us Grace to Fast in the same holy Spirit.*

O God, who didst spare *Esther* and her People, solliciting for thy Help in Prayer and Fasting.   R. *Give us Grace to Fast in the same holy Spirit.*

O God, who didst mercifully assist the *Maccabees*, calling upon Thee in Fasting, Sackcloth and Ashes.   R. *Give us Grace to Fast in the same holy Spirit.*

O God, who, by thy Prophets, didst call upon thy sinful People to return to Thee in Fasting, Weeping and Mourning. R. *Give us Grace to Fast in the same holy Spirit.*

O God, by whose Holy Will thy only Son, our Lord Jesus Christ, did Fast Forty Days and Forty Nights in the Desart.   R. *Give us Grace to Fast in the same holy Spirit.*

Be merciful to us.   R. *Spare us, O Lord.*

Be merciful to us.   R. *Graciously bear us, O Lord.*

From all Niceness in Eating, ⎤   *O Lord,*
From seeking to please our ⎥   *deliver us.*
Appetite, ⎦

From

Aſh-wedneſday.   5

From all kind of Exceſs,
From all Abuſes of this holy Time,
From all unbecoming Liberties,
From all the undue Contrivances
of Appetite,
From Sloth and Self-love,
From Tepidity and Coldneſs,
From deferring Repentance,
By thy holy Incarnation,
By thy Faſting in the Deſart,
By whatever thou ſuffer'dſt in
thoſe forty Days,
By that infinite Love, which mo-
ved thee to become our Example,
By that bitter Cup, which was gi-
ven Thee to drink by thy Eternal
Father,
By that bitter Cup, which was gi-
ven thee by thy Enemies,
By all, whatever thou ſuffer'dſt for
our Redemption,

O Lord, deliver us.

We Sinners, R. *We beſeech Thee hear us.*
That the earneſt Deſire of finding Mercy may be our Motive for undertaking
this Faſt. R. *We beſeech Thee hear us.*
That the Multitude of our Sins, and
the Senſe of our Unworthineſs, may
oblige us to be faithful in it. R. *We beſeech Thee hear us.*
That the Fear of thy Judgments upon
unrepenting Sinners may preſs us to it.
R. *We beſeech Thee hear us.*

That

6 *Aſh-wedneſday.*

That the Memory of our being Duſt and Aſhes may make us chearfully ſubmit to all the Difficulties of it. R. *We beſeech Thee hear us.*

That the Uncertainty of our Life, and Certainty of never more returning, may be a daily Motive to us to do now, whatever is in our Power to do. R. *We beſeech Thee hear us.*

That we may not neglect this Acceptable Time, this Time of Mercy and Salvation. R. *We beſeech Thee hear us.*

That we may wiſely lay hold of this Time, which thou now offer'ſt us; and bringing forth worthy Fruits of Penance, find Mercy with thee. R. *We beſeech Thee hear us.*

That thou vouchſafe graciouſly to hear us. R. *We beſeech Thee hear us.*

Son of God, R. *We beſeech Thee hear us.*

Lamb of God, who tak'ſt away the Sins of the World. R. *Spare us, O Lord.*

Lamb of God, who tak'ſt away the Sins of the World. R. *Hear us, O Lord.*

Lamb of God, who tak'ſt away the Sins of the World. R. *Have Mercy on us.*

Let

Aſh-wedneſday. 7

Let us Pray.

BEhold, O God, we lay open our Deſires before thee. We know, in
this Time of *Lent*, we have a fair Opportunity of moving thee to Mercy;
and 'tis our ſincere Deſire to lay hold of
this Time, and ſo to employ it, as to
obtain the Mercy we want. But behold,
O God, we confeſs both the Falſeneſs of
our Nature and our Weakneſs. There is
but very little we can do; and in that
Little we are very much in Danger of
deceiving our ſelves, to the Diſappoint-
ment of all that Good which thou haſt
deſign'd for us. Wherefore we beſeech
thee in thy Mercy to help us. Have
Compaſſion on our Infirmity, and give
us Strength to follow that Spirit which
ought to guide us at this Holy Time:
Secure us likewiſe againſt all Deluſion,
that we may not be impos'd on by the
falſe reaſoning of Sloth or Self-love. Let
the Horrour of our Sins, and the true
Love of thee, our God, work ſtrongly
in us, that where, of our ſelves, we are
ſubject to great Miſcarriages, we may be
enabled thro' thy Grace, and do all to
thy Glory, and our own everlaſting
Good.

Q

8 *Aſh-wedneſday.*

O God, give a Bleſſing to what we begin this Day : We undertake it in thy Name, in Obedience to thy Church, which, by thy own Ordinance, being put over us, thou haſt commanded us to hear : We undertake it as a Means, which by thy own Declaration, is powerful for caſting out Devils, and inclining thee to Mercy : We undertake it as a juſt Puniſhment due to our Sins. Sanctifie this our Undertaking, we beſeech thee, and enable us ſo to perform it, that we may find the Fruit of our Labours.

Give us Courage not to be afraid to ſuffer : Rather let us rejoyce under whatever Difficulties we meet, whilſt we know this Temporal Scourge may be a Means for preventing that which is Eternal ; and that nothing can be more pleaſing to thee, than to ſee Sinners humbled under the Senſe of their Guilt.

But then, O God, give us Diſcretion too ; that while we correct Nature, we may not diſable it ; and while we puniſh the Sinner, we may not make the Chriſtian uſeleſs. Secure us by thy heavenly Light againſt all Extremes, and mercifully lead us on by ſuch a Spirit, as may not ſpare Sin, and yet not be injurious to the Sinner.

Help

Thurſday *before*, &c. 9

Help us, O God, in both theſe Particulars . To thee all our Neceſſities are known ; and according to theſe, ſo we now beſeech thee in thy Mercy ;to ſupply our Wants. In thee is all our Truſt ; but as for our ſelves, we only propoſe to find Mercy in thy Sight by ſuch Methods, as thou haſt approv'd ; and even in theſe our Truſt is not in our ſelves, but in thee. Help us therefore, O God, and by thy Grace may we happily finiſh, what by thy Mercy we now begin.

Grant, O Lord, to thy Faithful, that they may enter upon this ſolemn Faſt with a due Piety, and go thro' it with a ſecure Devotion. Look mercifully, O Lord, upon us bowing down before thy Majeſty, that having been refreſh'd by thy heavenly Banquet, we may be always ſtrengthen'd from above. Thro' our Lord Jeſus Chriſt, thy Son.

Thurſday before Firſt *Sunday* in L E N T.

Haveing *enter'd upon this ſolemn Faſt of* Lent, *let us now beg of Almighty God that we may obſerve it, not only outwardly, by abſtaining from Meat ; but likewiſe inwardly, in our Hearts, by fighting againſt*
Sin,

10   *Thurſday* before

*Sin, and carefully avoiding whatever we can
diſcover in our ſelves to be diſpleaſing to
him.*

Let us Pray.

GRant, O merciful God, this Grace to
us thy Servants, that we may obſerve this *Lent* in ſuch a manner, as to
make it a Chriſtian Faſt ; even ſuch a
Faſt, as thou haſt choſen. Hence, O
Bleſſed Lord, let it be the Effect of thy
Mercy to us, while we keep a Guard upon our Lips, as to what we eat, we may
keep a much ſtricter Watch upon all our
Ways, in withdrawing our Feet from all
the Paths of Sin, and tolerating nothing
in us, which can provoke thy Diſpleaſure
againſt us.

We confeſs, O God, it is thy Sum-
mons to Sinners to be converted to thee
with all their Hearts, in Faſting, Weeping and Mourning ; to rend their Hearts,
and not their Garments.

We confeſs that this is thy Call to Sinners ; *Let the wicked Man forſake his Way,
and the unrighteous Man his Thoughts, and
let him return to his Lord, and he will have
Compaſſion on him, and to his God, for he is
full of Mercy to forgive.*

We confeſs again, thou haſt declar'd
thy Diſlike of all ſuch Faſts, wherein
Men

First *Sunday* in *Lent*. 11

Men feek to do their own Wills, are full of Strife and Contention, are fevere and exacting upon their Neighbours. Nay, thou haft pofitively pronounc'd, That while Men do thefe Things, tho' they afflict themfelves by Fafting, tho' they fpread Sackcloth and Afhes under them, yet thou wilt have no Regard to them.

Thefe Particulars we confefs; and therefore from thy own Mouth, O God, we are bound to acknowledge, That if we keep a ftrict Faft from Meat, and are not converted from our evil Ways; if we do not walk in the Ways of Charity and Peace, our Fafting will be rejected by thee, and we are to expect no Benefit by it.

Wherefore behold now, O God, we make our Addreffes to thee, imploring thy Goodnefs to have Compaffion on us, and to give us fuch Grace, whereby we may difcern all our Evils, and with Refolution labour to overcome them, that fo our Faft may find Acceptance with thee. For this End we now join in our Petitions, and with one Voice befeech thee to hear us.

Lord, have Mercy on us.
Chrift, have Mercy on us.
Lord, have Mercy on us.

God,

12   *Thurfday* before

God, the Father of Heaven,⎫
God, the Son, Redeemer⎪
of the World,   ⎬ Have Mer-
God, the Holy Ghoft,   ⎪ cy on us.
Holy Trinity, One God,   ⎭

Grant, O merciful God, that we may now carefully fee into all our Ways, and forfake all thofe, which are difpleafing to thee. R. *We befeech Thee hear us.*

That we may in earneft break off all thofe finful Cuftoms, by which we have hitherto provok'd thee. R. *We befeech Thee hear us.*

That we may faithfully refift all thofe Inclinations in us, which lead to Evil. R. *We befeech Thee hear us.*

That we may vigoroufly fupprefs all fuch Paffions or Affections, as are contrary to thy Law. R. *We befeech Thee hear us.*

That we may no more follow our own Ways, or our own Will, whenever they put us in Danger of Sin. R. *We befeech Thee hear us.*

That we keep a Watch upon our Lips, fo as to avoid all finful Difcourfe, or Words. R. *We befeech Thee hear us.*

That we ftrictly obferve our Converfation, fo as to decline all Company and Entertainments, which are not agreeable to the Sanctity of this Holy Time. R. *We befeech Thee hear us.*

That

Firſt *Sunday* in *Lent.* 13

That we renounce all the common Methods of Pride, Vanity and Prodigality. R. *We beſeech Thee hear us.*

That we carefully fly all Degrees of Intemperance, Gluttony, and of all Exceſs. R. *We beſeech Thee hear us.*

That we indulge not our Senſes or Thoughts in any ſinful Liberties. R. *We beſeech Thee hear us.*

That we miſ-ſpend not our Time, by yielding to Idleneſs, Sloth, or to immoderate Sleep or Gaming. R. *We beſeech Thee hear us.*

That we may no more go on careleſs or luke-warm in the Affairs of Salvation. R. *We beſeech Thee hear us.*

That we may no more Neglect, or Perform with Coldneſs, the Duties of Eternity. R. *We beſeech Thee hear us.*

That we may no more ſet our Hearts upon the Things of this World, nor by any immoderate Sollicitude prejudice that Love, which is due to thee. R. *We beſeech Thee hear us.*

Hear us, O God, we beſeech thee, and mercifully grant theſe our Petitions, becauſe we know all our Faſting is but Vain, if with our Faſts we join not our beſt Endeavours, for reforming our Lives.

B

Help

14   *Thurſday* before

Help us therefore in this Work, and,
by the Power of thy Grace, make us Zealous in it.

Let us join all our Forces againſt Sin,
and with all the Earneſtneſs of our Souls
make Oppoſition againſt it.

Let us obſerve all our Diſorders, in
whatever kind they be, and now give no
Quarter to them.

It is now a Time wherein we ſeek for
Mercy ; and how can we hope for this, if
we live on in his Diſpleaſure, who is to
grant it ?

God hears not Sinners ; it muſt therefore be in Vain, if, with our unforſaken
Sins, we pretend to gain his Favour.

God is the Searcher of Hearts, and it
is not with our Lips only, but with all
our Hearts, we muſt be converted to
him.

Thus, O God, we are convinc'd ; thus,
O God, may we do by the Effect of
thy Grace.   Aſſiſt us therefore now, we
beſeech thee ; and ſince we are now in
the Time of Mercy, direct us ſo to make
uſe of it, that no ill Management of ours
may diſappoint us of that Mercy, which
we want.

Confirm us, O Bleſſed Lord, in this
Deſign, and let it not paſs away, like
barren Purpoſes, without Effect.   Let
us every Day conſider what our Failings
are,

First *Sunday* in *Lent.*   L 5

are, and every Day study to amend them. Let us look upon that Day lost, with its Fast, wherein we keep not a Watch upon our usual Infirmities, and strive not in good earnest to overcome them.

For this End, we beseech thee, O God, to give us Perseverance, that we may not be tir'd with any Difficulties, nor want Patience in doing that Work, which cannot be left undone, but with the Danger of our Souls. Let us go on with Constancy, notwithstanding all the Discouragements we meet in our Way; and never cease, till we have gain'd the Victory over all our Disorders, and purified our Souls, as this Time requires Grant this, O God, we beseech thee, for the Glory of thy Name, and our own everlasting Good, and let no Unworthiness of ours turn away this Mercy from us.

O God, who by Sin art offended, and by Penance pacified, mercifully regard the Prayers of thy People, who make Supplication to thee, and turn away the Scourges of thy Anger, which we deserve for our Sins. Spare, O Lord, spare thy people, that having been justly punish'd for their Sins, they may find Comfort in thy Mercy. Thro' our Lord Jesus Christ thy Son.

16   *Friday* before

░░░░░░░░░░░░░░░░░░░░░░░░░░░░░░░░░░░

Friday before Firſt *Sunday* in LENT.

BEing now enter'd upon the Faſt of Lent, *let us both reſolve, and uſe our beſt Endeavours, this Day, for making it a Faſt Acceptable to God. And ſince nothing can more contribute to this good Effect, than a true Repentance of all our Sins, proceeding from an humble and contrite Heart ; let us both ask this now in Prayer, and by true Contrition endeavour to make our Peace with God, that ſo the Guilt of our paſt Sins may not make void all we do.*

Let us Pray.

O God, who wilt not the Death of a Sinner, but that he repent and live, have regard, we beſeech thee, to the Sighs of as many as are here preſent ; and to all thoſe who ſincerely deſire to repent from their Heart of all their Sins, mercifully grant what they ask ; that being reſtor'd to thy Favour, there may be nothing found in them, to hinder the Effects of that Mercy, which they ſeek at this Time.

That

First *Sunday* in *Lent*.　17

That we may all be restor'd to this State of Life, behold, we all join in the Acknowledgment of our Unworthiness and Sins, and humbly sue for Mercy.

To thee, O Heavenly Father, we confess our Iniquities ; our Sins have been multiplied above the Hairs of our Head. We have departed from thee, our God, and have done Evil before thee. We have been ungrateful under all thy Favours, we have abus'd thy Blessings, and turned thy own Gifts against thy self. We have call'd thee our Lord, but have not serv'd thee : We have made Profession of being thy Disciples, but have not followed thee : We have promis'd to renounce the Devil, the World, with all their Pomps and Works ; and what has the great Part of our Life been, but following these, and a Homage in their Service ?

Hence, O God, when we look back, and take a Review of our Lives, how little, how very little, can we see that is truly Christian, and answerable to the Sanctity of our Profession ? The great Bulk of what appears is a monstrous Heap of Ingratitude and Treachery, a horrid Mixture of Pride and Sensuality, of Sloth and Self-love, of Impatience and Passion, of Tepidity and Dulness ; with a Thousand other like Ingredients, such

B 3　　　　　　　as

as we cannot look at, without Confufion, upon the Sight of our Infidelity and Folly.

And now, O God, while we know the great Hatred thou bear'ft to Sinners, and the Severity of thy Judgment againft thofe who have forfaken thy Law, what could we do but lie down in Defpair under the Weight of our Sins, if thy Goodnefs did not prevent it ? who calling upon Sinners to forfake their evil Ways, haft promis'd Mercy to thofe, who heartily feek it, and to be a God to as many as truly return to thee their God.

Upon this Encouragement of thy Goodnefs, and the Fidelity of thy Promifes, behold, we all here humble our felves before thee, in the Confeffion of our Sins ; and now this Day defiring to obtain Pardon of all our paft Iniquities, and confiding in the Merits of Chrift our Redeemer, we with one Voice call upon thee for Mercy.

Lord, have Mercy on us.
Chrift, have Mercy on us.
Lord, have Mercy on us.
God the Father of Heaven,
God the Son, Redeemer of the World, *Have Mercy on us.*
God the Holy Ghoft,
Holy Trinity, One God,

O

Firſt *Sunday* in *Lent.* 19

O God, who wilt not the Death of Sinners, but that they be converted and live.

O God, who didſt bring *Adam*, after his Fall, to the Confeſſion of his Sin, and to Repentance,

O God, who didſt caſt *Cain*, deſpairing of thy Mercy, from before thy Face.

O God, who didſt mercifully deliver *Noah* from the general Deſtruction of Sinners.

O God, who didſt pardon the *Iſraelites*, humbling themſelves before thee in the Confeſſion of their Sins,

O God, who didſt forgive *David*, with true Repentance, acknowledging his Guilt,

O God, who didſt ſpare *Achab*, Humbled and Penitent,

O God, who ſhew'dſt Mercy to *Manaſſes* upon his Repentance,

Bleſſed Jeſus,

Jeſus, who cam'ſt into this World to ſave Sinners,

Jeſus, who cam'ſt into the World to ſeek the Loſt-Sheep,

Jeſus, who cam'ſt into the World to call Sinners to Repentance,

Jeſus, who call'dſt *Matthew* from a Publican, to be of the Number of thy Apoſtles,

Have Mercy on us.

B 4

Jeſus,

20   *Friday* before

Jefus, who forgav'ft *Mary Magda-len*, and becam'ft her Advocate,

Jefus, who didft pardon *Peter*, having thrice denied thee.

Jefus, who promis'd Mercy to the Thief repenting on the Crofs,

(right margin: Have Mercy on us O)

Be merciful to us.   R. *Spare us,* O *Lord.*

Be merciful to us.   R. *O Lord, deliver us.*

By thy Fafting in the Defart,

By all thy Labours in feeking loft Man,

By all thy Suffering for our Redemption.

By thy bloody Sweat,

By thy Scourging at the Pillar,

By thy facred Blood, fhed for the Remiffion of Sin,

By the Sacrifice thou offer'dft on the Crofs, for making our Peace with God,

(right margin: O Lord, deliver us.)

We Sinners ;   *We befeech Thee hear* us.

That we may now heartily repent of all our Sins,

That we may renounce all Impiety and worldly Defires,

That Sin may no more reign in our mortal Body,

That we may no more be conform'd to this World,

(right margin: We befeech thee hear us.)

                                    That

First *Sunday* in *Lent*.   21

That we may crucifie our Flesh, with its Affections and Lusts,

That no more evil Words may come out of our Mouth,

That all Bitterness, Anger and Impatience, be taken from us,

That we may put off the old Man, with his Acts,

That we may not live according to the Flesh,

That having put on the Armour of God, we may be able to stand against the Snares of the Enemy,

That being dead to Sin, we may live to Justice,

That thou vouchsafe graciously to hear us,

Son of God,

We beseech thee hear us.

Lamb of God, that tak'st away the Sins of the World. R. *Spare us, O Lord.*

Lamb of God, that tak'st away the Sins of the World. R. *Hear us, O Lord.*

Lamb of God, that tak'st away the Sins of the World. R. *Have Mercy on us.*

Have Mercy on us, O God, we be-seech thee, and by thy Grace now puri-fie us from all our Sins, that being re-ceiv'd into thy Favour, our Prayers and Fast may find Acceptance in thy Sight.

Despise not, O God, the Prayers and Sighs of those that seek for Mercy; and
since

22   *Friday* before, *&c.*

fince we defire to find Mercy by a true Repentance, and call upon thee to help us, hear us, we befeech thee, and grant that our Repentance be fincere.

Grant we may now keep a ftrict Watch upon our felves, a ftrict Watch againft our ufual Infirmities, and in the Amendment of our Lives, fee the good Effect of our Endeavours, and the Fruit of our Prayers. Then, O God, fhall we have Comfort in the Exercifes of this Holy Time, and hope that what we offer to thee, fhall be accepted as a grateful Sacrifice, and afcend like Incenfe in thy Sight. Wherefore,

We befeech thee, O Lord, gracioufly to favour us in the Faft we have begun ; that what we obferve outwardly, we may perform with fincere Minds. Defend thy People, O Lord, and in thy Mercy purifie them from all their Sins ; becaufe no Adverfity will hurt them, if no Iniquity has Power over them. Thro our Lord Jefus Chrift, thy Son.

Saturday

(23)

Saturday before Firſt *Sunday* in L E N T

IT being a Principal Concern at this Time to keep ſuch a Faſt as is well-pleaſing in the Sight of God ; and God himſelf having manifeſted his Will in this Point, that the Faſt he has choſen, is *not only to Faſt from* Meat *and from Sin, but likewiſe to abound in good Works, eſpecially in the Works of Charity, Piety, Mercy and Compaſſion towards our Neighbour ;* in pouring forth our Soul to the Hungry, and ſatisfying the Soul that is afflicted ; in breaking the Bonds of Wickedneſs, looſing the Burthens that are Oppreſſing, ſetting the Diſtreſs'd at Liberty, and undoing every Burthen ; in breaking our Bread to the Hungry, and bringing the Poor and Harbourleſs into our Houſe ; in Cloathing the Naked, and not Deſpiſing our own Fleſh . *God himſelf having thus manifeſted his Will, let us now join in Prayer, and ask his Grace, that we may keep this* Lent *by his own Direction, and make it ſuch a Faſt as he has choſen.*

24. *Saturday* before

Let us Pray.

O God, who know'ſt all our Miſeries, our Neceſſities, and our Sins, and haſt not only appointed us a Time, wherein in a particular Manner we may ſeek for Help; but likewiſe mercifully inform'd us, by what Means we may obtain all the Help we want : Grant, we beſeech thee, that being now in this Holy Time, we may zealouſly follow thy Directions, and ſeek thy Mercy, as we have been taught by thee to find it.

We muſt here confeſs it, O God, a wonderful Effect of thy Goodneſs, to be thus particular in ſhewing us the Means by which we miſerable, unhappy Sinners may make our Peace with thee, and unlock thoſe Treaſures of thy Mercy, which our Sins have ſhut up againſt us.

But what Benefit will this be to us, if we ſtill go on our own Ways, Blind and Confident, and neglect to follow thine! Can we go to Heaven by any Way of our own ? Can we obtain thy Bleſſings, without obſerving thy Orders ? Can we recover the Robe of Juſtice, or turn away thy Anger from us, if we take not thy Directions for effecting it ?

We.

Firſt *Sunday* in *Lent.*   25

We confeſs, O God, we acknowledge it here before thee, we cannot; we can have no Hopes but by obſerving thy Preſcriptions. To follow our own Ways, when thou haſt told us thine, is certainly to go out of the Way: For thy Word is our Rule, thy Will is our Law, and thy Way muſt be ours, if we expect to ſee the Fruit of our Endeavours.

Wherefore, O God, we beſeech thee, as thou haſt in thy Mercy taught us thy Ways, ſo in thy Mercy give us Grace to walk in them, and never let us think our ſelves ſafe, if we decline from them. Eſtabliſh us, O Lord, in this Principle, and ſo confirm it in us, that we may never truſt in any Thing which pretends to diſpenſe with it.

Come therefore, Chriſtians, ſince we have ſo great an Intereſt in this, and eſpecially at this Time, for making our *Lent* Acceptable to God, let us Repent and Confeſs before him, what are the Particulars he requires of us, for rendring our Faſt Beneficial to us, and to be that Faſt, to which he has made the Promiſe of many Bleſſings, the Faſt which he has choſen.

We confeſs, O Lord, that in the Day of our Faſt thou requir'ſt us to Relieve the Diſtreſſed, to Break our Bread to the Hungry, to Cloath the Poor, and
bring

26 *Saturday* before

bring them into Shelter. R. *Thus, O Lord, we confeſs it ought to be in the Faſt, which thou haſt choſen.*

We confeſs, O Lord, in the Day of our Faſt, thou requir'ſt us to looſe the Burthens that are oppreſſing ; to ſet the Diſtreſs'd at Liberty, and undo every Burthen. R. *Thus, O Lord, we confeſs it ought to be in the Faſt, which thou haſt choſen.*

We confeſs, O Lord, in the Day of our Faſt, thou requir'ſt us to keep Peace with every Neighbour, and ſtrictly to avoid all Debates, Contentions and Quarrels. R. *Thus, O Lord, we confeſs it ought to be in the Faſt, which thou haſt choſen.*

We confeſs, O Lord, in the Day of our Faſt, thou requir'ſt us not to ſpeak our own Words, nor do our own Will ; but to govern both our Words and our Will by thy holy Will. R. *Thus, O Lord, we confeſs it ought to be in the Faſt, which, thou haſt choſen.*

We confeſs, O Lord, in the Day of our Faſt, thou requir'ſt us to break the Bonds of Wickedneſs, to renounce all our evil Ways and Cuſtoms, and in all Things to obſerve thy Law, and keep thy Commandments. R. *Thus, O Lord, we confeſs it ought to be in the Faſt, which thou haſt choſen.*

Thus,

First *Sunday* in *Lent.* 27

Thus, O Lord, we all confess it ought to be; and therefore being now in this Solemn Fast, we most earnestly implore thy Grace, that at this Time we may live in all Holiness and Justice, and be constant in the daily Practices of such Exercises as thou, O God, hast recommended to us, and without which our Fast cannot be well-pleasing in thy Sight.

But then, O most merciful Father, remember what our Weakness, and what our Corruption is; and according as thou know'st these to abound, so, we beseech thee, let thy Grace abound in us; that by this Help of thy Mercy we may overcome the Corruption of our Nature, resist all Evil, and be sollicitous to walk as thy Children, in doing those Things which thou hast so expresly required of us. Hear us, O God, we beseech thee, and mercifully grant this our Petition.

Christ hear us.

Christ graciously hear us.

That at this Time we may live soberly, justly and piously. R. *We beseech thee hear us.*

That we may work Good while we have Time. R. *We beseech thee hear us.*

That we may walk worthy of our Vocation. R. *We beseech thee hear us.*

That

28 *Saturday* before

That we may put on the New Man, which is created according to God, in Juſtice, and Holineſs of Truth. R. *We beſeech thee hear us.*

That we may bear with one another in Charity, ſollicitous to keep the Unity of the Spirit in the Bond of Peace. R. *We beſeech thee hear us.*

That we return none Evil for Evil, but do Good for Evil. R. *We beſeech thee hear us.*

That we may endeavour to bear one another's Burthens, ſo to fulfil the Law of Chriſt. R. *We beſeech thee hear us.*

That we may be ever ready to do good, and communicate what we have to the Diſtreſs'd, becauſe with ſuch Sacrifices thou art well-pleas'd. R. *We beſeech thee hear us.*

That by Good Works we may ſtrive to make our Election ſure. R. *We beſeech thee hear us.*

That doing Good, we may not faint or be tir'd. R. *We beſeech thee hear us.*

That we may live according to the Spirit of Chriſt. R. *We beſeech thee hear us.*

Hear us, O God, we beſeech thee, and mercifully grant our Requeſts, that we here aſſembled, tho' Poor and Miſerable of our ſelves, may by thy Grace walk in ſuch Holineſs as to become grateful to thee. Grant.

First *Sunday* in *Lent.*   29

Grant we may sanctifie every Day of our Fast with such Practices of Charity, Piety and Mercy, that notwithstanding all our Infirmities, we may become a holy People, and find thy Acceptance in the Plenty of heavenly Blessings.

Direct us, O God, in this Particular, that following thy own Prescriptions, we may make an Advantage of this present Time, and by an holy Fast make some Attonement for our past Offences.

Confirm us, we beseech thee, in these our good Desires, and let not our usual Weaknesses prevail against us : If Nature and Custom be strong in us, let the Strength of thy Grace likewise appear in standing against them, that we overcoming, thou may'st be glorified in our Weakness.

Give Ear, O Lord, to our Prayers, that with a true Devotion we may observe this solemn Fast, which is piously instituted for giving Health both to our Soul and Body. May thy Faithful, O God, be strengthen'd by thy Gifts, that they may ever thirst after them, and have their Desires satisfied in the everlasting Possession of them. Through our Lord Jesus Christ.

[Anon.], *The Primer, or, Office of the B. Virgin Mary, Revis'd: With a New and Approv'd Version of the Church-Hymns throughout the Year: To which Are Added the Remaining Hymns of the Roman Breviary* (London, T. Meighan, 1717), pp. 116–31

In the seventeenth century *The Primer, or, Office of the B[lessed] Virgin* regularly came off overseas presses, being published in Antwerp (1650, 1658, 1685) and St Omer (1651, 1673, 1685). In the eighteenth century the text had regular runs from presses in England and Ireland. It was published in London in 1706, and in 1717 Thomas Meighan issued the present edition. With slight variations in its title, it was published again in London (1732 and twice in 1780), in Dublin (1767 and 1796) and Cork (1789).Through this series of reissues, *The Primer* offered lay people continuous access, in English, to a key feature of the office of the breviary.[1]

1.   J. M. Blom, *The Post-Tridentine English Primer* (London, Catholic Record Society Monograph Series, vol. 3, 1982), pp. 168–75.

THE

PRIMER,

OR,

OFFICE

OF THE

B. Virgin *MARY*,

REVIS'D:

With a New and Approv'd

VERSION

OF THE

CHURCH-HYMNS

Throughout the Year:

To which

Are Added the Remaining HYMNS
of the Roman Breviary.

Faithfully Corrected.

Printed in the Year, 1717.

The Office of our B. Lady.

To be said from the Even Song of Chriftmafs-Eve,
to the Feaft of the Purification *Inclufive.*

At *MATTINS.*

All is to be said as before Advent, *pag.* 1.

At *LAUDS.*

INcline unto my Aid, O God.
R. O Lord, make hafte to help me.
Glory be to the Father, *&c.*
As it was in, *&c. Alleluja.*
The Anth. O Admiral Intercourfe.

P s a l m 92. **Dominus regnavit.**

OUR Lord has reign'd, he has put on
Beauty; our Lord has put on Strength,
and girded himfelf.

For he has eftablifh'd the Globe of the
Earth, which fhall not be mov'd.

From that Time was thy Seat prepar'd,
thou art from Eternity.

The Rivers, O Lord, have lifted up,
the Rivers have lifted up their Voice.

The Rivers have lifted up their Waves
from the Voice of many Waters.

Marvellous are the Rifings of the Sea:
marvellous is our Lord on High.

Thy Teftimonies are made very Credible : Holinefs becomes thy Houfe, O Lord,
for Length of Days.

Glory be to the Father, *&c.*

The

after Advent, at Lauds. 117

The Anth. O Admirable Intercourse, the Creator of Mankind taking a Living Body, vouchsafed to be born of a Virgin ; and coming forth Man, without Seed, has given to us his Godhead.

The Anth. When thou waſt unſpeakably.

P s a l m 99. Jubilate Deo.

MAke ye Joy to God all the Earth, ſerve our Lord in Gladneſs.

Enter in before his Sight with Joy.

Know, that the Lord is God, he made us, and not we our ſelves.

His People, and the Sheep of his Paſture, enter into his Gates in Confeſſion, his Courts with Hymns, confeſs ye to him.

Praiſe his Name, becauſe our Lord is ſweet, his Mercy for ever, and his Truth even from Generation to Generation.

Glory be to the Father, &c.

The Anth. When thou waſt unſpeakably Born of a Virgin, then were the Scriptures fulfill'd ; thou didſt deſcend like Rain into the Fleece, that thou might'ſt ſave Mankind : we Praiſe our God.

The Anth. The Buſh which *Moſes* ſaw.

P s a l m 62. Deus Deus meus, ad te de luce vigilo.

O God my God : to thee I watch from the Morning Light.

My Soul has thirſted after thee : my Fleſh alſo very many Ways.

As

118 *The Office of our B. Lady,*

As in a Defart Land, and inacceffible, and without Water : fo in the Holy Place have I appear'd to thee, that I might behold thy Strength and thy Glory.

Becaufe thy Mercy is better than Life, my Lips fhall praife thee.

So will I blefs thee in my Life, and in thy Name I will lift up my Hands.

As with Marrow and Fatnefs let my Soul be fill'd, and my Mouth fhall praife with Lips of Joy.

If I have been mindful of thee on my Bed ; in the Morning I will meditate on thee ; becaufe thou haft been my Helper.

And under the Cover of thy Wings I will rejoice, my Soul has cleav'd after thee ; thy Right Hand has taken me under it's Protection.

But they in vain have fought my Soul, they fhall enter into the lower Parts of the Earth : they fhall be deliver'd into the Power of the Sword ; they fhall be the Portions of Foxes.

But the King fhall rejoice in God, all fhall be prais'd, that fwear on him ; becaufe the Mouth of thofe, that fpeak wicked things, is ftop'd.

PSALM 66. Deus mifereatur noftri.

GOD have Mercy on us, and blefs us, caufe his Countenance to fhine upon us, and have Mercy on us.

That

after Advent, at Lauds. 119

That we may know thy Way, on Earth, thy Salvation, in all Nations.

Let People, O God, confefs to thee, let all People praife thee.

Let Nations be glad, and rejoice, becaufe thou judgeft People with Equity, and directeft the Nations on the Earth.

Let People, O God, confefs to thee; let all People praife thee : the Earth has yielded her Fruit.

May God, our God, blefs us ; may God blefs us, and may all the Ends of the Earth fear him.

Glory be to the Father, &c.

The Anth. The Bufh which *Mofes* faw burn, without confuming, we acknowledge thy Laudable Virginity preferv'd ; O Mother of God, make Interceffion for us.

The Anth. The Root of *Jeffe* has Budded.

The Song of the Three Children, Dan. 3.

ALL the Works of our Lord blefs our Lord ; praife and extol him for ever.

Blefs our Lord ye Angels of our Lord ; ye Heavens blefs our Lord.

All Waters, that are above the Heavens, blefs ye our Lord ; blefs our Lord all ye Powers of our Lord.

Sun and Moon blefs our Lord : Stars of Heaven blefs our Lord.

Showers and Dew blefs our Lord : all Spirits of God blefs our Lord.

Fire

120   *The Office of our B. Lady,*

Fire and Heat blefs our Lord : Cold and Summer blefs our Lord.

Dews and Hoary Froft blefs our Lord: Froft and Cold blefs our Lord.

Ice and Snow blefs our Lord : Nights and Days blefs our Lord.

Light and Darknefs blefs our Lord : Lightnings and Clouds blefs our Lord.

Let the Earth blefs our Lord ; let it praife and extol him for ever.

Mountains and Hills blefs our Lord : all Thing:s that Spring in the Earth blefs our Lord

Blefs our Lord ye Fountains : Seas and Rivers blefs our Lord.

Whales, and all that move in the Waters, blefs our Lord : blefs our Lord all ye Fowls of the Air.

All Beafts and Cattle blefs our Lord : Sons of Men blefs our Lord:

Let *Ifrael* blefs our Lord ; praife and extol him for ever.

Priefts of our Lord blefs our Lord: Servants of our Lord blefs our Lord.

Spirits and Souls of the Juft blefs our Lord: ye Holy and Humble of Heart blefs our Lord.

Ananias, Azarias, Mifael, blefs our Lord; praife and extol him for ever.

Let us blefs the Father and the Son, with the Holy Ghoft: Let us praife and magnifie him for ever.

Bleffed

after Advent, at Lauds. 121

Bleſſed art thou, Lord, in the Firmament of Heaven; and prais'd, and glorified and extoll'd for ever.

The Anth. The Root of *Jeſſe* has Budded out, a Star is riſen from *Jacob*, a Virgin hath brought forth a Savionr : We praiſe thee our God.

The Anth. Behold *Mary.*

PSALM 148. Laudate Dominum de Cælis.

PRaiſe our Lord from the Heavens, praiſe him in the high Places.

Praiſe him all his Angels, praiſe him all his Powers.

Praiſe him Sun and Moon, praiſe him all ye Stars and Light.

Praiſe him O Heavens of Heavens! and let the Waters, that are above the Heavens, praiſe the Name of our Lord.

Becauſe he ſpoke, and they were made; he commanded, and they were created.

He eſtabliſh'd them for ever, World without end: He made a Precept, and it ſhall not be annull'd.

Praiſe our Lord from the Earth, ye Dragons, and all Depths.

Fire, Hail, Snow, Ice, Tempeſtuous Winds, which obey his Word.

Mountains and all Hills, Trees that bear Fruit and all Cedars.

Beaſts and all Cattle: Serpents and winged Fowls.

G   Kings

122 *The Office of our B. Lady,*

Kings of the Earth, and all People, Princes, and all Judges of the Earth.

Young Men and Virgins, the Old with the Young ; let them praife the Name of our Lord, becaufe his Name alone is ex. alted.

The Confeffion of him is above Hea. ven and Earth, and he has exalted the Horn of his People.

A Hymn to all his Saints, to the Sons of *Ifrael*; a People that approaches to him.

PSALM 149.

SING to our Lord a new Song, let his Praife be in the Church of Saints.

Let *Ifrael* be joyful in him that made him, and the Children of *Sion* rejoice in their King.

Let them praife his Name in Quire: On Timbrel and Pfalter let them fing to him.

Becaufe our Lord is well pleas'd with his People, and he will exalt the Meek to Salvation.

The Saints fhall rejoice in Glory, they fhall be joyful in their Beds.

The Praife of God fhall be in their Mouths, and two-edg'd Swords in their Hands.

To execute Revenge on the Nations, Chaftifements among the People.

To bind their Kings in Fetters, and their Nobles in Chains of Iron.

That they may execute on them the Judg-

after Advent, at Lauds. 123

Judgment that is written : this Glory is to all his Saints.

PSALM 150. Laudate Dominum in Sanctis.

PRaise our Lord in his Saints, praise him in the Firmament of his Strength.

Praise him in his Powers, praise him according to the Multitude of his Greatness.

Praise him in the Sound of Trumpet, praise him on Psalter and Harp.

Praise him on Timbrel, and in Quire, praise him on Strings and Organs.

Praise him on well-sounding Cymbals, praise him on Cymbals of Joy, let every Spirit praise our Lord.

Glory be to the Father, &c.

The Anth. Behold, *Mary* has brought forth to us a Saviour, whom *John* seeing, cry'd out, saying, Behold the Lamb of God, behold him, who takes away the Sins of the World. *Alleluja.*

The Chapter, Cant. 1.

THE Daughters of *Sion* beheld her, and declared her most Blessed ; and Queens did praise her.

R. Thanks be to God.

The HYMN, *O gloriosa Virginum.*

O *Mary* ! whilst thy Maker blest Is nourish'd at thy Virgin Breast, Such Glory shines, that Stars less bright Behold thy Face, and lose their Light.

G 2

The

124 *The Office of our B. Lady,*

The Lofs that Man in *Eve* deplores
Thy Fruitful Womb in Chrift reftores,
And makes the Way to Heaven free
For them that mourn to follow thee.

By thee the Heavenly Gates difplay
And fhew the Light of endlefs Day :
Sing ranfom'd Nations, fing and own
Your Ranfom was a Virgin's Son.

May Age to Age for ever fing
The Virgin's Son and Angels King ;
And praife with the Celeftial Hoft
The Father, Son, and Holy Ghoft. *Amen.*

V. Bleffed art thou among Women.
R. And bleffed is the Fruit of thy Womb.
The Anth. A Wonderful Myftery.

The Song of Zach. Luke 1.

BLeffed be our Lord God of *Ifrael*, becaufe he has vifited and wrought the
Redemption of his People.

And rais'd up a Kingdom of Salvation,
to us, in the Houfe of *David*, his Servant.

As he fpoke by the Mouth of his Holy
Prophets, that are from the Beginning.

Salvation from our Enemies, and from
the Hand of all that hate us.

To work Mercy with our Fathers, and
to remember his Holy Covenant.

The Oath, which he fwore to *Abraham* our Father, that he would grant
to us.

That without Fear, being deliver'd from
the Hand of our Enemies, we may ferve
him   In

after Advent, at Lauds. 125

In Holiness and Justice before him all our Days.

And thou, Child, shalt be call'd the Prophet of the Highest : For thou shalt go before the Face of our Lord to prepare his Ways.

To give Knowledge of Salvation to his People, for Remission of their Sins.

Through the Bowels of the Mercy of our God; in which the Rising Sun from on high has visited us.

To enlighten them that sit in Darkness, and in the Shadow of Death : To direct our Feet in the Way of Peace.

Glory be to the Father, &c.

The Anth. A Wonderful Mystery is declar'd this Day : Natures are renew'd, God is made Man ; he remain'd what he was, and assum'd what he was not, suffering neither Mixture nor Division.

Lord have Mercy on us.

Christ have Mercy on us.

Lord have Mercy on us.

V. Lord hear my Prayer.

R. And let my Cry come to thee.

Let us Pray.

O God, who by the Fruitful Virginity of the Blessed Virgin *Mary*, hast given to Mankind the Rewards of Eternal Salvation : Grant, we beseech thee, that we may be sensible of the Benefit of her Intercession, by whom we have receiv'd the

G 3   Au-

126 *The Office of our B. Lady,*

Author of Life, our Lord Jesus Christ thy Son, who liveth and reigneth one God with thee, &c. R. Amen.

For the Saints.

The Anth. All ye Saints of God, vouchsafe to make Interceffion for the Salvation of us, and of all. V. Ye Juft rejoice in our Lord, and be exceeding glad. R. And glory all ye right of Heart.

Let us Pray.

Protect, O Lord, thy People, and let the Confidence we have in the Interceffion of the Bleffed Apoftles, *Peter* and *Paul*, and of thy other Apoftles, prevail with thee, to preferve and defend us for Ever.

May all thy Saints, O Lord, we befeech thee, every where affift us, that whilft we celebrate their Merits, we may be fenfible of their Protection : Grant us thy Peace in our Times, and repel all Wickednefs from thy Church ; profperoufly guide the Steps, Actions and Defires of us and all thy Servants in the Way of Salvation : Give eternal Bleffings to thofe who have done good to us, and everlafting Reft to the Faithful departed : Thro' our Lord Jefus Chrift thy Son, &c. R. Amen.

V. Lord hear my Prayer.

R. And let my Cry come to thee.

V. Blefs we our Lord.

R. Thanks be to God.

V. May

after Advent at Lauds. 127

V. May the Souls of the Faithful, thro the Mercy of God, reſt in Peace. *R.* Amen.

This being done, the Anthem *following is to be ſaid Kneeling.*

The Anthem. *Alma Redemptoris Mater.*

B Right Parent of our Lord, whoſe Pray'rs diſplay
The Heav'nly Gates, whoſe Light directs our Way;
Bright Ocean's Star, with ſacred Influence guide
Our ſtraggling Courſe in Spite of Nature's Tide.

Thou in whom Nature ſtood amaz'd to ſee
Both God and Man, thy Maker born of thee
In whom alone the Maid and Mother meet,
Remember Sinners at thy Infant's Feet,

V. Thou didſt remain an inviolate Virgin after thy Child-bearing.

R. O Mother of God, make Interceſſion for us.

Let us Pray.

O God, who by the Fruitful Virginity
as before. *R.* Amen.

V. May the Divine Help ever remain with us. *R.* Amen.

The aforeſaid Anth. *is ſaid in the End of* Complin *till the Day of the* Purification *incluſive.*

The Anthem. *Ave Regina Cælorum.*

H Ail ſhining Queen of the Celeſtial Train,
O'er Angel-Pow'rs extend thy brighter Reign.
Hail fruitful Root of Life, Hail Orient Gate,
From whom Earth's better Light derives its Date.
O glorious Maid *!* rejoice alone poſſeſs
The higheſt Seat of Creatures Happineſs.

And

128 *The Office of our B. Lady,*

And crown'd with Beauty, thence, implore thy Son
To grant our Prayers from his indulgent Throne.

V. Vouchfafe that I may praife thee, O
Sacred Virgin, *R.* Give me Force againft
thy Enemies.

Let us Pray.

STrengthen us, O God of Mercy, againft
all our Weaknefs, and grant that we
who celebrate the Memory of the Bleffed
Virgin *Mary*, Mother of our Lord, may
by the Affiftance of her Prayers forfake all
our Iniquities. Thro' the fame Chrift our
Lord. *R.* Amen.

V. May the Divine Help always remain with us. *R.* Amen.

At P R I M E.

Hail *Mary*.

INcline unto my Aid, O God.
R. O Lord make hafte to help me.
Glory be to the Father, &c.
As it was in the Beginning, &c.
The HYMN. *Memento rerum Conditor.*

REmember, You, O Gracious Lord,
Th' eternal God's Co-equal Word,
In Virgin's Womb a Creature made
Our Nature wore for Nature's Aid.

O happy *Mary* chofe to be
Mother of Grace and Clemency !
Protect us at the Hour of Death,
And bear to Heav'n our parting Breath.

May

May Age to Age for ever fing
The Virgin's Son and Angels King,
And praife with the Celeftial Hoft
The Father, Son, and Holy Ghoft. *Amen.*

The Anth. O Admiral Intercourfe !

Psalm 53. Deus in nomine tuo.

O God, fave me by thy Name, and by
thy Strength judge me.

O God, hear my Prayer; with thy
Ears receive the Words of my Mouth.

Becaufe Strangers have rifen up againft
me, and the Strong have fought my Soul:
and they have not fet God before their Eyes.

For behold, God helps me, and our Lord
is the Protector of my Soul.

Turn away the Evils to my Enemies,
and in thy Truth deftroy them.

I will freely facrifice to thee, and will
confefs to thy Name, O Lord, becaufe it
is good.

Becaufe thou haft deliver'd me out of
all Tribulation : and my Eyes have look'd
down upon my Enemies.

Glory be to the Father, &c.

Psalm 84. Benedixfti Domine.

O Lord, thou haft bleffed thy Land :
thou haft turn'd away the Captivity
of Jacob.

Thou haft forgiven the Iniquity of thy
People, thou haft cover'd all their Sins.

Thou haft moderated all thy Wrath, thou
haft

130 *The Office of our B. Lady,*

haft turn'd away from the Wrath of thy Indignation.

Convert us, O God our Saviour, and turn away thy Anger from us.

Wilt thou be angry with us for Ever? Or wilt thou extend thy Wrath from Generation to Generation?

O God, thou being reconcil'd, fhalt quicken us; and thy People fhall rejoice in thee.

Shew us, O Lord, thy Mercy, and give us thy Salvation.

I will hear what our Lord God fhall fpeak in me, becaufe he will fpeak Peace to his People.

And to his Saints, and to them that are converted to the Heart.

But his Salvation is near to them that fear him, that Glory may inhabit our Land.

Mercy and Truth have met each other, Juftice and Peace have kiffed.

Truth is rifen out of the Earth, and Juftice has look'd down from Heaven.

For our Lord will give Plenty, and our Land fhall yield its Fruit.

Juftice fhall walk before him, and fet her Steps in the Way.

Glory be to the Father, &c.

PSALM 116. Laudate Dominum.

PRaife our Lord all Gentiles, praife him all People.

Becaufe

after Advent, at Prime. **131**

Becaufe his Mercy is confirm'd on us ;
and his Truth remains for Ever.

Glory be to the Father, &c.

The Anth. O Admiral Intercourfe ! the
Creator of Mankind, taking a living
Body, vouchfafed to be Born of a Virgin,
and coming forth Man without Seed,
has given to us his Godhead.

The Chapter. Cant. 6.

WHo is She, that comes forth as the
Morning Rifing, fair as the Moon,
elect as the Sun, terrible as the Front of
an Army fet in order of Battle. *R.* Thanks
be to God.

V. Vouchfafe that I may praife thee, O
Sacred Virgin.

R. Give me Force againft thy Enemies.

Lord have Mercy on us. Chrift have
Mercy on us. Lord have Mercy on us.

V. Lord hear my Prayer.

R. And let my Cry come to thee.

Let us Pray.

[William Crathorne (ed.)], *Mr Gother's Spiritual Works. Tome X. Instructions for Particular States and Conditions of Life. There Are Added General Indexes and Tables to each Tome. Faithfully Corrected* (London, T. Meighan, 1718), pp. 284–300, 314–27

This volume was first produced in 1689, around the time when Gother effected his own transformation from English Catholicism's leading published controversialist to the foremost ethical, devotional, catechetical and liturgical guide to the English Catholic community at large. It offers a good example of Gother's pastoral and moral directions on the duties of the various social strata in an English Catholic community emerging into a new age, when aristocratic leadership was still crucially important, while the Catholic element in English society was also acquiring an increasingly important 'plebeian' and broadly middle-class component. For the Catholic body living in an England whose values, as Bossy writes, were 'regularity, rationality and work',[1] Gother provided a convincing 'work ethic'. His identification of 'Working Christians' as 'a kind of Religious Order, in which God himself has Instituted their Rule', while 'their daily Toil will be as much an Act of Religion and Obedience, as what those do, who live in a Cloyster, and observe the Rules of their Founder', at first sight may seem to relegate the lay condition to an emulative shadow of the religious life, the most authentic calling for Catholic Christians. However, by describing in considerable detail and, indeed, occasional vivid colour, lives of planned and disciplined labour willingly accepted, Gother can be seen as having put forward a cogent code of 'inner-worldly asceticism' for his lay co-religionists.

In this moral system, servants owed duties of conscientious service to those who hired them, while employers had reciprocal obligations to those in their employ. In particular, Gother decreed there lay on the latter a duty to provide for the religious education of employees, even at the expense of some time lost to work (though, as Bossy writes, 'on the whole the [recusant] gentry were not very enthusiastic supporters of intensive religious instruction for everyone'[2]). Having in mind the traditional, religiously homogeneous Catholic gentry household, with its own elaborate aristocratic regime of domestic maintenance, cleaning, hospitality, socializing, and the preparation of opulent meals (particularly on Sundays and feast-days), Gother analysed the tension between the hard work necessary to uphold such amenities and the need to allow the servants time for their own religious nurture. He strongly advised an organization of a household's timetables to create space for the religious lives of its staff, indeed requiring masters and mistresses to monitor their domestics' morals, as well as their religious performance, especially in attending the sacraments. Clearly, then, Gother had before him an ideal vision of the Catholic head of household as the exemplary president of a religious community, a person selfless over his or her own creature comforts when their provision ate into religious concerns; again, such a master or mistress would be admonitory when necessary, but not censorious, as well as stable, prudent and mild, avoiding 'an Uneasy, or too Nice a Temper': a contrast, perhaps, with his own employer at Warkworth Manor, the 'melancholy and bigoted' George Holman.[3]

1.　　John Bossy, *The English Catholic Community 1570–1850* (London, Darton, Longman & Todd, 1975), p. 286.

2.　　Bossy, *English Catholic Community*, p. 276.

3.　　Eamon Duffy, 'Richard Challoner 1691–1781: A Memoir', in Duffy (ed.), *Challoner and his Church: A Catholic Bishop in Georgian England* (London, Darton, Longman & Todd, 1981), p. 1.

Mr. *GOTHER's*

Spiritual Works.

TOME X.

Inſtructions for particular States and Conditions of Life.

Theſe are added,

General *Indexes* and *Talles* to each TOME.

Faithfully Corrected.

LONDON:

Printed in the Year 1718.

Inſtructions

For Particular

STATES.

Printed in the Year, 1718.

284

C H A P. XIII.

Instructions for Laborious or Working Christians.

'TIS generally reputed an Unhappinefs to be oblig'd to work for
Bread ; but fince the Advocates, that
plead thus againft it, are Self-Love,
Sloth and Pride, there is Reafon to
Hope, it deferves a better Character,
fince they, that thus render it Contemptible, are too Infamous, to have
their Opinion pafs for Juft amongft
Chriftians ; who may rather conclude
it to be Honourable and Holy, becaufe
thefe think fo ill of it.

'Tis true, all Labour may be efteem'd
an Unhappinefs, if it be confider'd, as
the Mark and Punifhment of Sin ;
but if we look on it, as the Penance
impos'd by God himfelf on Sinners,
and as the Remedy of many Evils, to
which thro' their Natural Corruption,
they are fubject, it muft then have a
better Name, and be reputed a Happinefs belonging to this State : Even
fuch a Happinefs, as it is for one, who
is very much in Debt, to have wherewith to Difcarge it ; or for one, who
being expos'd to many Dangers, is
pro-

Inſtruƈtions for Working, &c.   285

provided with ſufficient Means for his Security. For ſince by Sin, all Chriſtians are Indebted to God, the ſureſt Way to ſatisfy it, muſt be by chearfully ſubmitting to the Puniſhment of the Sin: And ſince Idleneſs is the Root of many Evils; he that is oblig'd to daily Work, has by the Circumſtances of his State, the Ax laid to this Root, for preventing its unhappy Growth.

Hence the Firſt Inſtruƈtion for this ſort of Chriſtians, is to undertake their daily Work in the Spirit of Obedience, that is, in Obedience to the Order of God. They are to conſider themſelves, as in a kind of Religious Order, in which God himſelf has Inſtituted their Rule: He has expreſly Commanded, that they ſhall Eat their Bread in the Sweat of their Brows; and if in Submiſſion to this Command, they undertake their Work, it is certain, their daily Toil will be as much an Aƈt of Religion and Obedience, as what thoſe do, who live in a Cloyſter, and obſerve the Rules of their Founder.

II. They are to conſider their Work as Part of that Penance, which the Juſtice of God has impos'd upon Sin. And if upon this Conſideration, they humbly ſubmit to all the Trouble of it;

289　Instructions for Laborious

it; if, in this Spirit, they chearfully quit their Beds in the Morning, and with Fidelity go thro' all the Uneasiness of the Day, 'tis certain, their daily Work will thus become a continued Act of Penance; and in this they will have another Resemblance with the best Religious; whose daily Endeavours are by repeated Mortifications to do Penance for their Sins. And what better Penance, than that which God has fixt on Sin? Even that, which the Primitive Hermits undertook, and those now follow, whose Eminent Sanctity turns upon them the Eyes of our present World.

III. They are to consider their daily Labour, as a Means to preserve their Souls Pure from that general Corruption, which is the Effect of Idleness. Infinite are the Evils of an Idle Life; this opens the Way to all manner of Vice, and leads directly into the Broad Way. Now if these would consider the Danger they are in, arising from the common Weakness of a Corrupt Nature, and undertake their daily Work, as the best Preservative against this Corruption; willingly embracing it, for their better Security against the Evils, which Idleness might otherwise lead them into: they would in this act according to Christian Prudence, and concur in the

first

firſt Deſign of the Beſt Religious, who obſerving the Dangers of the World, reſolve upon withdrawing from it, that ſo by their diſtance, they may not be expos'd to the Occaſions of Sin. Now, if what Religious do by retiring, theſe do by Working, the End in both is the ſame, tho' the Means be different, and the Act in both may be truly ſaid Religious.

IV. They are to conſider their daily Labour, as a Means to provide for themſelves and Family ; and this being what the Obligation of their State lays upon them, whatever they do, upon this Motive, is an Act of Juſtice ; and thus may be made an Offering acceptable to God ; ſo as not only to Work for Bread in all they do, but likewiſe for Eternity ; ſince whatever is here undertaken on the Motive of Juſtice, muſt be available to everlaſting Life. Now in this Part again they may concur with the beſt Religious ; for ſince the Deſign of theſe in their Retirement is to make a Sacrifice of their Lives to God; will not Working Chriſtians do ſo too, if they ſanctify all their Labours by the Motives of Juſtice, and offer them all to God, in Compliance with the Obligations of their State ? It cannot be queſtion'd, but thus they will be well-pleaſing

288   *Inſtructions for Laborious*

pleaſing in the Sight of God, and that
their Labours may be hallow'd by Juſtice, as theirs were heretofore by Faith,
who for being Chriſtians were condemned to dig in Mines.

By obſerving theſe few Inſtructions,
all Labouring Chriſtians may render
their Lives truly Chriſtian, Holy and
Religious. 'Tis true, they have not
that Opportunity for frequent Prayer;
but yet they may Pray ſtill. They
ought to begin the Day with Prayers;
ſo to Conſecrate their Labours and
themſelves to God; if this cannot be
long, becauſe Buſineſs preſſes, yet if
faithfully perform'd, as Circumſtances
will allow, it may, like the Widows
Mite, find as good Acceptance, as the
longer Exerciſes of thoſe, who have
their Time at Command. Other Prayers they may ſay, even at their Work,
by raiſing up their Hearts to God in
ſhort Ejaculations; by acknowledging
their Miſery, aſking for Mercy, Grace
and Protection from Sin, &c. This may
be done in Shops, in the Field, in the
Kitchin, with the Needle, Broom, or
Hammer in the Hand; there being
ſcarce any Exerciſe of Corporal Labour,
but where the Mind has Liberty enough
of raiſing it ſelf above the Employment
of the Hands. And this ought to be
                                    much

or Working Christians. 291

much recommended t o all, who by neceffary Bufinefs being ftraitn'd in their
Time, fcarce find Leifure to begin or
end the Day, by bending their Knees to
God in Prayer : Becaufe by help of
fuch Thoughts, they live mindful of
God, and give proof of their Dependance on him. Befides thefe accidental
Flights, they may be Conftant, at the
Beginning of every Action to Offer it
to God, defiring him to accept it, in
Union with the Labours of Jefus Chrift
on Earth, and in the difcharge of their
Duty. 'Tis thus the Apoftle gives Directions to Chriftians to do all in the
Name of our Lord Jefus Chrift ; that
fo whatever they do, may be fanctify'd
thro' him, and by this holy Expedient,
they have it in their Power, to make
all their Actions Prayer.

I could wifh likewife, thofe, who
have Families would meet, with all under their Care, and conclude the Day
with Prayer : If their early Rifing and
hard Labour, render their tir'd Spirits
unfit for the common Exercifes of
Night, let them take fhorter Prayers,
which God, knowing their Circumftances, will not fail to accept. And
on *Sundays* and Holy-days, they ought to
be exact in fatisfying the Duties of thofe
Days, if they have not the Opportuni-

N   ties

292 *Inſtructions for Laborious*

ties of a Publick Aſſembly, they muſt do it in the beſt manner they are able at home ; always taking ſome Time both Morning and Afternoon for Reading ſome Good Books, which may revive in them the Memory of their Duty, and quicken in them the Deſire of complying with it ; and if this can be done in Common, it will be more Exemplary and Beneficial.

In this manner may labouring Chriſtians, even amidſt the Toil and Diſtraction of their Lives, anſwer all the Obligations, which the Goſpel lays upon them, and prepare for dying happily. There are however ſome Points, in which they are to be careful : Firſt, In not going to their Work, like Brutes, without thinking of thoſe Motives, which may make their Labours available to Salvation. Secondly, If they work for Hire, to be Faithful in what they undertake, and not favour themſelves in his Wrong, who employs them. Thirdly, Not to let Covetouſneſs make them Diligent, but Duty. Fourthly, To ſuppreſs all immoderate Sollicitude, and to truſt in Providence, that if they are truly Induſtrious, they ſhall find help in all Neceſſities. Fifthly, If they work in Company, to avoid all ſinful Diſcourſe and Songs, as likewiſe Animoſities

ties and Quarrels. Sixthly to accuſtom themſelves to no ſort of Prophane Ex-preſſions, as of Curſing, Swearing, &c. And ſince Mirth is commendable in them, to confine it to what is Innocent, and not ſeek Diverſion, in what will pleaſe the Devil, but make God their Enemy. Seventhly, To keep Peace in their Families. Eightly, If they want ſome Relief in the Evening, to make their own Homes the place of it, and not go to ſuch Houſes, where they will be tempted to ſpend Extravagantly in the Night, what they gain with Toil in the Day. Where there is a Wife, it is her Part to contribute to this, by ma-king Home Eaſy and Comfortable ; for it is a Temptation to a Man, who has been labouring all Day, to ſeek Relief abroad, if he cannot find it in his own Houſe ; and on this Conſideration, be-ſides others, ſhe is oblig'd to govern her Paſſions and Tongue, and connive at many Things, which ſhe cannot try to mend, but by making them worſe. Ninthly, To be moderate in their Ex-penſes, and not ſpend Extravagantly in Drink, Diet or Cloaths, what ſhould be their Support in Sickneſs or Age, or the Proviſion of Children. Laſtly, If ſome more than ordinary Reſt be taken on *Sundays* or Holy-days, not to ſpend them,

294 *Inftruftions for Laborious*

at leaft, in Idlenefs; and if they ufe
fome Diverfion, after the Duties of fuch
Days are fatisfy'd for the Relief of their
Spirits, not to make this the Principal
Bufinefs of them, by going into Idle
Company, and committing greater Sins
on Days, that ought to be Sanctify'd,
than in all the Week befide. Thofe,
who Labour hard all the Week, are under great Temptations on all Days,
wherein they do not Work, of running
into fome Folly, Extravagance or Excefs:
For while Diverfion feems neceffary for
them, they have no Scruple in feeking
it; and while the World is fo Corrupt
as it is, they cannot eafily find it, but
with the Danger of being drawn into
fome Diforder; and hence is often Dated the Ruin of themfelves and Families. Wherefore, I think it a very Important Point for this Rank of Chriftians, to fee, how they keep thefe Days,
and particularly in all their Recreations, to make choice of fuch Company,
whofe Principles of Sobriety, Piety,
and Modefty, may fecure them againft
the Common Evils of Idlenefs, and to
avoid fuch Places, where they know
they cannot divert themfelves, but with
the evident hazard of Sin.

Thefe

or Working Chriſtians.   295

Theſe Cautions I preſs to Labouring Chriſtians, that ſo while their Circumſtances exempt them from many Occaſions of Sin, and oblige them to ſpend the great Part of their Lives in ſuch a Way, as is capable of being Sanctify'd, even like that of the Hermit, and ſtricteſt Religious, they may not loſe the Fruit of all their Labours for want of a little Care : It being truly a Matter of Pity, to think, that they, who take ſuch Pains, ſhould make no Advantage of what they do; but after having born the Burthen of the Day, ſhould at the Evening be depriv'd of what was deſign'd for their Hire, and as the Reward of their Labours: Which Unhappineſs can no otherwiſe be prevented, but by a due Care in theſe Particulars; and a Neglect here will likely prove the Loſs of all.

Could they bring their Lives to theſe Rules, I ſhould think them the Happieſt of all Degrees of Chriſtians, that are in the World ; and a little Reflection will teach them to think ſo, notwithſtanding all the Hardſhip they undergo, and the mean Opinion the World has of them. For when I conſider their daily Toil in Working for Bread, I ſee in this the Happineſs of

N 3   being

being deliver'd from that Idleness, which
leads the great Part of the World into
Hell. I follow after the Rich, whom
the World calls Happy, and see them at
their Bottles and Cards, at their Entertainments, Musick, Park, Plays, &c.
and while they are here spending their
Souls, their Lives and Money, I turn
to the Labouring Man, and seeing him
Sweating with the Hammer, Ax or
Spade ; I presently say, How much
better art thou Employ'd, than those,
whom Plenty makes Idle : Happy is
that Necessity, which obliges thee to
Labour, and happy that Labour, which
delivers thee from Idleness. I then
turn to his Table, and seeing, how
Sparing it is, I am inclin'd to think
him unfortunate, because he is no better provided, but when I consider, he
has enough for the Subsistence and Support of Nature, and what he wants,
is only wanting to the demands of
Gluttony and Intemperance ; I here
proclaim him happy again, who Eats
according to the Design of Providence,
that is, for Life and Strength, and not
as an Unbeliever, for Sensuality and
Vice. I look again on his Furniture
and Cloaths, and begin to pity him ;
but when I see Necessity and Decency
                                                      suffi-

or Working Christians.   297

sufficiently provided for ; I then say,
Wherein art thou Unhappy ? Is it because thou haſt nothing to throw away
upon Curioſity and Vanity ? Rather,
the more Happy for this ; in being ty'd
by thy Circumſtances to Duty, and re-
ſtrain'd from what is Vicious.

Thus looking on Labouring Chriſtians, I ſee many Advantages in their
State ; Firſt, In their Labour, which is a
Daily Sacrifice, and Atonement for
Sin. Secondly, In their Wants, in not
having wherewith to feed Pride, Ambition, Luxury, and Extravagance. It
is in theſe Wants only they are diſtinguiſh'd from Men of Plenty :: And if
Pride, Luxury and Extravagance are
Evil, there can be no more Misfortune,
in not having wherewith to feed and
ſtrengthen theſe, than it is to a Sick
Man, not to have Opportunities of
increaſing his Diſtemper. Hence, if
Things are meaſur'd by the Goſpel, it
muſt be acknowledg'd that the Labouring Man at the Anvil, has much the
Preference to the Rich Man at his Entertainments and Games: That his
ſpare Diet anſwerable to Neceſſity, is
better than the other's Abundance, by
which he courts Appetite and Senſe :
That his plain and courſe Dreſs, which
Nature and Modeſty demand, is more

com-

298 *Inftructions for Laborious*

commendable than the other's Coft and Flutter, which are only to gratify his own Vain Humour, or to Complement a Diftemper'd World. 'Tis plain from the firft Rudiments of the Gofpel, which of thefe is in the more Chriftian Way; and therefore plain, which Condition is the more Evangelical. The Cafe is fo clear, that it muft be concluded; if the Rich Man does not bring himfelf, by Self-denials, to live according to the Method of the Labourer, he will be but ill prepar'd to Appear at the Day of Accounts: And hence it is, thofe Pious Souls, who feeing the Extravagencies of the World, are afraid of having a part in them, retire from it, and feek both Security and Perfection in obferving the Rules of the Labouring Man; both in his Daily Employment, and Spare Diet, and Mean Drefs. And as for thofe, that ftay behind, engag'd in a Worldly Life, 'tis moft evident, if they propofe not the fame Rules, overcoming Idlenefs by Bufinefs, and the Excefs of Table and Cloaths by Moderation, they will neither be fecure from Dangers, nor come up to that Perfection which the Gofpel requires as neceffary in all the Followers of Chrift

ſ

If there be any Truth in this, the Labouring Christians may then see the Advantage of their Condition, in being oblig'd to such a Method, which is most conformable to the Gospel, and most helpful to Salvation; and that for the effectual obtaining this Happiness, they need do no more than what their State obliges them to, but only do it in that Holy Disposition of Spirit, as to make their Labours Christian, and a Sacrifice acceptable to God. In this the foregoing Instructions will be some help; but because their Business may not allow the reading them often, I here add a short Prayer, as an Abridgment of them, and if said every Day, before they begin their Work, may be a means of Sanctifying all their Labours.

HERE in Thy Presence, O God, I acknowledge Thy Justice in Commanding us to Labour, in Punishment of Sin; and in Obedience to Thy Command, I willingly undertake the Work of this Day, and submit to all the Trouble of it, as a Penance justly due to my Sins: Accept it, I beseech Thee, in Union with all the Labours of Christ, in the Work of my Redemption, and in Virtue of his Sacred Passion, may it be available for the Discharge of that great Debt I have contracted by my manifold Offences.   N 5

300 *Instructions for Laborious,* &c.

I Confess likewise before Thee, my great Weakness and Corruption, and being sensible, how dangerous Idleness would be to me, in leading me into the Occasion of many Sins, I chearfully undertake the Labour of this Day, as what Thou, knowing my Infirmities, haft mercifully appointed for me, as the best Preservative from Evil: I thank Thee for it, and Hope, by thy Grace, it will have that Effect in me, which thou propofest for my Good.

I acknowledge it again my Duty to provide Neceffaries for Life, both for my felf, and thofe that belong to me; this is an Obligation which Justice lays upon me, to fatisfy this Duty, I willingly undertake the Work of this Day, give thou a Blessing to it, and since doing Justice is my Motive, may it be available, not only for gaining Bread, but likewife in order to Eternal Life. Preferve me this Day from all Sin, give me Grace to refift all the Occasions of it: Govern my Tongue, and all my Passions, abide with me this Day and for Ever.

CHAP.

3:4

CHAP. XV.

Inftructions for Mafters, &c.

THE firft Duty of Mafters to Servants, is Juftice, in the exact Payment of what is their Due, according to
the Agreement made with them, and
to be wanting in this, is a moft finful
Oppreffion. And if Sicknefs difables
them for a Time, here Juftice preffes
in regard of fome, and Charity in regard of others, that due Care be had of
them for their Recovery. 'Tis a Point,
in which many are wanting ; and is an
Argument of a moft Subftantial Defect,
fince the Principles of the Gofpel are
fuch, that 'tis not to be apprehended,
how thofe can be good Chriftians, who
have not due Care and Compaffion in
Time of their Servants Diftrefs.

A Second Day is that of Inftruction,
becaufe being under the Mafter's Care,
and in fome manner to be efteem'd as
Children, as the Scripture Terms them,
it is their Obligation, to fee, they be
duly Taught whatever is neceffary for
Salvation. For this End, upon their
Admittance Examen ought to be made,
how far they know, and Care taken for
their being Inftructed, as fhallbe found
necceffary

Masters, &c. 315

And becaufe many of them are under great Difadvantages, becaufe of their E-ducation, it is not fufficient to have them once inform'd of their Duty, but they are to be often call'd to an Account, to fee, what Improvement they make, or how much they retain of what has been taught them, and fuch Means pro-vided, as may be anfwerable to their Neceffities. Whence it muft certainly be condemn'd as a Fault in thofe, who allow no Time to their Servants, in which they may learn at Home or be In-ftructed Abroad. The Number of thefe, if one may guefs by the general Igno-rance of Servants, is very great. And tho' the common Plea for their Defence, Is the Multiplicity of Bufinefs, which will not allow them Time ; yet this Point ought to be well examin'd, to fee, whe-ther it will pafs with him, who is to be the Judge of all. They are to confider, whether all that Bufinefs, in which they engage their Servants, be of that great Concern, that none of it can be excus'd at any Time, upon the Confideration of providing for their Eternal Good, who are under their Charge. Is all their Work of Neceffity ? Is not fome to fa-fisfy Nicenefs and Humour ? If fome of it, upon occafion were omitted, would

O the

316 *Inſtruĉtions for*

the Conſequence be ſo bad, as the want of Inſtruĉtion in their Servants? In the one Caſe, they cannot be ſatisfy'd, if ſuch Work be not duly done by their Servants. On the other Side, their Servants Souls are in Hazard, if Time be not found for Inſtruĉtion. Which is of the greateſt Concern? Which ought to give place to the other? The Cauſe would ſoon be decided, were Charity and the Spirit of the Goſpel to ſpeak their Sentiments; and where 'tis not thus determin'd, is it not becauſe their Suggeſtions are ſtifled by a Covetous, Worldly, or Humourſom Spirit, which being bent with too much Eagerneſs, on its own Ways, thinks theſe of the greateſt Concern, and cannot apprehend any thing beſides of ſo much Weight, as to oblige them to give it Place. Hence the leaſt Intereſt and moſt inconſiderable things have the Preference to their Servants Souls; and they can have more Peace with their Servants Souls, than their Walls or Boards being in Diſorder.

Now I do not preſs in this, that the Work, for which Servants are hir'd, ſhould be left undone; but that, with ſome good Contrivance, Time be found for their Inſtruĉtion; becauſe this is an Obligation, which God lays on them, in

Re-

Masters, &c.   317

Regard of their Servants, and therefore ought to be satisfy'd: And it being a Point of Concern, if sometimes some other Work, which is not of Necessity, were adjourn'd, or let alone, it would be no more, than what the Order of Charity requires, which having Compassion on Servants, will provide for their Eternal Welfare, and esteem it no Loss, if some other Business of an inferiour Concern, be omitted on this Account: And the same Charity will give Direction to Christians, (if she be admitted to the Consult) when they determine, *What Work is necessary*, not to consider only the Earnestness, with which they are bent upon it; but rather, what will be the real Harm, if for once it be left undone.

This Sollicitude, which Masters, &c. should have for their Servants Instruction, should be extended something farther, that is, in seeing they have time for saying their Prayers, for frequenting the Sacraments at due times, and for keeping *Sundays* and Holy-days; so that they lose not the Benefit, which God and his Church have design'd for them in these Institutions 'Tis a hard Case to think, that those, who by their ill Circumstances, are oblig'd to Toil for Bread, should have such Advantage ta-

O 2   ken

ken of their neceſſitous Condition, as
to be tied to Work like Beaſts, without having Time allow'd them, for aſking God to have Mercy on them ; but
to live on, as if they had neither Faith,
nor Souls, nor Eternity to provide for.
'Tis again as hard, that being exercis'd
with Difficult Trials, and ſubjeƈt to
many Weakneſſes, they cannot have
Opportunities of ſeeking Help and
Strength from God, in the Sacraments,
which by the Divine Bounty, are ordain'd as much for their Relief, as for
others of a better Condition : But that
by a kind of Spiritual Oppreſſion, they
are ſo ſtreighten'd, as ſeldom to have
leiſure to go to them, and when they
go, are forced to do all in ſuch a Hurry,
ſo as to have neither time to prepare, as
they ought, nor to make any Recolle-
ƈion for receiving the Benefit of what
they do. There is little leſs Unhappineſs, in having no Days of Reſt, either
for Soul or Body, but that, on all Days,
they are ſo buſied with this World, as
to have no time to think of the next.

Theſe are their greateſt Misfortune,
who are in ſuch ill Circumſtances, and
have no help for themſelves ; but as to
the Guilt, I cannot but think, Maſters,
&c. have generally a greater ſhare in it,
than the Servants ; and that 'tis their
Duty

Duty to Remedy it, what they can: All cannot be as eafily done, as could be defir'd; but fomething may be, by fuch as truly confider, how valuable a Soul is, and how much ought to be done for its Salvation. Thefe will examine the Hours of going to Bed and Rifing; and fee, whether Servants have time for beginning the Day with Prayer: And if it be then wanting, to fupply it at leaft by Family-Prayer, when all meet in common, for paying a Common Homage to God. They will obferve, what order Servants keep in going to the Sacraments, and to contrive it, that they have due time for the well performing thofe Duties: As likewife, that they have fome leifure on *Sundays* and Holy days, for applying their Thoughts to the Work of their Salvation.

This they will effect, by abating fomething of the ufual Duties of other Days, and keeping to the Rule, of doing nothing on fuch Days, but what is really neceffary. They will confider fuch Days, to be Days for Souls, and not for Houfes; and that if Walls and Boards are taken Care of all the Week, Souls ought to be taken Care of on *Sundays* and Holy-days: And on this Confideration, will excufe all that can

be of the uſual Work. This many
cannot eaſily perſwade themſelves to,
becauſe of Education and Cuſtom, that
prevail upon them, and they know not
how to omit, what a long Practice
makes them duly expect: But when
they conſider, that the great Work on
Sundays and Holy-days, is chiefly occaſion'd by Vanity, Pride, Gluttony, and
Niceneſs; and that, were not Servants
taken up in providing for theſe, they
would have time enough for their more
important Duties : When they reflect
again, how little this Anſwers the deſign of keeping ſuch Days Holy; and
that it muſt be a great Abuſe, to have
theſe Days diſtinguiſh'd from others,
by making better Proviſion for the
Houſe, Belly and Back, and the Buſineſs of Salvation (for which they were
principally inſtituted) to be neglected
on this Account; hence they may conclude upon changing this Method, and
in the firſt place, begin to take Care,
that ſomething be retrench'd of that
uſual Work, which Vanity, &c. find
for Servants on *Saturday* Nights and Vi-
gils, to keep them up ſo late, as not
only to labour beyond the Time pre-
ſcrib'd, but to oblige them to ſpend a
great part of the next Morning in Bed,
to recover the Sleep, that was loſt.

They

They may take another Step, in reforming Vanity, in being contented themselves to serve God in what is Clean and Decent, without employing the Morning, in being set out for a shew; for as this is not suitable to the Humility of the Gospel, nor to the Worship of a Crucifyed Redeemer, so it muſt be injurious to the Day, and to Servants, to take up their time in such Preparations. Again, they may abate something of Sweeping and Cleaning the House; for this having been done the Day before, it is more agreeable to the Time, to be then busy in purifying their Souls. Then, as for the Table, they may contrive what is neceſſary for Subſiſtance, in such a manner, as requires the leaſt attendance of Servants, that so, that time may not be given to Senſuality or Gluttony, which God has reserv'd to himself: Therefore they ought not to make these Days of Entertainments, except only for such, who will be content with a Dinner, without spending the Afternoon at the Table. And as for what is to be Clean'd, this may be reserv'd for the Buſineſs of the following Day, that those Servants, who have been employ'd in the Morning, may have time for Prayer and Inſtruction in the Afternoon, which they ge-

O 4. nerally

nerally want more than others. They
may contrive again more time for Servants, by not admitting Visits, nor going themselves abroad on those Days,
at least, till the Duties, which belong
to them are Discharg'd: For tho' doing otherwise, brings no Labour with
it, yet it is a hindrance to Servants, and
puts by what might be more for their
Advantage.

By these, and such other Ways, Christians, whose Charity makes them Sollicitous for the Salvation of all under
Care, find time for their Servants,
wherein they may look into the State of
their Souls, and make all necessary Provision for them. And tho' this be effected, by departing from the common
Method of the World, yet since 'tis departing from nothing, but the Corruption of
it, in favour of those Rules, which the Gospel prescribes; since 'tis departing from
Pride and Excess, for the Improvement of
Virtue, they think it very well becoming
their Profession, who believing the next
Life to be Eternal, ought to be more
zealous in preparing for Eternity, than
in complimenting Self-love, and the
World, with the Hazard of all that is
to come.

A Third Duty is Admonition, by
which Masters are oblig'd to be watchful over their Servants; and if they
ob-

Masters, &c. 323

obferve any thing Diforderly, to give them Reproof, according to Defert. The greateft part are fharp enough in Faults; wherein they are concern'd; but few exprefs a Zeal for God, in reprehending what is difpleafing to him. And yet thus it ought to be; for fince Mafters, &c. have not only the Charge, but alfo Command of their Family under God, 'tis moft certain, they are accountable for all the Sins, which are the Effect of their Connivance or Neglect. Wherefore, upon perceiving any Diforder, whether in Words or Actions, they muft confider it their Duty to reform it; they are to try all Means, firft of Charitable and Repeated Advice, then of Reproof, Threats, and Difcouragements, and whatever other Expedients may be fuitable to their Circumftances: And if, after fufficient Trial, fuch as Charity prefcribes for their Amendment, they prove Obftinate, the Family ought to be clear'd of their ill Example, by a Removal. The Change is often of thofe, who are not found fit for Service; and is there not more Reafon, when Prophanenefs or notorious Irregularities difturb all Difcipline, and may be an Infection to the whole Family?

In this Caſe therefore, Chriſtian Zeal allows of ſome Severity ; but in all others, Moderation is more to be Encourag'd, at leaſt, in ſuch a manner, that tho' Servants may have their Overſights and Neglects, and for theſe may deſerve Reproof, they be not however treated like Brutes or Slaves. This Rule is neceſſary for ſome, whoſe Paſſion is ſo eaſily provok'd, that they ſeem to think no others to have any feeling beſides themſelves, and therefore beſtow their Irreligious Threats and Blows ſo freely, as if reſolv'd, that none ſhould be in Peace, while they themſelves are in Diſorder. This is a Temper ſo contrary to the Chriſtian Spirit, and ſo pernicious in its Effects, by deſtroying all Peace, and putting all concern'd in an Incapacity of doing any Duty well, that thoſe, who are ſubject to it, have Reaſon to labour for Moderation, for their own and others ſakes, who Live under their Roof. 'Tis likewiſe neceſſary for thoſe, who being of an Uneaſy, or too Nice a Temper, can look no where, but they find matter of Reproof, and hence are ſo fruitful in their chiding Lectures, that they either keep Servants upon a continual Fret, or Oblige them, for their own Peace,

Masters, &c. 325

Peace, not to value what they Hear.
This is a Way convenient for neither
Side, by making all Uneafy, and particularly tempting Servants to be Carelefs, whilft they fee, nothing gives
Content, whatever they do. But however I do not except, in this, againft
all Reproofs, but only defire, they may
be Seafonable : Faults and Neglects
ought to be reprehended ; and yet For-
bearance is fometimes Advifable ; one
Word is Spur enough to many ; and
peaceably fhewing a Fault will go farther with moft, than an Angry and
Publick Reproof. If fome deferve this,
it ought not to be us'd with all : Becaufe Paffion raifes Averfion, and Moderation caufes Efteem and Love, and
the Effects of thefe are the more la-
fting Wherefore, fince Meeknefs is
fo much advis'd by the Gofpel, it ought
to be the general Rule, and great Dependance ought to be on his Bleffing,
who gives the Advice. And if all
things are not exact according to Wifh,
yet there will be Peace in a Family,
which of all other things is moft defi-
rable, and has much the Preference, to
all Impatience, Fretfulnefs and Paffion,
which undertaking to Remedy what is
Diflik'd, have one certain Effect, of
putting all into Diforder, but commonly

ly fail in what they otherwife propofe.
One thing I can fay with certainty, that
where Servants live under the Government of Paffion, they are feldom in a
good Humour, which is a great hindrance in their Service, and makes way
for New Faults; and as for the Affairs
of their Souls, they are under a general Neglect, becaufe of the Difcompo-
fure of Mind, which renders them unfit for all Spiritual Duties. And tho'
they are not to be wholly excus'd in
this; yet Chriftian Charity ought to
have fome Compaffion on their Weaknefs, and ftudy fuch a peaceable Way
of Reproving Faults, as not to put
them out of the Way of being Chriftians, whilft it endeavours to make them
good Servants. This I fay in regard of
thofe, who are to be wrought upon by
fair means, as I hope moft are; but as
to thofe whofe Obftinate or Slothful
Temper makes void all Admonitions,
after a fufficient Experience of them,
'tis better they be remov'd, than to let
a Family be in a perpetual Diforder
upon their Account.

A Fourth Duty is Good Example,
which is the fureft way for keeping
Order in a Family, and will give the
beft Authority to all Reproofs. The
want of this is the Ruin of many Servants,

vants, who considering those over them as their Head, naturally receive Impressions from whatever they do. Whence all Heads of Families, as they are Christians, and have a Concern for their own Souls, ought to be very Regular in all they do; because the Post, in which they are, makes them Remarkable; and the Weakness of those under their Care is such, as to be inclin'd to follow without Scruple where they see the Track made by those, who should Guide. And hence, who can imagine how their Sins are multiply'd in their Servants, who give ill Example to them? How is Prophaneness, Luxury, Intemperance, Passion, Vanity, &c. by this way Propagated? How is a Neglect of God, and of all Christian Duties by this Method encourag'd? And to what a Sum must the Account soon rise, which is Daily Multiply'd by so many Additions? Let those consider it, who are concern'd, and, for their own sakes, learn to be Watchful, since they must needs see their Example to be so Fruitful. And if their Servants are better than they, let them remember, 'tis a very unbecoming Privilege of Masters, &c, in orderly Families, to be the only Persons, that observe no Order.

CHAP.

[William Crathorne (ed.)], *Mr Gother's Spiritual Works.*
Tome XII. A Practical Catechism divided into Fifty-
two Lessons for each Sunday in the Year. There are added,
General Indexes and Tables to each Tome. Faithfully
Corrected (London, [T. Meighan], 1718), pp. 246–85

Working at the heart of an English Catholic community whose legal pre-
cariousness still made the regular provision of Sunday Masses unreliable,
Gother was aware of the need to sanctify the Lord's Day, if necessary by
alternative religious means: 'in the best manner they are able at home;
always taking some Time both Morning and Afternoon for reading some
Good Books' (see above, Gother's *Instructions for Particular States*, p. 276).
Gother's volumes of *Afternoon Instructions for Sundays, Holy-Days, and*
Other Feasts, from Low-Sunday to Advent and *Afternoon Instructions for*
Sundays, and Holy-Days, from Advent to Low-Sunday between them set out
a programme of homiletic reflections patterned to accompany the entirety
of the Church's year.

Similarly scheduled on a Sunday-by-Sunday basis, Gother's *Practical*
Catechism was not intended to be linked to the liturgical cycle as such,
but, as he announced in his preface 'To the READER', he simply and for
purposes of convenience '*distributed the whole matter into fifty-two lessons,*
that one being read or expounded every Sunday, *the whole duty of a Christian*
may be examined and considered every year'. He also explained the point
of his title '*Practical Catechism*': a moral manual, or 'practical catechism,
as well as speculative', that is to say doctrinal. His provision of a conduct
guide aligned his work with then current English books of recommended
Christian behaviour, the best-known of which was *The Whole Duty of Man*,
attributed to Richard Allestree (1619–81) – so that it is perhaps more than
a coincidence that Gother himself used the phrase 'the whole duty of a
Christian' to describe the didactic purpose of his own work.

Within his own community, Gother's exhaustive pedagogic activity
may have been partly responsible for a growing perception of the role of
the Catholic priest as being, in Bossy's words, 'primarily to teach'[2]. Cat-
echisms as texts might have been used either directly for lay reading or

as source books on the basis of which priests could carry out their own teaching syllabuses. Staple works of instruction included: the *Catechism, or Christian Doctrine necessary for Children and Ignorant People* (Louvain, 1567) by the priest Laurence Vaux (1519–85), out of print by the earlier seventeenth century; English translations of standard catechetical works by Bellarmino; the 1556 'Large Catechism', specifically designed for popular lay consumption in the version by Bellarmino's fellow-Jesuit Peter Canisius (1521–97); and the priests' bulky manual influenced by Bellarmino, Henry Turberville's (d. 1678) *An Abridgment of Christian Doctrine* of *c.* 1649, which came to be known as the *Doway Catechism*. Bossy suggests that a résumé of Turberville may have been made by Gother, in the summary called the *Doway Abstract*.[2] Whatever the case, his own contribution to English Catholic literary catechesis clearly fell within an extant tradition within which he could both operate and, if necessary, innovate – though 'To the READER' warned: 'WHERE *the practice of the Gospel is the subject, nothing new can be expected: To look for this here, would be to forget the undertaking; since novelty, which, in other cases, is so inviting, in this is a scandal.*'

In catechetical texts, there was indeed room for some choice, if not for innovation, in the adoption or not of the interrogative dialogue form: if it was not invariable, it was certainly customary in this genre. Such a form, when used with relatively brief question-and-answer alternations, might lend itself to memorization of material. However, that is unlikely to have been the case with Gother's quite lengthy dialogues: instead his messages might have been intended to sink in through the annual repetition of his cycle. Interestingly, his questioner is not a mere interviewer, but has a relatively opinionated stance.

In the material excerpted here, Gother is seen to be concerned not so much with doctrinal orthodoxy as with Christian behaviour and, within that area, with having a proper disposition – one combining moderation, detachment, reserve, self-restraint and self-observation, along with a kind of cheerful stoicism and a 'Docil Temper'. Given this emphasis on states of mind and temperament, the questions are directed to a moral adviser or confessor rather than to a dogmatic authority, and the cast of the discourse between counsellor and counselled helps give it a genuine conversational flavour.

Gother's sharply observed portraits of the various human types who spurn advice (pp. 321–3) may have been drawn from his own experience of intractable cases in administering the sacrament of Penance.

1.   Bossy, *English Catholic Community*, p. 273.
2.   Bossy, *English Catholic Community*, p. 272.

Mr. *GOTHER*'s

Spiritual Works.

TOME XII.

A Practical Catechifm divided into Fifty-two Leffons for each Sunday in the Year.

There are added,

General *Indexes* and *Tables* to each TOME.

Faithfully Correded.

LONDON:

Printed in the Year 1718.

A

Practical Catechism:

In Fifty Two

LESSONS:

One for every

SUNDAY

IN THE

YEAR.

WITH

An APPENDIX

FOR

Particular States.

Printed in the Year, 1718.

246

C H A P. XXXVIII.

Of Troubles and Afflictions.

Q. ARE the Troubles and Afflictions of this Life always the Punifhment of Sin?

A. They are not always fo: For
tho' *Cain* was Afflicted for his Sin, and
Pharaoh, and the Children of *Ifrael*
in the Defert, and *Saul* and *David*,
and other Kings of *Ifrael*; yet we find
many others Vifited with fevere Afflictions, who were the Faithful Servants of God, and not Punifh'd for
Sin, as *Abraham, Elias, Job, Toby,* the
Apoftles, the Man born Blind, and all
the Primitive Martyrs.

Q. What then may be the Defign of
Providence, in afflicting the Juft?

A. The Scripture mentions fome;
As Firft, For the Trial of their Fidelity, as in *Abraham, Job,* and *Toby*.
2*ly*. For their Improvement in Virtue.
3*ly*. For their greater Refemblance to
Chrift their Head. 4*ly*. For the In-
creafe of their Crown. 5*ly*. For the manifefting the Power of God in fuch
weak Veffels. Laftly, That God may
be Glorify'd.

Q. In

Of Troubles and Afflictions. 247

Q. In what manner are Chriftians to bear Troubles, and go thro' the Afflictions of this Life?

A. With Patience.

Q. By what Motives are Chriftians to prevail with themfelves to be Patient?

A. They have many:

Firft, Becaufe nothing happens to them, but by the Appointment or Permiffion of God. Now God being alwife and ordering all for the beft, they have Reafon to Submit to whatever he Orders, as believing that to be beft for them. Again, God's Will is always Holy, and always Juft, and therefore always Adorable: God's Will then being manifeft in whatever happens, it ought always to be Submitted to, and by Submiffion Ador'd.

2*ly.* They every Day afk in the Lord's Prayer, that God's *Will* may *be done on Earth as it is in Heaven.* If they afk this daily, have not they Reafon to Submit to it, when they fee it done? To make Exceptions then and Grieve with Impatience, is to Unfay their own Prayers, and contradict in their Troubles, what they have been Petitioning all their Lives.

3*ly.* We know not what is Good for ourfelves; and that very often, which

M 4 we

248 *Of Trouble and Afflictions.*

we Grieve for, as our Misfortune, is the firſt Step to our Happineſs. Did not *Jacob* lament the Loſs of *Joſeph*; And *Joſeph* his being Falſly Accus'd, and his Impriſonment ; and yet were not all theſe the Steps, by which Providence manifeſted it ſelf wonderfully in their Behalf, and Uſher'd in their greateſt Good? The Nobleman (*Jo.* 4, 46.) griev'd at the Sickneſs and Danger of his Son ; and yet this, which he Lamented, as the Misfortune of his Family, was the Occaſion that brought both him and his Family to Chriſt.

4. We know not our ſelves, till we are exercis'd and prov'd by many Trials. We know not our Dependance on God, till we Experience our own Poverty and Wants. We know not the World, till we find the Uncertainty and Vanity of all its Goods. If then by Troubles, we are Inſtructed in theſe Three great Leſſons, there is Reaſon to have Patience, with what is ſo much to our Advantage.

5*ly.* The Love of the World and the great Value for its Goods, are the greateſt Impediments of Virtue, and what make Chriſtians not only moſt Unwilling, but moſt Unfit to Die. Afflictions are the ſureſt Remedy againſt both theſe Charms: The World being Uneaſy

Of Trouble and Afflictions. 249

eafy is more willingly left; and its Treachery being difcover'd, puts Chriftians upon feeking fomething more Solid. And is there not fome Patience due, where they are fo well Inftructed to Eternity?

6ly. Becaufe God Undertaking the Caufe of the Opprefs'd, to be the Comforter of the Afflicted, the Protector of the Orphan and Widow, and making many Promifes to fuch, as call upon him in thefe Troubles and put their Truft in him; Chriftians have Reafon to be Patient under Afflictions, which give them fuch a Title to the particular Protection of God.

7ly. Becaufe the Life of Chrift was a Life of all kinds of Afflictions; the way he walk'd in, was the Way of the Crofs: If Chriftians then Suffer; they are in this Affociated, or United to their Head. He was Scourg'd and Crown'd with Thorns: If they feel the Scourge and the Thorns; let them ftand by him, and fee if they cannot find Comfort in fuch Company. If they have their Crofs, let them follow their Leader; and fay, It is better to Suffer with Chrift, that we may be Glorify'd in him; than to Rejoice with the World, and have our Portion with it.

M 5 *8ly.*

250 *Of Troubles and Afflictions.*

8ly. Becaufe tho' all Troubles and Afflictions are Uneafy to Nature, which feeks prefent Peace; yet, if we confider them, as the Exercife, which God fends; that they are the Means to purify our Hearts from the Love of the World; that they are the Way, by which God has led his beft Servants, his Prophets, Apoftles and Martyrs; that he has promis'd Bleffings, and an Eternal Crown to fuch, as Suffer with Patience; and that their Sorrow fhall be turn'd into Joy: Upon this Confideration there is fomething very Valuable in the Troubles and Afflictions of this Life; and what Nature is Averfe to, which is guided by Senfe, Faith may Defire and Embrace, which is directed by the Reveal'd Will of God. For if a Chriftian remembers, that he was Born for Eternity, and that his greateft and only True Intereft is in gaining Everlafting Happinefs; he cannot but think that Valuable and Defireable, which is particularly Serviceable for obtaining this End: This he muft do, if he has the Life of Faith in him.

Thefe are fome Motives, amongft many others for Chriftians being Patient under all the Troubles of this Life.

Q. Are thefe proper, whatever the Reafon be of their Troubles?

A. Yes

Of Troubles and Afflictions.   201

A. Yes, Whether their Troubles be the Effect of God's Justice, for the Punishment of Sin : or of his Mercy, for the Trial and Improvement of Virtue, or the Increase of their Crown ; this is the Way, for making Advantage of them. Wherefore I cannot but disapprove their Method, who, upon falling under Trouble, and with great Curiosity or Anxiety enquiring, what may be the Occasion of their Misfortune, by this Sollicitude encrease their Disquiet, and indiscreetly lose the Opportunity of making the Right Use of their Troubles.

Q. What would you have them do ?

A. I would have them, upon their first Approach, endeavour to receive them with Patience ; because thus they will turn to their Good, whatever is the Occasion of them.

Q. And if they endeavour to be Patient is that enough ?

A. This will do very well ; but having gain'd this Point, they may take one Step farther, and endeavour to have Comfort and even to rejoice in their Troubles ?

Q. How can this be ?

A. S. *Paul* knew how to do this : *We Glory,* says he, *in Tribulation,* Rom. 5. 3. *As the Sufferings of Christ abound in us,*

so

252 *Of the best Method*

so our Confolatton alfo Aboundeth by Chrift,
2 Cor. 1. 5. *I take Pleafure in Infirmi-*
ties, in Reproaches, in Neceffities, in Perfecu-
tions, in Diftreffes for Chrift's Sake ; for when
I am Weak, then am I Strong, 2 Cor. 12.
10. Here he mentions all kinds of
Troubles, and owns his Comfort in
them.

Q. Upon what Motives do you think ?
A. In the Accomplifhment of God's
Will ; in communicating with Chrift's
Paffion ; in the Hopes of that Eternal
weight of Glory, which light Tribulation Worketh in us. And why
may not we do fo too ? We Rejoice in
our own Will being done. Why not
much more in God's ? Our whole dependance is in Chrift's Paffion, and is it
not Matter of Comfort, to be more
nearly affociated to it ? We Rejoice, in
Temporal Intereft ; and why not much
more, when we are in the beft Way of
fecuring what is Eternal ?

C H A P. XXXIX.

Of the beft Method in time of Trouble.

Q. WHat would you advife a Chriftian, upon the firft Approach of
any Trouble ?

A. I

A. I would advise him, immediately to retire, and in private to make his application to God.

Firſt, Bowing down, as under the Hand of God.

2*ly*, Offering himſelf, with an entire Surrender of his own Will, of all his Inclinations, and Worldly Intereſts, to the Will and Diſpoſal of God.

3*ly*, Beſeeching Almighty God, to Direct, and Support and Strengthen him by his Grace, that he may entirely comply with his Holy Will; not Offend him by Impatience, but make a good uſe of his Troubles.

4*ly*, Confeſſing the Will of God to be Juſt and Holy, in his preſent Appointments; and that, as for himſelf, he is a Sinner, and Suffers nothing, in Compariſon of what he deſerves.

5*ly*, Caſting his whole Care upon God, with an entire Confidence, that he, who has ſo many Ways Signalized his Goodneſs to the Afflicted, will now manifeſt his Mercy to him, by ſupporting him under his Affliction, or delivering him from it.

Laſtly, Acknowledging his own Weakneſs, and again repeating his moſt earneſt Petitions, that God will be his Protector, and enable him to

bear

254   *Of the best Method*

bear the Crofs, which is laid upon his
Shoulders.

Q. This is very well, but how fhall
a Perfon do thus, that is furpriz'd with
a fuddain Affliction ?

A. If this could not be done, why
fhould Chrift call upon all, who Labour
and are Heavy-Loaden, to come to him,
that from him, they may receive Re-
frefhment ? He that calls them, knows
what is beft for them, and what they
can do, if they will. Affliction puts
People in Mind, that they want Comfort and Help ; and fince God alone is
he, who is able and willing both to
Comfort and Help them, it ought not
to be afk'd, how they can go to him in
Trouble ; but rather how they can be
fo much their own Enemies; as not to
go to him ?

Q. I have feen fome fo overcome with
Grief, as not to know, what they do,
nor to have any Concern for whatever
belongs to them.

A. It may be fo, but can you fay,
They could do no better ? Are you
fure, there was no Affectation or Sullen-
nefs in this ? Nature being ftruck in a
tender Part, or rob'd of what is moft
Dear to it, inclines fome Tempers very
ftrongly to this fullen or defpairing
Grief; But, whatever the Inclination
be

in time of Trouble.   255

be, it is certain, a Chriſtian muſt be ſenſible of the Unreaſonableneſs and Rebellion of it, and that if he would be Reſolute, he might follow this Senſe of Reaſon and Faith, and apply himſelf to God for Remedy, inſtead of lying down under the Burthen.

Q. What is the Unreaſonableneſs of this kind of Grief?

A. It is in the firſt Place, very prejudicial to Health; and if it be indulg'd for any Time, it changes the whole Conſtitution, and inſenſibly cauſes ſuch an Habitual Diſorder, as is not in the Power of Art to Remedy, but will likely be their Exerciſe and Puniſhment all their Lives.

2*ly*, This ſort of Trouble diſables thoſe, that yield to it, and makes them either Careleſs or Unfit for whatever Buſineſs belongs to them. And is not this an unreaſonable Method, that Chriſtians being under a Weight, which, they complain is too Heavy for them, ſhould however ſo manage it, as to add more weight to that Burthen, and encreaſe their own Miſery?

3*ly*, It ſets them at a Diſtance from God, and ſhuts out his Comforts, who is the only Comforter in the Time of Affliction. For what part can they have in him, who thus, not only ſhew a diſlike

256 *Of the best Method*

like of his Orders, but likewise set
themselves in Opposition against them,
and wilfully persist in this Rebellion?

4*ly*, It unqualifies them for Prayer
and other Exercises, by which they
are to ask Help for themselves, and prevail with God to come in to their Relief; and, thus by ill Management,
they confirm themselves in Misery.

Q. Then I see, you have no Patience
with those, who lie under sullen or af-
fected Grief?

A. These certainly take the wrong
Way, and are their own greatest Enemies, doing themselves much more Injury, than that can possibly do them,
which is the Occasion of their Complaint.

Q. What then do you advise them?

A. To take the contrary Way; that
is, whatever their Trouble be, I would
have them stand Resolutely, against
this sort of Grief, as being Unreasona-
ble and Sinful; I would have them resist Inclination, and not take that for
their Guide, which being Corrupt,
Treacherous and Blind, will lead them
into irrevocable Ruin. I would have
them Labour to keep up their Spirits
inwardly, whatever Decency may exact
of them outwardly, and as often as they
begin to Sink, to be upon the Watch,

and

and ftill raife them up, by the Help of a Vigorous Faith and Hearty Submiſſion to God. Becauſe in ſuch difficult Circumſtances they want a good Heart, and to let their Spirits then Sink, when they are in greateſt Need of them, is what, in any other Cafe, would be eſteem'd Folly or Madneſs.

You fee here then, I advife all under Trouble, to keep up as Chearful a Spirit, as they poſſibly can ; becauſe, by this Means, they will be better difpos'd for making their Addreſſes to God and having a more Firm Hope in him ; as likewiſe for ſtruggling better with the Difficulties of this World : On which Two Points all depends.

To help them in this, it may be proper to admit of ſome Charitable and Experienc'd Perſon, by whoſe Difcourfe and Direction, the Darkneſs of Grief may be diſſipated, and the Light of Reaſon and Faith be Reſtor'd ; and if Reading in ſome Choice Book be made a part of their Daily Exerciſe, it may contribute to the more Speedy Recovery of the Mind.

When the Soul is recover'd from the firſt Surprize, it muſt be its beſt Expedient, by a hearty Repentance, to endeavour to make its Peace with God ; that ſo, the Scourge may be Moderated

258　　*Of the best Method*

or Remov'd, if it be the Chaſtiſement
of Sin ; or God's Goodneſs more powerfully engag'd to its Help, if there has
been no ſuch Provocation given.

But it cannot be approv'd, what too
many Practiſe, to drown Cares with
Drink, and by Sottiſhneſs to blunt the
Sharpneſs of Grief; for this is not to
cûre the Evil; but by undue Means,
to leſſen the preſent Senſe of it, and
(as Folly generally puniſhes it ſelf) to
add new Tortures to the Rack, as ſoon
as the Mind begins to think, and reflect upon the Ill Method it has taken,
in going to *Belzebub,* as if there was not
a God in *Iſrael.*

Q. The adviſe you give is plain ; but
how few will take Care to follow it ?

A. All will endeavour to follow it, that
are Wiſe in the Management of their
Eternal Concerns.

Q. How ſo ?

A. Becauſe, if a Chriſtian takes this
Method, when he is in Trouble, he
makes a great Advantage of it, even ſo,
as to render it very ſerviceable to Salvation : And if, thro' Paſſion, Sullen-
neſs or Impatience, he forſakes this
Way, he is ſo far from gaining, that he
is a great loſer by all his Afflictions.
And is not that a remarkable Indiſcretion, to be there a Looſer by ill Management,

nagement, where he had a fair Opportunity of being a Gainer? We call it Folly, if a Man parts with a Piece of Money at half the Value ; and we laugh at the *Indians*, who exchange their Jewels for Trifles: And what muſt it be call'd, when a Chriſtian lets that go for nothing, which might have gone a great Way in the Purchaſe of Heaven? Afflictions are ſuch, if rightly manag'd by a Spirit ſkill'd in the Goſpel ; and they are ſo much Worſe than nothing, as to ſet him at a greater Diſtance from it, if they are left to Impatience to put them off. How great Reaſon then have Chriſtians to Study this Point, ſince meeting with ſome Difficulty or other, every Day of their Lives, they would, by this Art, have Opportunity of taking every Day large ſteps towards Heaven?

C H A P. XLI.

Of Docility, or being Eaſy in taking Advice.

Q. I Obſerve there are many and great Difficulties in a Chriſtian Life, can you tell me, what may be a good Help to Overcome them ?

A. The

260 *Of Docility, or being Easy*

A. The Grace of God is the only Help; but since God is pleas'd to make use of Humane Means, and likewise to require our Concurrence, I think, among other Things, it very much depends upon our being of a Docil Temper, which is easy in being Advis'd, takes the Admonitions and even Reproof of Friends in good Part, and by a general Sweetness encourages all to be thus Friendly to him.

Q. To whom do's this belong in Particular?

A. I know of no Body exempted from it.

In the first Place, it is a great Happiness in Children, to be of a Tractable and Docil Temper, by which they will be Easy in receiving the Instructions of their Parents, and be shap'd by their Care, who have the Inspection over them.

2*ly*, It is a very considerable Advantage to Youth, who being willing to hear Advice, and shewing a Desire of being inform'd of what is for their Good, will by this be deliver'd from many Evils, which otherwise cannot fail of attending the Resolutions of their Rash and Unexperienc'd Years; and in all their Undertakings, will proceed

ceed with a Conduct far above their Age.

3*ly,* It is very Serviceable in all States of Life; becaufe in all there are many Difficulties, which are beft manag'd and overcome by Counfel; there are many Advantages, which may be made, and thefe are beft laid hold of by fuch, who make ufe of more Heads, than their own.

Laftly, There are none, even the moft Learned, Experienc'd and Wife, but what are Subject to Overfights and Miftakes in what they know; and meet many Things, in which others are better Skill'd. and more Quick-fighted than themfelves. Now where the Temper is Docile, it not only confiders, what Help they can have in all Affairs, but likewife encourages all Friends, even unafk'd, to give their Opinion, to Fore-warn, and by Inftances of Succefs and Mifcarriages, to inform them, which Way to take with moft Security.

Q. The Advantages are obvious enough, and I think, fo great, that, I Queftion, whether there be any Tempers, who will not make Ufe of them, if not by Inclination, at leaft by Choice.

A. There are many, who will not: There are fome fo Self-conceited, that they cannot imagine any to know better

262   *Of Docility, or being Easy*

ter than themselves, and hence Despise all Advice.

There are others, who dispute every Thing, that is said to them, and take it as an Affront, if their Judgment be Question'd. Others receive all Advice with a Scornful Smile.

Others cannot be spoken to, but they are presently mov'd, Swell, and discover Anger in their Looks.

Others run into the other Extreme, and instead of being Angry fall into Dejection, and cry, They are Unhappy, who cannot please, nor do any Thing well.

Others thro' Jealousy, Suspect all Advice and dare not follow it, for fear of some Design.

Others are so Morose or Reserv'd, that either they will not be spoken to, or will not own their Design.

Others are so Proud, that they will not do, what they know is for the best. because it is not their own Thoughts, and think it beneath them to follow others.

Others are so Stiff and Self-will'd, that they will not be put out of their Way, whatever they Suffer.

Others are over-rul'd by Affection, and will hear none, but those, whom
                                                                they

in taking Advice. 263

they like, without confidering, whether they are Wife or no.

Others are fo Govern'd by their
Paffions or Intereft, that they cannot
approve of any Thing, that do's not
Favour thefe, and to oppofe them is
argument enough of the Wrong.

Others are fo Inconftant, that hearing and refolving to follow the beft
Advice, they prefently change their Refolutions, upon Hearing the next, that
is but of another Mind.

Others hear and know the beft, but
thro' Fear, Perfwafion, Ill Company,
Vice, Sloth, Love of Eafe or Compliance with the World, Act contrary to
what they know.

Others thro' a certain Lightnefs of
Mind or Vain Humour, have no regard
to any Thing, but as it is agreeable or
difagreeable to this Inclination; and
therefore cannot approve Advice, that
is not Favourable to it.

By thefe, and many other Ways, are
Chriftians hinder'd from reciving the
Benefit of Friends and their Good Advice; and this feldom without their
own Fault; it being generally, you fee,
fome Pride or Paffion or ill Humour,
which is the Occafion of their being depriv'd of this Good.

Q. But

264   *Of Docility or being Eafy.*

Q. But are not they punifh'd for their Fault ?

A. Pride, Morofenefs, Paffion and Ill-Humour have generally this Juftice accompanying them, that they punifh themfelves. And, befides many others, this is one general Punifhment, that not bearing Advice, they are depriv'd of it; and thofe Friends, who obferve their Indifcretions, Follies and ill Ways, look on with Pity and Silence; as thinking it to no Purpofe to fpeak to fuch, who have not Humility enough to be advis'd. And by this Means, whatever Friends they have, yet they have not the Benefit of them.

Q. If the Injury they do themfelves, be fo Great, have they not Reafon, to amend this Ill Way, which is the Occafion of it ?

A. They have great Reafon; and therefore I cannot but wifh, that fuch Chriftians who obferve this in themfelves; that they cannot be advis'd of any Fault, or juftly Reprov'd, but it is generally with fome Difturbance in them, either of Pride, that fwells, or of Anger, that makes them Peevifh, or of Melancholy, that Dejects; would take Pains in overcoming themfelves, in fuppreffing all fuch inward Motions; and till this be gain'd, to prevent thefe

Di-

in taking Advice. 26**5**

Diſturbances appearing in their Word**s**
or Looks. For ſince *Advice* and *Re-*
proof are the great Benefit we can
make of Friends; and theſe are particularly recommended in the Goſpel.
to ſuch as are over us, as the proper
Means for doing us Good; *Be Inſtant*
in Seaſon, out of Seaſon; Reprove, Rebuke,
Exhort, 2 Tim. 4. 2. They, who do
no not thus endeavour to Govern themſelves, cannot fail of being great Lo-
ſers by it, by the Diſcouragements given to thoſe, who, otherwiſe, would
be willing to do them Good, both for
this World and the next.

Q. Well, but are not ſome too eaſy in
their Temper, ſo as to be impos'd on,
and led out of the Way?

A. None can be too Eaſy in receiving
juſt Reproof, or Advice of their Faults,
or Counſel from the Wiſe and Good;
for this ought fo be receiv'd with Satisfaction and Thanks. And as for
others, who are not Good, or have any
Deſign of drawing them into a Snare;
there are very few ſo Weak, but they
have Senſe enough to Diſcern or Su-
ſpect it at leaſt; and if then they yield,
this muſt not be call'd Eaſineſs of
Temper, but a Great Weakneſs of
Mind, who ſeeing or ſuſpecting Evil
before them, will be contented to be

N   led

led into it. This is almost the only Case, in which Roughness is commendable in a Christian. At other Times he is to be Easy, Affable, Complying and Sweet, and be as a Lamb : But when Evil is propos'd, he ought then to put on the Lion, and by an Heroick Anger strike Terrour in the Proposers.

C H A P. XLI.

Of the Love of Worldly Things.

Q. YOU have propos'd many Christian Duties, both as to what is to be follow'd, and what avoided; tell me now, What you think of the Love of Creatures, or of any Thing in this World?

A. I think it a very difficult Point in Practice, such as requires great Grace and Discretion in the Management of it.

Q. Is then the Love of Creatures lawful in any Case?

A. Yes, in many; as between Parents and Children, Husband and Wife, &c. Any Thing that is Lawful, Innocent, and Good, may be lov'd.

Q. Where then is the Difficulty?

A. The same as in Physick; a due Quantity do's well, but take too much

of

Worldly Things. 267

of it and it do's Injury; nay, in many Cafes, is Poifon. The Difficulty then is in being Moderate, and avoiding Excefs.

Q. Is all Excefs then in the Love of Creatures, evil?

A. Yes; but as there are different Degrees of Excefs; fo there are in the Evil of it.

Q. As how?

A. Firft, If a Perfon be bent, with an immoderate Love, upon what is Lawful, as it may be in Parents towards their Childen; this is fo far Evil, as to leffen the Concern and Love for God; it takes up the Heart too much, it poffeffes the Mind with too much Violence; fo that it has not due Liberty to think of God, nor to be fo follicitous for Eternity as it ought to be.

2*dly*, This Love may arife to another Degree; fo as to indulge Children in many indifcreet and hurtful Things, rather than difpleafe them; to connive at their Faults, their Prodigality, their Vanity, *&c.* to hope all to be well, contrary to what they fee; and thus let them go on, till they are out of their Reach and Government.

3*dly*, It may ftill grow to another Degree, fo as to favour their Childen in

what

268   *Of the Love of*

what is evidently Sinful; to do what
is Unjuft, for making Provifion or gaining Preferment for them ; to renounce
Confcience and Faith, rather than fuffer them to be expos'd to Want.
Thefe, and many other Evils may be
the Effects of immoderate Love ; and
what the Sin of this is, Chrift himfelf has declar'd ; *He that loveth Father*
or Mother more than me, is not worthy of
me: and he that loveth Son or Daughter
more than me, is not worthy of me, Mat.
10. 37.

Q. I fee this ; and may the like be
in all other Cafes ?

A. Yes ; the fame may be in every
thing that is lov'd immoderately.

First, It diminifhes the Love of God,
fo that a Chriftian do's not, in fuch
Cafe. love God with all his Heart.

2*dly*, If it prevails on him fo far, as
to be Carelefs in his Duty, to venture
what is Hurtful, to be Bold in the
Dangers of Sin, to take Indifcreet Liberties, to hufh Confcience by particular Opinions, to lofe Refpect where it
is due, to caft off Difcipline, *&c.* there
is ftill another Degree of Evil in it.

3*dly*, If it go's fo far, that a Chriftian, for the Sake of what he loves,
tranfgreffes the Law of God, defpifes
his Precepts, lays afide, regards not,
                                    or

Worldly Things. 269

or omits Duty, gives Scandal to his Neighbour, neglects his Family, waftes his Eftate, ruins his Health, gives Ill Example, makes the Enemies of God blafpheme, &c. It is evident here is fomething lov'd more than God ; and confequently, that fuch an one is not a Difciple, who, in Fact, has forfaken God.

Q. And this, you fay, may be in e-very thing ?

A. Yes, in every Thing, tho' in it felf never fo Indifferent, Innocent, or Lawful. For if it be thus in regard of fuch Objects, where Love is a Duty, and according to the Command of God, as in the Inftances already mention'd, of Parents and Children, Husband and Wife ; that a Chriftian may, in thefe, arife to that Excefs of Love, as to be-come Guilty of Forfaking God, and Lofing the Character of Chrift's Difci-ple ; how much more may this be in other Things, where if any Degree of Love be tolerated, yet there is none Commanded ? It is certain, in regard of thefe, the Excefs cannot be lefs Criminal, than of the former.

Q. What may thefe Things be ?

A. I have already told you, All Things which are capable of being lov'd by Man; as Company, Recreati-

270   *Of the Love of*

or, Gaming, Divertifement, Enter-
tainments, Eating, Drinking, Dreffing,
Gain, Money, Eafe, Senfual Satisfa-
ctions, Revenge, Idlenefs, Goffiping,
Honour, State, Reputation, Party,
Friends, &c. All thefe, with many
other Particulars, are capable of the
Excefs mention'd, and may be made
the Occafions of departing from the
Commandments, and from God.

Q. Then thefe may be lov'd in fome
Degree, tho' not in Excefs?

A. Some of them are Evil, as *Revenge,* &c. The reft being appointed
or permitted by God, for the Ufe,
Convenience or Help of Man, fo far
they may be approv'd and lov'd, as
they are ferviceable to thefe Ends,
which God approves; but if the Love
exceeds thefe Bounds, and Satisfaction
is fought in them not now with Regard to the real Ufe and Service of
Man, as God allows, but to gratify
Inclination or Senfe, to comply with
Self-Love, Vanity, or the World, &c.
All this Love is Immoderate, and as
far as it becomes the Occafion of
Neglecting any Duty, or Running into
Danger of Sin, or Tranfgreffing any
Commandment of God, fo far in Proportion, it muft be own'd to be evil
and finful.

Q. As

Worldly Things.   271

Q. As how, in Particular?

A. I have already inftanc'd Particulars; but for more Clearnefs I add others.

Firft, A Chriftian may love a Friend and Company, as far as they are ferviceable, for the Profitable or Innocent Entertainment of Seafonable Times: but if the Love of thefe be fo great, that for the Sake or Satisfaction of them, he neglects his Duty, expcfes himfelf to the Dangers of Sin, or breaks any Commandment, fuch Love is Immodeate and Sinful.

2*dly,* A Chriftian may love any lawful Divertifement, as far as it is ferviceable for Health, or for the Relaxation of the Mind; but if it be lov'd fo far, that for the Sake or Satisfaction of any Divertifement he neglects his Duty to God or his Family, fpends or hazzards unreafonably, engages in ill Company, is averfe to what is Serious, loves to be Idle, and makes his Life but a Change or Succeffion of Idlenefs, fuch Love is immoderate and finful.

3*dly,* A Chriftian may love Cloaths, as they are ferviceable againft Cold and Shame; but if this Love go's fo far, that with them he gratifies his own Vanity, complies with an extra-

N 4   vagant

vagant World, and for them spends un-
reasonably, such Love is immoderate
and sinful. And thus it is in all other
Things : And the Reason is ; because,
tho' it be no Fault to make use of any
Thing Created, as far as it serves for
that End for which it is ordain'd or
permitted by God ; yet to employ it
beyond or contrary to that End, and
to the Offence of the Creator, is to
pervert the Order of Providence, to
abuse Blessings, and to turn them un-
gratefully against the Giver. Great
Discretion therefore, and good Management, is necessary in whatever we love ;
so as not to exceed the Bounds which
God has set. He that keeps within
these, obeys God ; but he that exceeds
them is disobedient.

CHAP. XLII.

Of the Love of Created Things.

Q. WHat is the great Perfection of
a Christian in this Life ?

A. The same as in the next ; that is,
To love God with all his Heart.

Q. Can a Christian thus love God,
if he loves any Thing Created ?

A. The Love of our Neighbour, such
as God requires of us, is an Extension

of

Created Things.   273

of the Love of God, and therefore very confiftent with it. But where Love
is not a Duty, the Rule is this : The
nearer a Chriftian can come to be Indifferent, as to all Things in this World,
the more is the Soul at Liberty for
Seeking and Loving God. For the Faculties of the Soul being Narrow, and
Limited in their Operations, they cannot with Earneftnefs be bent on any
one Thing, but by Leffening their Application to others. And hence it is,
that Worldly Concerns take off the
Soul from the Concern of Heaven, by
employing the Thoughts, and poffef-
fing them with a Sollicitude which has
no relation to Eternity. Whence thofe
Chriftians have the greateft Advantage
in order to love God, who are moft
feparated from this World, or who ufe
this World as if they did not ufe it,
that is, without Concern or Sollicitude
for it. Hence St. *Paul's* Defire is, *I would
have you be without Carefulnefs*, 1 Cor. 7. 32.
that the Heart may not be divided,
which God demands Entire to him-
felf. *Thou fha't love the Lord thy God with
thy whole Heart.* For this Reafon the
fame Apoftle prefers a fingle Life before that of Marriage. *He that is unmarried*, fays he, *careth for the things that be-*

274 *Of the Love of*

ong to the Lord, how he may please God: but he that is married, is careful for the things that belong to the World, how he may please his Wife, and is divided. And the unmarried Woman thinketh on the things of our Lord, how she may be holy both in Body and in Spirit: but she that is married careth for the things of the World, how she may please her Husband. And then concludes thus: *He that gives his Virgin in Marriage, does well; but he that gives her not in Marriage, does better,* 1 Cor. 7. v. 32. 38.

Q. If the Love of Creatures be thus ensnaring, what do you say of Fondness?

A. Love is a Passion, and what then must I say of Fondness, which is the Passion of a Passion? I say, this is still so much more Injurious, as possessing the Soul with greater Violence, more enslaving the Thoughts, encreasing the Sollicitude of the Mind, and subjecting the Heart to a Succession of anxious and perplexing Disquiets, whilst all that pleases or displeases is all upon Extremes. All this is Injurious to that Liberty of Spirit and Interiour Calm, in which the Soul ought to seek God; besides the Variety of other Passions that are annext to it, and the great Blindness and Indiscretion that at-

Created Things. 275

tend it: And therefore it is what a Chriſtian has Reaſon to be afraid of.

Q. But if it be the Effeсt of Temper, and a Chriſtian knows not how to prevent or remedy it?

A. He has ſo much more Unhappineſs to lament in himſelf; he has ſo much more Reaſon to keep a ſtriсter Watch upon himſelf; he has ſo much more to try his Diſcretion and exerciſe his Patience.

Q. But what muſt he do?

A. The ſame as with all other Natural Weakneſſes; he ought, in Prudence, to remove or moderate it as much as he can; and what he cannot at preſent overcome, he muſt bear with Patience, till Endeavours and Time have made it yield.

Q. Do you mean this of all States?

A. Yes, of all; for where Love is a Duty, yet Fondneſs is not; but is rather to be eſteem'd an Exceſs, a Weakneſs, a Paſſion, and ſubjeсt to ſo many Inconveniencies, that it muſt be Wiſdom to overcome it, and to ſuppreſs the Suggeſtions of it, till it can be overcome.

Q. But what do you ſay of it, in regard of other States?

A.

276 *Of the Love of*

A. I fay it is a dangerous Paffion.

Q. But if nothing be propos'd or thought on but what is Innocent?

A. How many Evils follow, where nothing was at firft thought on, but what was Innocent?

A. Then you are not for trufting it?

Q. As I would do Sparks of Fire among dry and combuftible Matter; they fometimes take Fire, and fometimes not; and it is Difcretion not to truft them, but to put them out, as foon as one can. No fort of Paffions ought to be trufted; for it is the Nature of them to be Blind and Rafh; and who can be Secure, when he is under fuch Conduct?

Q. Then, it may be, you will not allow of Friendfhip?

A. Yes, if there be great Difcretion in the Choice; otherwife it may prove the Way to Ruin: But, with the beft Choice, ftill the Foolifh Part of Friendfhip is not to be allow'd, which is Paffion; for this cannot well be, but with Mifchiefs attending it, even where they are not propos'd, fore-feen or apprehended; befides that unavoidable one of foftning the Soul, and bringing it to a Temper unbecoming a Soldier of Chrift.

Q. But if a Perfon finds this Paffion feizing him?   *A.* He

Created Things.   277

A. He ought to confider who is capable of giving the beft Advice, and there make timely Application; for he certainly ftands in need of the beft, which being to be determined by particular Circumftances, cannot here have Place; except only in General, and that is,

Firft, That he confider well, and take good Advice; for that this Paffion being Blind, runs confidently into irrecoverable Mifchiefs.

2*dly*, That, if there be no Profpect of Good, he ufe all poffible Means for fuppreffing it.

3*dly*, That he remove from all Occafion of feeding it, by Separation, if it be in his Power.

4*thly*, That, if this cannot be, he inpuftrioufly avoid all particular Communication, and be very watchful in the Government of all his Senfes.

5*thly*, That he allow no kind of Addreffes or Freedoms, which only ferve to encreafe the Paffion.

Thefe are difficult Prefcriptions, but being to prevent greater Difficulties, it muft be reafonable to fubmit to them. When a Tyrant threatens Slavery, it is worth the Pains to labour in difpoffeffing him, for the Securing of Liberty; and he that do's not, muft not afterwards complain of his Misfortunes which he faw coming on, and would not take the Pains to prevent them.

C H A P. XLIII.

Of a clean Heart.

Q. WHat do you mean by a Clean Heart?

A. I mean a Heart that loves nothing, but according to the Order and Will of God ; for whatever is beyond this, defiles.

Q. How do you fhew this ?

A. Becaufe God's Will is the Meafure and Rule of all Holinefs ; and therefore, as that cannot be holy which is difagreeable to the Divine Will ; fo if it be lov'd, it muft neceffarily defile ; becaufe it carries the Heart, and fixes it on that which fo far departs from the Rule of Holinefs and from God.

Q. But what is it that is chiefly underftood to defile the Heart, and render it Unclean ?

A. All Senfual and Carnal Defires: Hence St. *Peter* calls upon all Believers ; *I befeech you as Strangers and Pilgrims, abftain from flefhy Defires, which war againft the Soul,* 1 Pet. 2. 11. And St. *Paul* declares

Of a clean Heart.   279

clares to them, *To be carnally minded is
Death : The Carnal Man is Enmity against
God : If you live after the Flesh, you shall
die*, Rom. 8. 6. 7. 13.

Q. What then is the Christian to do?

A. He is always to remember what
the Apostle has told him, That *to be
Carnally minded is Death*; and his Salvation depending upon his avoiding
whatever brings Death to the Soul, he
is consequently to be very careful in
avoiding whatever is Carnal or Sensual, and thus fatally wars against the
Soul.

First, He is to keep a strict Watch
upon his Heart, so as to give no Admittance to any sinful Desires, nor to
entertain or please himself with any
kind of Thoughts, which are contrary to that Purity which the Gospel
requires, and ought to be abhor'd by
those who hope for the Blessing promis'd to the Clean of Heart. To such
Thoughts he ought not to open his
Heart, but start with Fear at the very
first Approach of them, as at the Appearance of Traitors who have a Design against hisLife; of Monsters which
come to devour him, and of Evil
Spirits, who, by pleasing Snares, in-
tend to draw him into Hell. And this
not only at Thoughts, which are directly

rectly sinful but at all others which have any Relation to them, and attempting him at a greater Distance, pretend to be Innocent, that they may destroy more securely, and without a Suspicion of their Design. Where there is not this Care, there cannot be long a Clean Heart.

2. He is to keep a like Guard upon all his Outward Senses: His Eyes are to be shut against all Evil Objects, and to be turn'd from all that which invites to Sin. He ought not to entertain himself with Books which are either Obscene, or by Amorous Subjects help to soften and effeminate the Soul. He ought to shut his Ears against all sinful Discourse, and not to bear their Company, who thus take upon them to act the Devil's Part. He ought to avoid all Publick Shews, in which such Liberties are taken, as betray a notorious Corruption, where they are pleasing; and cannot give Satisfaction, but what must be abhor'd by a Clean Heart.

3. He ought to put a strict Watch upon his Tongue, so as never to speak an Immodest or Unseemly Word; for so St. *Paul* gives the Charge, saying, *Let it not be once nam'd amongst you,* Eph. 5. 3. And this is not only to be
avoided

avoiding in *Plain Terms*, but likewife as to all fuch Words, which bearing a *double Meaning*, may be taken in an Ill Senfe ; for it being from the Abundance of the Heart, the Mouth fpeaks, there is a plain Difcovery of the Heart not being Clean, where the Lips utter fuch Expreffions, as are fo prejudicial to that Purity, which is enjoin'd the Followers of the Gofpel. The fame Care muft be us'd in avoiding all Immodeft Jefts or Songs ; becaufe all thefe fpeak what the Heart is. And if it be Clean, it muft have a Horrour of all fuch Entertainment : It muft be confounded, to think, how Chriftians, who fay, they Love and Fear God, can make that their Paftime, which is fo very Difpleafing to him; how they can Sport themfelves in that, which brings Death to their own Souls, and to all theirs, who are pleas'd with Hearing them. For what is this, but playing with Poifon, and Singing one another into Hell ?

A like Care is to be obferv'd, in making Reports or relating what has happen'd to others, to avoid fuch Paffages and Expreffions, as are not agreeable to Chriftian Modefty : For tho' it be no Participation of the Guilt, to relate it ; yet fuch as are frequent in
this

282   *Of a clean Heart.*

this Matter, and have Satisfaction in it, shew but too evidently, what their Heart is; besides the Mischief they do, by entertaining others with this Filth and giving Youth (if any happen to be present) an early Knowledge of this Subject, which they cannot Learn too late.

4. He is to be very strict in taking no Liberties with himself or others, which can bear the Construction of this Guilt. I except against nothing, that is really Innocent; and yet this ought not to be a Plea, to justify the Attempts, in any kind, of a Sensual Heart; for whatever is done upon such a Suggestion, will certainly be condemn'd, in the Sight of God, of Sin, however there may be nothing Visible to prove the Guilt of it before Men. Whence I cannot but admire at what Custom has made too Common, and that is, the great Freedom us'd both in Words and Actions, where Sensuality is rather Profess'd than Hid. For tho' there be no Evil propos'd or intended, yet while it is in Compliance with an Interiour Corruption, and to Gratify a Sensual Mind, there can be no Excuse for it, but it must be Condemn'd as the Liberty of Unbelievers, such as either know

not,

Of a clean Heart.   283

not, or defpife, the Promifes made to
the Clean of Heart.

And if fuch Freedoms are to be thus
Cenfur'd in the Aggreffors. Let thofe
confider, how far they partake in the
Guilt, who, by Looks, Smiles, Words or
other Hints of Carriage, give any Encouragement to them ; all that is fo underftood, is equal to the Confent of
Words ; and if the Heart be Confenting
to it, there needs no other Proof at the
Tribunal of Chrift. Let thofe too confider it, who feem to Difcourage it, and
exprefs their Diflike ; but do it in fuch
a manner, that they plainly difcover
themfelves not to be in Earneft. What
would thefe do, if any fhould attempt
to take away their Money? What, if
their Life? In thefe Cafes they would
omit nothing, that could poffibly be a
Means of refcuing them from the Violence, and would foon fhew themfelves
to be in Earneft. And why not fo here,
where the Concern is very often greater
than of Money or Life?

Here I have told you at length, what
the Chriftian is to do, for ftanding a-
gainft the Dangers of Natural Corruption, for avoiding all, that can Defile,
and for preferving a Clean Heart. And
however the Practice of Chriftians is
fuch, that one would Guefs this to be a
Matter,

284   *Of Self-denial.*

Matter, wherein God has given no Precept, but left them to the Liberty of their own Defires ; yet whoever will or has read the New Teftament, muft obferve there all the Sins under this Head, to be mark'd out, as the Sins of Unbelievers, even of thofe, who have no Knowledge of God ; that they are fuch, as exclude them from the King-dom of Heaven, and from which all the Followers of the Gofpel ought to be wafh'd and purify'd ; for that the Sight of God, which they believe and Hope for, can be expected only by thofe, to whom it is promis'd, that is, to the Clean of Heart : For *They, that are Chrift's have Crucify'd the Flefh, with the Affections and Lufts,* Gal. 5. 24.

C H A P. XLIV.

Of Self-denial.

Q. IF this be the Rule of a Chrifti-an Life, as you have hitherto de-clar'd, is there not great Self-denial neceffary for coming to the Practice of it ?

A. Yes, Self-denial is abfolutely ne-ceffary.

Q. From what Head do's this Necef-fity of Self-denial arife?

A. From

Of Self-denial. 285

A. From the Corruption of Nature, which fpreading it felf thro' all the Faculties of our Soul and Body, inclines them all, with a fort of Violence, to Evil; fo that if they have the Liberty of following their own Bent, they will all run into Sin, and feek Satisfaction in it.

Q. How do's this Corruption oblige us to Self-denia 1?

A. Becaufe the Will and Law of God and the Gofpel are Holy : and we cannot walk according to thefe, except we Check and Supprefs in us all thofe Inclinations, which carry us out of the Way of this Holinefs, and lead us to Evil. If we follow that, which is Juft and Good; we muft of Neceffity, ftand againft and refift that, which bends us to Sin.

Q. Is it thus declar'd in the Gopel?

A. It is by Chrift himfelf, who thus fays to his Difciples; *If any Man will come after me, let him deny himfelf, and take up his Crofs and follow me,* Mat. 16. 24. And again; *Whofoever will come after me, let him deny himfelf, and take up his Crofs and follow me,* Mar. 8. 34. Here Self-denial is exprefly declar'd a Neceffary Condition, for becoming Chrift's Diciple.

Q. How

[John Anselm Mannock], *The Poor Man's Catechism: Or, The Christian Doctrine Explained. With Short Admonitions* (1752), pp. 243–67

Another example of a text from a productive period of English Catholic catechesis is *The Poor Man's Catechism*, published anonymously in this variant in 1752, without place of publication or publisher and, apparently, edited or facilitated by George Bishop (1695–1766), Vicar General in Oxfordshire to the Vicar Apostolic John Talbot Stonor (1678–1756). Another edition was published in the same year by Gibson and the work was reissued in 1762 (London), 1767 (Dublin), 1770 (London), 1792 (London), 1794 (Dublin) and 1797 (London).

The author was the Benedictine John, in religion Anselm, Mannock (1677–1764), from a Suffolk recusant gentry family. Mannock was educated at St Gregory's in Douai where, in 1700 he made his profession as a monk and in 1709 returned to England. For half a century he acted as chaplain to the Canning family in Warwickshire, being appointed Procurator of the Southern Province of the English Benedictine congregation in 1729. He later served John Wright in Essex, where he died in 1764.

Mannock's many writings in manuscript are preserved at Downside Abbey and include his three-volume English Benedictine hagiography, *Annus Sacer Brittanicus, or Short Lives of the English Saints* (1747–50), as well as other works on the saints, a compilation of reflections for the days of the year, and a similar production for Sundays, a commentary on the epistles and gospels for feast-days, a catechism of the Old Testament and a catechism on the life of Christ, a nine-volume commentary on the bible intended for preacher, *Thesaurus Praedicatorum*, and *The Poor Man's Companion, or some Moral Collections upon the Commandments*.

In 1726, under gentry patronage, Mannock published a commentary on the Mass, *The Christian Sacrifice*, and in 1752 the more popular *The Poor Man's Catechism*. *The Poor Man's Controversy*, a posthumous work of 1769, reflected the growing acceptance of Catholics in English society and the influence of the Catholicism of the Enlightenment – it showed a comparatively conciliatory approach to Protestantism in citing Protestant authors and in playing down alleged Catholic exaggerations of belief over the papacy and veneration of Mary.

Certainly as far as *The Poor Man's Catechism* is concerned, and despite the publisher's claim for the author's *'Intent of imparting himself clearly to the Ignorant'*, the overall approach and style seem somewhat recondite, or even Scholastic, rather than elementary. Perhaps this work was part of Mannock's output designed for Benedictines training to go on the English Mission as well as for those already engaged on it. Indeed, much of Mannock's *oeuvre*, while popular to an extent, did tend to have a restricted appeal, as with his spiritual writings which were composed, writes Dom Gregory Scott, 'for a small circle of Warwickshire gentry some of whom had been educated by the Benedictines and maintained monks as chaplains.'[1]

Even so, the appeal of *The Poor Man's Catechism* was popular in the sense that it was, as with Gother's writings of a similar nature, intensely practical and useful, dealing with such issues as the Church's marriage laws and the avoidance of manual labour on Sundays, as well as laying stress on justice towards tenants and employees. This catechism enjoyed a lasting vogue in the United States in the nineteenth century, with numerous editions published in Baltimore, Maryland, and New York.[2]

1.   Geoffrey Scott, *Gothic Rage Undone. English Monks in the Age of the Enlightenment* (Bath, Downside Abbey, 1992), p. 84.
2.   Oliver L. Kapsner, OSB, *A Benedictine Bibliography. An Author–Subject Union List* (2nd edn, Collegeville, MN, St John's Abbey Press, 1962), p. 363.

THE

Poor Man's CATECHISM:

OR, THE

Chriſtian Doctrine

EXPLAINED,

WITH

Short ADMONITIONS.

Bleſſed are the Poor in Spirit, for theirs is the Kingdom of Heaven, MAT. v. 3.

Hath not God choſen the Poor in this World, rich in Faith, and Heirs of the Kingdom, which he hath promiſed to thoſe that love him, JAMES ii. 5.

Printed in the YEAR MDCC LII.

THE

Publisher to the READER,

HE *Author of the following Work has modestly intitled it,* The Poor Man's Catechism: *He addresses not himself to the Rich and the Great ; he supposes them sufficiently instructed already by a superior Education. He presumes not to write to the Learned ; he knows how hard it is to content them, and instruct the Ignorant at the same Time. To the Poor he dedicates his Work, since they in Scripture are declared* Heirs of the Kingdom of Heaven, *thro' their Docility and Obedience. If he has condescended to write in a plain intelligible Style, this certainly best answers his Intent of imparting himself clearly to the Ignorant : I beg Leave to add, that the many fine spiritual Thoughts, the understanding Reader will discern dispersed throughout the whole Work, will make a good Amends for the Deficiency of a higher Style.*

THE

The CHRISTIAN DOCTRINE *Explained.* 243

Of VIRTUE *and* VICE.

Q. HOW many *Cardinal Virtues* are there? *A.* Four; *Prudence, Justice, Fortitude* and *Temperance.* They are call'd *Cardinal,* because they are the Principal, and other moral Virtues branch from them.

INSTRUCTION. The End of Religion is Virtue, without which we cannot be beloved of God, or come to the Enjoyment of him. Virtue is a Power that reigns in the Soul, which directs and inclines us to do Good, and avoid Evil, both with Regard to the Happiness of this Life and the next. In acting virtuously we cannot do ill; because Virtue is essentially good, and renders those who obey its Power, good, and their Actions good. There are some common inbred Principles of Truth, and the Light of Reason in all Men, which contain the Seeds of some Virtues; we have a natural Light to discern Truth from Error, and some Inclination to follow Reason, which will ever remain in a rational Nature ; so that by repeating good Acts, we may get a Habit of doing them, and acquire moral Virtues as the Heathens did   But this did not render them truly good and wise to Salvation ; it only fitted them for the Society of Men, and made them good Citizens of this World, not of Heaven.   There is a great Disparity between the Virtue of one who is temperate, merely because Reason dictates that Intemperance is prejudicial to Health, and hinders Reason from working, and one who is temperate because God teaches that it is necessary for subjecting the Body to the Soul, in order to overcome Sin, and be saved: This is true Virtue, which has God for its Principle, and Salvation its End. The Power of Virtue is all through Grace : God has given to every one a Free-will to embrace Virtue or follow Vice ; 'tis through his Grace, that in our weak Nature and fallen State, we practise Virtue ; 'tis through our perverse Will, we practise Evil : A good Will, which we cannot have without Grace, is the Original of all good Things; on the contrary, a bad Will is the Original of all Evil and Vice.

M 2   SECT.

SECT. I.

Of PRUDENCE.

Q. WHAT is Prudence ? *A.* 'Tis a Virtue that guards us against Ignorance, and directs us in a right Choice, that we deceive not ourselves, nor deceive others.

INSTRUCTION. *Prudence* is the Key to true Knowledge; 'tis what makes us wise in our own Actions, and capable to counsel others, even in the most difficult Occurrences. 'Tis the Part of Prudence to examine well before we determine : To suspend our own Judgment in Doubts, and rather submit to others, and learn Knowledge from them who have had more Experience ; to lay up the Memory of what has happen'd to others ; to be circumspect in weighing all Circumstances; to be provident in foreseeing the Event ; to be cautious in considering what Obstacles we are likely to meet with. To this Virtue the holy Scripture very frequently exhorts us; *Son do nothing without Counsel, and after the Fact thou shalt not repent*, Ecclef. xxxii. 24. To this our Saviour encourages his Disciples, *Be prudent as Serpents, and simple as Doves,* Mat. x. 16. innocent and mild as Doves, but cautious how to proceed to a right Undertaking. To this St. *Paul* admonishes all Christians, *Take heed how you walk warily, not as unwise, but as wise, redeeming the Time, because the Days are evil,* Ephef. v. 15. Of this the wise Man says, *The Law of a prudent Man is a Source of Life, by which he may decline from the Ruin of Death,* Prov. xiii. 14. In a word, 'tis Prudence that directs us in all our Ways and Doings to Good, and diverts us from all Evil ; it guides us in Truth, and diverts us from Error. By this great Virtue Kings and Magistrates rule, and People obey ; Armies are commanded, Families governed, and every one's private Life, and all our Actions, directed to our last End.

EXHORTATION. Think, O Christian, what Need you have of this great Virtue, considering the Ignorance you are born with, and the Corruption you bring with you into the World ; then pray that God would infuse it into your Soul. It is highly necessary to guide you both in

M anners

The CHRISTIAN DOCTRINE *Explained.* 245

Manners and Religion:———1. As to Manners; how many are carried away with the World, how many go aftray by its alluring Delights, and the falfe Maxims of the Perverfe? How many by this Means are ruin'd to Eternity? 'Tis Prudence muft there direct our Steps; and this will foon difcover the Miftake, in taking falfe for true Joys; falfe Pleafure for true Delight; and will fhew this is no where to be found, but in the Love of God and a good Confcience. Then as to Religion, how ne ceffary is Prudence to direct you in a right Choice, amidft the Errors of the Age? This, laying Prejudice afide, will foon difcover Truth from Falfehood : 'Tis certainly the greateft Prudence to find out, amidft the confufed Opinions of Men, the only fure and fecure Way to Salvation. There is but one Way to Heaven; feek then to be inftructed in it, rather than to follow your own Inventions.

SECT. II.

Of JUSTICE.

2. WHAT is Juftice? *A.* 'Tis a Virtue which gives to every one his Due : *To whom Tribute, Tribute; to whom Fear, Fear; to whom Honour, Honour,* Rom. xiii. 7.

INSTRUCTION. *Juftice* is threefold; to God, to our Neighbour, and to ourfelves. God claims his Due in the firft Place, and what we owe him is Religion, Love, Fear, Honour, Service, Adoration; and this is fo high a Duty, that we can never render to God an Equality to what we owe him. Juftice to our Neighbour, is a fix'd Principle to give every one his own, and to wrong no Man : Hence a juft Man is honeft in all his Dealings and Bargains of any kind. This Virtue, in Kings and Princes, is an univerfal Good; as Injuftice in them is an univerfal Evil. 'Tis a Virtue alfo which runs through the whole Courfe of every Man's Life; as we continually have Dealings with others; fo that, of all moral Virtues, this is the moft beneficial to Society; and for this Reafon it is remark'd, that in all States, the *Juft* and the *Brave* are the moft honour'd by the Publick; as from them the Publick receives the moft Service. Befides this general Honefty to all Men, there is a Juftice

M 3

in

246 *The* POOR MAN'S CATECHISM: *Or,*

in honouring our Parents, in the next Place under God ;
to whom we can never return fo much as we have receiv'd, (*Pietas in Parentes.*) A Juftice in loving our Country, in which we are born and educated, (*Pietas in Pa-
triam.*) A Juftice in refpecting the Good and the Great,
(*Obfervantia Majorum.*) A Juftice in being grateful to our
Benefactors ; in fpeaking Truth to thofe we live with,
and not deceiving them ; in living friendly with our
Neighbours : It is juft alfo in fome Cafes to be generous ;
there is Juftice in rewarding, and Juftice in punifhing.
Thefe are Virtues of a fecond Rank, which branch
from this Cardinal Virtue, and belong to it, as having
all fomething of Juftice in them.

3. There is a kind of Juftice to ourfelves ; for tho',
ftrictly fpeaking, there can be no Juftice but between
two Perfons ; yet, as in every one there is Soul and
Body, fuperior Powers of the Soul, and inferior, it is juft
that the inferior fhould obey the fuperior Part ; and therefore Juftice to ourfelves is to take care of the Charge
God has entrufted us with, the Salvation of our Souls ; that
we watch and guard it by Grace, from the Enemy, the
World and our own Concupifcence ; fo to fecure, by our
Virtues, its future Happinefs. The Reward of this great
Virtue is exprefs'd in thefe Words, *Bleffed are they that
hunger and thirft after Juftice, for they fhall be filled,*
Mat. v. 6.

EXHORTATION. To render your Life comfortable, and
your End happy, practife, O Chriftian, this divine Virtue : Be juft to Heaven and Earth, and perfect Peace will
poffefs your Soul : *Juftice and Peace have embrac'd each
other.* Follow then the general Rule of Juftice ; *Give unto
every one his Due* ; whether it be due by the Law of God,
or by the Law of Man. Alas ! what is it but a want of
this that creates fo much Mifchief and Confufion upon
Earth ? So much Rebellion againft God by Sin ; fo much
Fraud, Injuftice, and even Murders, with other innumerable Evils done to others ? What is it but Want of
Juftice has carried Multitudes of all Countries to Hell ?
Juftice does no Wrong ; Injuftice knows no Good : A
juft Man gives Glory to God, Obedience to his Superiors ; Love to his Equals, and Affiftance to his Inferiors ; he does no Injury to others, in Word or Deed ;
no, not even in Thought. Thus a juft Man is dear
both

The CHRISTIAN DOCTRINE *Explained.* 247

both to God and Men ; to God, who, as he *is just, loves Justice*; and to Men, because without Justice we can't live one by another. Whatever then be your State of Life, O Christian, let Justice attend it; for God is just, *and with him the Just shall live for ever*; that is, such as are just both to God and Man.

S E C T. III.

Of F O R T I T U D E.

Q. WHAT is Fortitude ? *A.* 'Tis a Virtue that gives us Power to face all the Evils of Life, and to withstand even Death itself, rather than abandon our Duty.

INSTRUCTION. *Fortitude* is the Armour and Fence of a Christian Life; without it Virtue is never secure : There is a *bad Fear*, sufficient of itself, without any other Crime, to ruin our Souls, and to make us abandon our Faith and Duty in Time of Danger; especially when we are threaten'd with Death, which is the most terrible of all Things in this World ; of this it is said: *Woe to those that fear*. Apoc. xxi. 8. that is, who, through Fear, abandon their Duty ; *Their Portion shall be in the Lake that burneth with Fire and Brimstone, which is the second Death :* 'Tis Fortitude that sustains us against these Terrors, which will otherwise force us from a good Life ; and vanquishes all the Dangers that oppose our eternal Felicity. It learns us *Patience*, to endure the Evils of Life willingly, rather than forsake Good : *Constancy*, to persist in Virtue, against all Difficulties, from whatever Hand they come : And *Perseverance*, to remain firm to the End in Good, against that Tediousness which arises from the Length of Suffering, which has wrought on many to abandon Virtue.

'Tis Fortitude to face Death in a just War, in Defence of one's Country ; this the Heathens had. But to die voluntarily for God, in Defence of the true Faith, or in Defence of Virtue, or to avoid Sin, is Christian Fortitude and Martyrdom. So many, in the Persecutions, died for their Faith ; and many holy Women were martyr'd for Chastity ; and St. *John Baptist*, for reprehending the Sin of Adultery. Blessed Fortitude, which has crown'd

M 4

248 *The* Poor Man's Catechism : *Or,*

so many with Glory! Whoever dies in such a Cause, has all Sin and Punishment forgiven him, and is immediately after Death received into the Joys of Heaven. Now, if Fortitude keeps the Soul steady and firm in the greatest Dangers, when we are threatened with Death, it cannot fail to fortify us against lesser ones, that we may never abandon any essential Duty, through Fear : To this Virtue Christ our Saviour encourages his Disciples in the Gospel ; *Fear not Man, who can only kill the Body ; but rather fear God, who can destroy both Soul and Body in Hell,* Mat. x. 28.

Exhortation. Great, O Christian, is the Necessity of this Virtue of Fortitude, if we only consider our miserable Weakness and Inconstancy on the one hand, and those powerful Enemies we have to combat, on the other : So weak, that of ourselves *we can do nothing,* (Jo. xv. 5.) at the same time, that *our Combat is not against Flesh and Blood, but against Principalities and Powers, against the Rulers of this World of Darkness, against evil Spirits which haunt the Air,* Eph. v. 12. Alas! we have Enemies both from within and without, Enemies watching Day and Night to devour us ; our own corrupt Nature, perverse Will, sensual Appetites, Malice of Man, and Envy of Devil, all conspiring our Ruin. And where can we find Relief, but from a divine Power, to support us ? As the Terror of Suffering, and the Fear of Persecution and Death, have a stronger Power to force us from Virtue and the Way of Life, than even sensual Pleasures have to allure us from it, hence we stand more in Need of Fortitude to withstand these Terrors. 'Twas this that supported the Martyrs, and is necessary to support every Christian in Good, *for every one that will live piously, will suffer Persecution,* 2 Tim. iii. 12. We have great Want of Fortitude, not only to vanquish our Enemies, and fight against Temptation, but to practise Virtue, and to surmount the Difficulty that lies in the Way of it : Depend not then upon your own Strength, but say: *My Help is only from our Lord, who made Heaven and Earth ;* and pray daily: O Lord, be thou my Strength, my Aid, my Power to conduct me, as thou didst the *Israelites,* thro' the Desart of this World, through the Dangers of Life and Death, to the true Land of Promise, the Land of the Living.

SECT.

The CHRISTIAN DOCTRINE *Explained.* 249

SECT. IV.

Of TEMPERANCE.

2. **W**HAT is Temperance ? *A.* 'Tis a Virtue that moderates our sensual Appetites, and keeps them within the Bounds of Reason, that they may not allure us from Virtue.

INSTRUCTION. Virtue has two great Enemies in this World ; 1. Terror and Persecution, which would force us from the Practice of it : 2. Sensual Pleasures, which, by their Power, too often allure us to what is contrary to it ; against the first, Fortitude is necessary ; against the second, *Temperance :* And as amongst all sensual Delights, carnal Pleasure and Gluttony are the most violent, we have in a particular Manner Need of Temperance, to contain those Appetites within the Bounds that Reason prescribes, that we neither commit Sin, nor abandon God for them. As every cardinal Virtue is attended with a Train of lesser Virtues, which, tho' they come not up to the full Perfection of their cardinal Virtue, yet have something of the Nature of it in them ; so Temperance, whose Perfection chiefly lies in moderating our Appetites to carnal Pleasure and Gluttony, which are the most violent, branches out into many lesser Virtues, which bridle us from Excess in Pleasures that are less violent : For Instance, there is Temperance not only in *Eating* and *Drinking*, but in *Dress, Furniture, Equipage*; *Moderation in all Things* ; in our *Mirth, Discourse* and *Recreation*; in our *Curiosity* after Knowledge ; in the Opinion we have of our own Abilities ; which are all Parts of Temperance ; as is also *Clemency*, which mitigates the Punishment due to others ; and *Mildness*, which moderates Anger ; *Abstemiousness* from certain Meats, at certain Times, called *Fasting*; *Sobriety* in Drinking ; *Chastity*, to refrain from all carnal Pleasures forbidden ; and *Continency*, to abstain even from lawful ones, and to withstand the most violent Attacks of them ; which have all something of Temperance in them, and spring from it. Temperance then relates both to Soul and Body ; 'tis a Virtue so necessary, that there is no Heaven for us without it : *He that is abstinent, shall taste Life.* ——Consider how many

M 5   Evils

250　*The* Poor Man's Catechism : *Or,*

Evils fpring from Intemperance? How many make a
God of their Belly, and Idols of themfelves? How
many, with the rich Glutton, damn themfelves by a
brutifh Intemperance in Diet and Clothing? How many
have no Bounds in the Liberty of the Tongue, and the
exorbitant Defires and Paffions of their Hearts? Temperance then is abfolutely neceffary to moderate all thefe
Extravagances; to regulate our interior, as well as exterior : Hence is that Leffon of St. *Paul, Let us live ho-
neftly, not in Rioting and Drunkennefs, but put on our Lord
Jefus Chrift,* Rom. xiii. 13.

　　Exhortation. What more neceffary Virtue for you,
O Chriftian, to live the fober, chafte and temperate
Life of Chrift and his Saints, then Temperance? Prayer,
Fafting and Penance, are the only Means to preferve it ;
Aufterities and Self-denials help and maintain it ; if you
fail in thefe, this Virtue is eafily and foon deftroyed.
Bleffed Temperance, that keeps us in Subjection to God,
and preferves us in all Good, againft the moft violent forbidden Pleafures! Temperance breeds Serenity of Mind,
and renders us happy, both in this World and the next :
Labour hard then to obtain of God this cardinal Virtue,
from whence fo much Good proceeds. Keep a Watch
over every Motion of your fenfual Appetite ; and if in
any Refpect you become irregular or immoderate in the
Offices of Life, correct yourfelf, and let Temperance
govern you ; let Temperance accompany all the Bleffings
of Nature you enjoy ; ufe them with Moderation, fuch as
God requires : Follow Neceffity, not Excefs and Super-
fluity ; whatever exceeds the Bounds of Neceffity, de-
generates into Luxury: Bridle your Appetite, that no
Gluttony proceed from Meat or Drink, which makes us
degenerate into Brutes : Let Temperance alfo govern
the inward Man, and bridle your exceffive Paffions, and
the immoderate Defires of your Heart. Let it govern
the outward Man, that nothing bad proceed from your
Lips : Let it teach you when, where, how much, and
in what Manner to fpeak. In a word, let it regulate
your whole Comportment, that nothing but Decency and
Modefty may be feen in it. Live *foberly* in this World,
and abftain from all forbidden Pleafures ; fo fhall you be
fatiated with the Torrent of eternal Pleafure in the next.

Of

The CHRISTIAN DOCTRINE *Explained.*   251

Of the GIFTS of the HOLY GHOST.

Q. WHAT are the Gifts of the Holy Ghoſt? *A.*
Wiſdom, Underſtanding, Counſel, Fortitude,
Knowledge, Piety, the Fear of our Lord.

INSTRUCTION. Theſe Gifts of the Holy Ghoſt are
ſet down by the Prophet *Iſaiah,* (c. lxi. 1.) Our Saviour was repleniſh'd with them; he brought them from
Heaven for us his Servants, and diſtributes them to the
Faithful, according as he pleaſes. They tranſcend moral
Virtues; moral Virtues are Habits that only incline us
to follow Reaſon in our Actions; but theſe Gifts incline
us to obey the Impulſe and Motion of the Holy Ghoſt,
by whom we are led to Life everlaſting. They are as ſo
many ſuperior Graces, to improve us in Virtue, and to
perfect us in a Chriſtian Life. They ſupply all the Neceſſities of our infirm State, in order to a bleſſed eternal one.

Wiſdom teaches us to order and direct all our Actions
to the Glory of God, and our laſt End: *Underſtanding,*
elevates us to penetrate and ſubmit to the Myſteries of
Faith: *Counſel,* diſcovers to us the Frauds and Deceits
of the Devil, the better to avoid them: *Fortitude,*
ſtrengthens us againſt the Perſecutions of the World:
Knowledge, teaches us to know and underſtand the Will
of God: *Piety,* makes us devout and zealous to put the
ſame in Execution: *Fear,* makes us cautious not to offend
ſo tremendous a Majeſty. Theſe Gifts are infuſed into
the Hearts of none but true Believers.

EXHORTATION. How much ought you, O Chriſtian,
to covet and preſerve theſe divine Gifts of the Holy
Ghoſt, ſo eſſential to Happineſs! O what are all the Gifts
of Nature to them! They raiſe us up, poor and miſerable
as we are in this World, to eternal Glory. They truly
come from God, and carry us to God. Behold now the
Aſſiſtance they give us, to advance and conduct us to
Happineſs everlaſting; to which ordinary Virtues, without theſe, would not be ſufficient in our infirm State; becauſe without theſe, Virtue is not long preſerved.——
As corrupt Nature carries us away to ſenſual Objects,
and to embrace falſe, for true Delights, to take Evil for
Good; *Wiſdom* corrects the Mind, and teaches us to
frame

frame a right Judgment, to afpire to higher Things ; to
purfue Virtue, and the Love and Knowledge of God :
This is the Wifdom of God, and produces Life ; the Wifdom of the World brings Death : O how neceffary is
this divine Gift amidft the dark Follies of Life !——As
we are all born with a natural Blindnefs, and Weaknefs
of Reafon, in refpect to the hidden Myfteries of God,
the Gift of *Underftanding* helps us to difcern the Truths
God has reveal'd to his Church ; enlightens us to fee
beyond Time into Eternity ; this is what we ought to pray
for : *Lord give me Underftanding to know thy Ways.* O what
is it, but the Want of this, makes fo many wife in their
own Conceits ; and to pafs Judgment upon what they are
not in the leaft able to comprehend ! Hence how many
walk in the Dark, and plunge themfelves into Error, Infidelity and Vice !—— *Counfel* helps the Ignorance of our
Minds, by embracing wholfome Inftructions given us ;
this teaches us to fhun Evil, and do Good ; it difcovers to
us the Snares of the Devil, and informs us of the many
Dangers a fpiritual Man is expofed to : To hear and follow *Counfel,* is the Way to be preferv'd from thofe Dangers which are the Overthrow of innumerable Souls :
—— *Fortitude* is the Armour of a Chriftian, and moft neceffary for him whofe Life is a Warfare and continual
Combat upon Earth ; 'tis only through Fortitude we can
be victorious over all, and fecure our Virtue here, and
Felicity hereafter. Through Fortitude, we are armed
againft the moft violent Affaults of the Devil, Malice
and Perfecution of wicked Men ; by it, we vanquifh
Self-will, Self-love, our greateft Enemy. So great is
this Gift, that of it the wife Man fays : *Better is he who
commands his Soul, than he who conquers Cities,* Prov. xvi.
32.—— *Knowledge* preferves us from the eager Purfuit of our
own Wills, and fhews us what is the Will of God, and what
our Duty to him ; many follow their own Fancies, and
have themfelves for their Guide ; what is this, but *the
Blind leading the Blind, till both fall into the Pit ?* Of whom
St. *Barnard* rightly fays, " He that has himfelf for his Mafter, has a Fool for his Scholar." Great is the Gift of *Knowledge,* which preferves us from fo great a Folly ; teaching
us to know God, and to know ourfelves ; to fee the Follies
of Life, and the Joys of Eternity. *If Knowledge pleafe
thy Soul, Counfel fhall guard thee, and Prudence preferve thee,*
from

The Christian Doctrine *Explained.* 253

from all Evil, Prov. ii. 10. *Piety* is a noble Gift, which inspires us with Zeal and Devotion, to serve the great God of Majesty, and with earnest Labour to work out our Salvation : We have certainly great Need of this Gift, who have hitherto been so lukewarm and indifferent in our Duty to God, and our spiritual Concerns.—*The Fear of our Lord is the Beginning of true Wisdom,* and inspires us with Reverence for God ; so adorable in Love and Goodness, that we dread nothing more, than the Evil of Sin, so displeasing and opposite to that infinite Good, which is in God. This Gift of the Holy Ghost is not a servile, but a filial Fear ; the Fear a Child has to offend a loving Parent : 'Tis like to that the Angels have in Heaven, who, with Trembling, fall down and adore their great-beloved God ; 'tis a Fear all just Men have on Earth, who, with this Fear and Trembling, work out their Salvation. This is the Fear, O Christian, you must pray for, as 'tis the Beginning of all Good ; alas ! 'tis the Want of it is the Beginning of all Folly and Wickedness : This is what all the Good, all the Saints desired : *Pierce, O Lord, my Flesh with thy Fear, for I have dreaded thy Judgments.* Let this holy Fear accompany you in all you do, and then you will not sin.

Of the Fruits *of the* Holy Ghost.

Q. WHAT are the Fruits of the Holy Ghost ? *A.* Charity, Joy, Peace, Patience, Longanimity, Goodness, Benignity, Mildness, Fidelity, Modesty, Continency, Chastity. So they are numbered by St. *Paul* to the *Galatians,* (c. v.) to which seems to answer, what is said in the Apocalypse, in the Description of the celestial *Jerusalem : On both Sides the River is a Tree of Life that bringeth twelve Fruits,* (c. ult.)

Instruction. The Fruit is the last Product we expect from the Tree ; and when it comes to its Perfection and Maturity, has a Sweetness in it, which delights the Taste : So the Acts of *Charity, Joy, Peace, Patience, &c.* above-mention'd, are what proceed in our Souls, through the Grace of the Holy Ghost, as the Fruits which are expected from that Grace, and are accompanied with all spiritual Delight. Amongst these, Charity has the first Place, as being the most excellent, from whence all the rest proceed : For by *Love,* the Soul having God always present, hence must follow *Joy :* Thence comes also
Peace

254 *The* POOR MAN'S CATECHISM : *Or* ,

Peace and Tranquility of Mind, while the fluctuating and restless Passions of the Soul are quieted by having our Hearts fixed upon only *one Object of Love* : But as we must know how to endure the Evils of this Life, as well as how to expect, with untired Minds, the good Things of the Life to come, in order to secure our *Peace*, hence the fourth Fruit of the Holy Ghost is *Patience* ; and the fifth, *Longanimity*. From the Love of God follows the Love of our Neighbour, which cannot be without a Will to do good to others; hence the sixth Fruit is *Goodness* ; and as this is not perfect, unless we do good to others, after a kind affable Manner, the seventh is *Benignity*. But since Charity is not yet perfect in us, unless, besides doing Good, we bear the morose and troublesome Manners of others, and allay all the Motions of our Anger and Passions against them, the eighth is *Mildness* : And of this Charity, we give a Proof, by our *Fidelity*, in every thing we undertake for others Service, and never deceiving them, which is the ninth. Thus far the Grace of the Holy Ghost disposes our Souls well, towards God and our Neighbour. As to ourselves, we are well disposed in our exterior Comportment, in our Words, Dress, &c. by *Modesty*, which permits nothing indecent about us ; and this therefore is the tenth Fruit of the Holy Ghost : And as to our interior Passions ; Concupiscence of the Flesh, which is the strongest, is quite suppressed by *Continency*; by which, we resist the most violent Temptations to Pleasure, which is the eleventh : And by *Chastity*, by which we abstain from all forbidden carnal Delight, which is sometimes brought to so great Perfection in the Soul, by the Grace of the Holy Ghost, as neither to be overcome by these Pleasures, or even much tempted by them.

EXHORTATION. These, Christian, are the Fruits which God expects from the Grace he has so abundantly bestow'd upon you ; these will make your Life comfortable, and your End glorious. *Charity* is the Main of them ; this must ever reign in your Heart, and work in your Life : Upon this all other Perfections are founded ; and our Virtues cease to be divine, when Charity fails. All Virtue must be ingrafted therein, as in a Vine, to bear Fruit. With this St. *Paul* begins, when he numbers up the Fruits of the Holy Ghost, as all proceeding from this first Fruit, Charity. All Things then become good and virtuous, where *Charity*, the Love of God and our Neighbour governs ;

The CHRISTIAN DOCTRINE *Explained.* 255

verns; *a good Tree cannot bear bad Fruit, nor a bad Tree good Fruit.* A good Chriftian, who has the Love of God, (while he fo remains in God) can do no Evil : A bad Chriftian, that is totally deprived of the Love of God, can do nothing, in that State, that is meritorious before God. Live then by the Grace of the Holy Ghoft, not by the Maxims of the World ; live fo, that the Fruits of the Holy Ghoft may appear vifibly in your Life, not the Works of the Flefh : Thofe are quite oppofite to thefe other ; becaufe one carries us to what is above ourfelves, the other to what is below ourfelves. Miftake not then, if you pretend to be *a Chriftian indeed. God will not be laughed at : What a Man fowes, that he fhall reap* ; *he that fowes in the Flefh, of the Flefh he fhall reap Corruption : He that fowes in the Spirit,* (he that works by the Grace of the Holy Ghoft) *fhall reap of the Spirit, Life everlafting,* Gal. viii. 6. One is the Work of Grace, the other of Sin and Corruption.

Of the EIGHT BEATITUDES.

Q. WHICH are the eight Beatitudes ? *A.* 1. Bleffed are the Poor in Spirit, for theirs is the Kingdom of Heaven. 2. Bleffed are the Meek, for they fhall poffefs the Land. 3. Bleffed are they that mourn, for they fhall be comforted. 4. Bleffed are they that hunger and thirft for Juftice, for they fhall be filled. 5. Bleffed are the Merciful, for they fhall find Mercy. 6. Bleffed are the Clean of Heart, for they fhall fee God. 7. Bleffed are the Peace-makers, for they fhall be call'd the Sons of God. 8. Bleffed are they that fuffer Perfecution for Juftice Sake, for theirs is the Kingdom of Heaven. *(Mat.* v. 3, *&c.)*

INSTRUCTION. Thefe great Virtues, which the World rejected and abhorred, our Saviour brought into Honour again, under the Name of *Beatitudes* ; becaufe we are to afcend, by thefe bleffed Steps, unto eternal Beatitude in the next Life, and to a kind of Beatitude here ; inafmuch as every one finds himfelf happy, in Proportion as he advances profperoufly, and approaches nearer to his eternal Beatitude. They were taught by our Saviour to his Apoftles on the Mountain ; to be by them deliver'd to all Chriftians, in oppofition to thofe, the World falfely ftiles Beatitudes ; which have deceiv'd many, and are a Hindrance to that true Beatitude we look for in Heaven.

1. As

256 *The* POOR MAN'S CATECHISM : *Or,*

1. As thofe, who place their Happinefs in their Pleafures, aim at Preheminence and Plenty, above others, in
Riches, and the Honours that attend them; in oppofition
to thefe, is the firft Beatitude : *Blefled are the Poor in Spirit;* who either actually forfake, or at leaft withdraw their
Affections and Heart from their Riches, even to a Contempt
of them : To them is promifed the Kingdom of Heaven;
where thatPreheminence ofHonour,and thatPlenty is found,
which others in their Riches and Greatnefs feek in vain.
2. As the Lovers of this World think to eftablifh their Security by Quarrels and Wars, the better to deftroy their Enemies ; in oppofition to thefe, is the fecond Beatitude : *Bleffed are the Meek;* who moderate Anger, and enjoy perfect
Tranquility interiorly, and fhew the fame exteriorly in
their Words, Countenance, and Behaviour; fpeaking affa-
bly when they are reviled, feeking no Revenge when in-
jured, but overcoming Evil with Good : To them is promifed, what the others often lofe, a quiet, fecure and
permanent Poffeffion of the Land ; the Land of the Living.
3. The Lovers of the World have a violent Paffion for
Delights and Pleafures ; imagining to find fome Shelter
and Confolation in them, againft the Sorrows of this
Life : In oppofition to thefe is the third Beatitude : *Blefled
are they that mourn;* who abftain from the Joys of the
World, bewail their own Sins with true Sorrow, and lament to fee God offended by fo much Wickednefs of
others, and figh in their Abfence from God and Heaven :
To them is promifed what the others look for, but never
find, true Confolation, which will have no End.
4. But as it is not fufficient to remove the Hindrances
to Beatitude, but we muft afcend unto it by Virtue ; hence
is the fourth Beatitude : *Blefled are they that hunger and
thirft for Juftice ;* that is, for Virtue, ftriving daily to in-
creafe in it, and to make others virtuous alfo : To them
is promifed, what the Wicked aim to acquire for themfelves by Wickednefs and Injuftice, *to be filled* and a-
bound. 5. As the Juft themfelves have ftill Need to
obtain Mercy of God, to deliver them from their Miferies,
both corporal and fpiritual; hence is the fifth Beatitude:
Blefled are the Merciful, who are ready and inclineable to
relieve all that fuffer, both corporally and fpiritually,
whether Friend or Enemy, without Regard to any Confideration, but their Wants : To them is promifed, what
the Unmerciful would have, but deferve it not ; to be
freed

The CHRISTIAN DOCTRINE *Explained.* 257

freed from all the Miseries both of this World and the
other, by the Mercy of God. 6. But as no one can see
God, but those who are defiled with no Sin or bad Paffions, and who have a holy and pure Conscience; to those is
promised the sixth Beatitude: *Bleſſed are the Clean of
Heart*; to them is promised what none of the Wicked,
defil'd with Sin, can have; *to see God* by the clear Vision
of him, for all Eternity. 7. As the Clean of Heart,
who are free from Sin, are at Peace with God, with
their own Consciences, and with all Men; hence is the
seventh Beatitude: *Bleſſed are the Peace-makers*; who
keep Peace with all, and seek not to create, but to
make up Differences and Quarrels amongst others: To
them is promised the Glory of being *the Sons of God*;
because by this they give Proof of their *Likeneſs to God*;
as those, who breed Quarrels and Difcord, are like the
Devil. Laſtly, when we are perfect in the foregoing
Beatitudes, and are well eftablish'd in thefe Virtues, the
Confequence will be, that we fhall fuffer Perfecution
for them; (which the Devils will procure out of their
Hatred againſt God and Virtue) but not departing from
them on that Trial, hence is the eighth Beatitude: *Bleſſed
are they that ſuffer Perfecution for Juſtice Sake*: To them
is promised a Remiſſion of all Sin and Punifhment, if
they die for it, and immediate Entrance, after Death,
into the Kingdom of Heaven, and greater Glory there
than to others.——Thefe Rewards are all one and the
fame in Subſtance, eternal Blifs; which is expreſſed in
different Words, and under different Notions, and a Reward adapted to every Beatitude, that it might be more
eafily comprehended: And as every Beatitude is a Step
that approaches nearer and nearer to the Enjoyment of
God, fo we may obferve different Steps and Degrees in
the Rewards promised: As to *have* the Kingdom of
Heaven is the firſt; to *poſſeſs* it is ftill more: To be *comforted* in it, feems ftill greater: To be *filled* with Comfort, is another Degree: To receive from the Mercy of God, what exceeds all Expečtation, is ftill greater:
To fee God and enjoy him, is the very Eſſence of Beatitude, and expreſſes more than any of the foregoing:
But to be *the Sons of God*, is the greateſt Dignity in his
Kingdom, next to the King himfelf: And all thefe are
comprehended *in the Glory* which is promised to thofe
who

258 *The* POOR MAN'S CATECHISM : *Or,*

who fuffer Perfecution for Juftice Sake ; for theirs is the greateft of all, in the Kingdom of Heaven. On the other hand, terrible Woes are pronounced againft thofe who have no Beatitudes but Riches, Honours, Delights, and Pleafures : *Woe to you Rich, becaufe you have your Confola-tion : Woe to you who are full, becaufe you fhall hunger : Woe to you who laugh now, becaufe you fhall weep and wail: Woe to you when Men fhall blefs you,* (with Praife, Flattery, Applaufe) (*Luke* vi. 24, *&c.*) *for fo their Fore-fathers did to the falfe Prophets.*

As our Saviour taught and fhewed his Difciples thefe bleffed Steps to Beatitude, he trod thofe Steps before them, to encourage them to follow after. Who was more poor and contemned by the World than he ? Who more meek, in bearing Injuries ? Who bewail'd the Sins of Mankind with greater Compaffion ? Who thirfted more after Juftice ? Who more merciful than he, who forgave thofe that crucified him, and relieved the pe-nitent Thief upon the Crofs, with the comfortable Pro-mife of Glory ? Who fo clean of Heart, and free from Sin ? Who a greater Peace-maker than he, who made Peace between God and Man ? Who more truly fuffered for Juftice, than he who died for teaching Virtue, repre-hending Sin and redeeming Mankind ?

EXHORTATION. Heaven, O Chriftian, is your defired End and Happinefs : All Things on Earth, the moft re-fined Pleafures and Delights of earthly Men, are Tor-ments in Comparifon of its Joys. Nothing but God can make the Soul of Man happy ; without him, all Things here are but Vanity, Mifery and Vexation of Spirit. Where is the Perfon who can deny it ? *Solomon,* the wifeft of all, confefs'd it : Live now the Life of *Jefus* and his Saints, that you may enjoy the Happinefs of the Saints ; and here fee by what Steps you are to afcend thither.— *Bleffed are the Poor in Spirit.* Bend not too much your Mind on Life, or any Thing in Life : Court not its Riches, State or Grandeur, which will foon have an End ; but fet your Heart upon Joys that are eternal. If you are rich, live not as *Dives* did ; remember he died, and was buried in Hell ; if you cannot actually forfake your Riches, to become Poor, forfake them at leaft with your Soul, and with your Reafon, and value them not ; this is true Wifdom.——*Bleffed are the Meek.*

Give

The CHRISTIAN DOCTRINE *Explained.* 259

Give not way to Paſſion ; Paſſion is the Deſtroyer of Reaſon, and takes away Underſtanding : Carry yourſelf with Lenity and Mildneſs towards your Fellow Creature ; this will juſtify your Cauſe before God and Man, more powerfully than Anger and Revenge.——*Bleſſed are they that mourn :* Sow in Tears, and you will reap in Joy : Bewail your Sins while you may, and Time is, with Tears of true Sorrow and Contrition : Confeſs, do Penance, leave off Sin ; one Hour of this Sorrow, will bring you more Conſolation, than all the vain Joys of the World. ——*Bleſſed are they that hunger and thirſt for Juſtice :* Be juſt to all, give every one his Due ; to God, in the firſt Place, give due Honour, Love and Service ; give your Neighbour alſo what is due to him, Obedience to Superiors, Love to your Equals, Aſſiſtance to Inferiors ; do Juſtice to yourſelf, in taking care of your Soul. —— *Bleſſed are the Merciful.* If you are merciful, you ſhall find Mercy : Be ever ready then to relieve thoſe that ſuffer, and have pity on them, as you are in conſtant Need of God's Mercy yourſelf ; and remember, if you are loſt, it will not be through any Deficiency of Mercy in God, but through Want of Mercy in yourſelf ; for if you had ſhewn Mercy to others, you might find Mercy at his Hands.—*Bleſſed are the Clean of Heart.* Keep your Soul pure from Sin ; let nothing defiled or offenſive to the moſt pure Eyes of God, harbour there ; you are the Temple of the Holy Ghoſt, nothing but Sanctity and Purity ought to be there : When any evil or impure Thought riſes in your Mind, turn your Heart to God, and ſay ; *Lead us not into Temptation.*——*Bleſſed are the Peace-makers.* Beware then of being the Occaſion of others Diſſentions, or widening the Breach, as many do. Seek Peace with God ; keep it with all Men, and ſtrive to reconcile and make up others Differences : Such are *the Sons of God.* ——*Bleſſed are they that ſuffer Perſecution for Juſtice.* They come the neareſt to their Lord and Saviour, who ſuffer unjuſtly from Men : They are his true and worthy Diſciples, who ſuffer Perſecution for his holy Religion : If we ought to embrace all the Evils of this Life, which we ſuffer juſtly for Sin, with the Patience of *Jeſus* on the Croſs, without Murmuring and Impatience ; how much in the Wrong are we to murmur and complain at ſuffering Perſecution for Juſtice ; in which

we

260. *The* POOR MAN'S CATECHISM: *Or,*

we ought ever to rejoice, becaufe to all fuch is promife
the higheft Reward in the Glory of the Kingdom o
Heaven. ——Thefe are the bleffed Steps we muft take in
this Life, and thefe will lead us unto the clear Sight and
Enjoyment of God.

SECT. I.

Of the WORKS *of* MERCY.

Q. WHAT are the Works of Mercy? *A.* They
are corporal and fpiritual. *Q.* Which are
the corporal Works of Mercy? *A.* To feed the Hungry;
to give Drink to the Thirfty; to clothe the Naked; to
harbour the Harbourlefs; to vifit the Sick; to vifit the
Imprifon'd; to bury the Dead. *Q.* Do thefe Works merit
a Reward? *A.* Yes: Chrift has promifed Heaven to fuch,
*Come, O ye Bleffed of my Father, and receive the Kingdom
prepared for you, from the Beginning of the World; becaufe
when I was hungry, you gave me to eat; when I was
thirfty, you gave me to drink, &c.* Mat. xxv.
   INSTRUCTION. Great is the Obligation of every
Chriftian to relieve, as in his Power, his diftreffed Brethren. 'Tis the Duty of Charity to love your Neighbour
as yourfelf; and this not in Word only, but in Work.
You can never truly love God, unlefs you thus love your
Neighbour: *He that hath the Subftance of this World, and
fhall fee his Brother in Need, and fhall fhut his Bowels a-
gainft him, how does the Love of God abide in him? My
little Children, let us love not in Word, and with our Tongue,
but in Deed and Truth,* 1 Jo. iii. 17.
   The corporal Works of Mercy are much recommended
in Scripture: *Break your Bread to the Needy; bring the
Harbourlefs into your Houfes; when you fee the Naked,
cover him, and defpife not your own Flefh; and this is the
Reward: Then fhall your Light break forth like the Morning,
and the Glory of God fhall encompafs you,* Ifaiah lvii. 7.
This Charity was much practifed by *Job, Toby* and
others, mention'd in holy Writ, and render'd them
well pleafing to God, and high in his Favour. The
Neglect of it, we fee punifh'd in *Dives*; who feafted
every Day fplendidly, but neglected poor *Lazarus: He
died, and was buried in Hell,* Luke xvi. 22. As many
Ways

The CHRISTIAN DOCTRINE *Explained.* 261

Ways as our Neighbour may be in Need, so many Way there are of relieving him, so many Works of Mercy; as to feed the Hungry, to give Drink to the Thirsty, to clothe the Naked, &c. Of the six first we read in St. *Matthew*, (c. xxv.) of the seventh much is said in the Book of *Toby*.

When you do a Work of Charity, do it with a good Intention, not to gain Applause, but to fulfil God's Commandment of loving your Neighbour as yourself; this is doing it for the Love of your Neighbour, and for the Love of God too : Let not your Left Hand then see what your Right Hand does ; and what you give, give willingly.——*God loves a chearful Giver.* Many, for want a right Intention, lose the Reward of their Charities ; and I fear there are some, who leave great Charities behind them at their Death, rather to perpetuate their vain Memories, than to benefit their Souls.

EXHORTATION. There is no more noble Virtue, than to give in Charities to others ; in this you resemble the great God of Nature, *who opens his Hand, and fills every Creature with Blessings.* Why has God given you Plenty, but to relieve those that want ? Why does he bless you with Riches, but to distribute of them to the Poor? Why does he give you Health, but to attend the Sick ? Why are you at Liberty, but to comfort those that are in Prison ? Consider the Reward of it ; *Come ye Blessed of my Father, and receive the Kingdom prepared for you, from the Beginning of the World*; *because when I was hungry, you gave me to eat,* &c. Mat. xxv. Our Saviour here declares, that in the Poor you relieve him ; that he takes it as done to himself, and rewards it accordingly, with no less Reward than Heaven ; where those who fed him in the Hungry here, shall themselves be fed, with all the Delights of the celestial Paradise : Those who gave him Drink in the Thirsty, shall themselves drink of the Torrent of eternal Pleasure : Those who cloth'd him in the Naked, shall be cloth'd with Robes of immortal Glory : And those who harbour'd him in the Harbourless, shall be receiv'd into the Mansions of Bliss ; and those who visited him in the Sick and Imprison'd, shall for ever be deliver'd from the Prison of Hell, from all Sickness and Pain, and from all the Miseries both of this World and the other. Shew Mercy then to others, that you may

find

find Mercy : When all Things fail, and there is none to assist you at the Day of Account, than those you assisted by your Charities, or at least these good Works themselves which you did, will intercede to God in your Favour; then you'll find you have *laid up Treasures in Heaven.*——Let the pious *Samaritan* be your Example, in doing Charities to the Distressed, though Strangers, and perhaps not deserving : Indeed, there is an Order in Charity, by which we should relieve those first who are the nearest allied to us in Blood, when they are in want; and next to them, those of the same Faith : Observe Order in your Charities, but let them at the same Time extend to all; *Let us do good to all, chiefly to those of the same Faith,* Gal. vi. 10. To all both good and bad, grateful and ungrateful, deserving and not deserving ; for in this Manner God does good to us.—— Exercise yourself then, O Christian, in all these corporal Works of Mercy, as your State, Condition and Power will allow; let no one go away empty.   Do all for the Love of God, who has lov'd you so, as to give his only Son, and *with him all Things :* Do it out of Charity to your Neighbour, who will plead for your Soul at our great Day of Judgment : Do it out of Charity to yourself; you will be the greatest Gainer ; Honour, Glory, and Benediction, will attend you : *To every one that does Good, Honour and Glory,* Rom. ii. 10. *you shall receive a Hundred-fold, and possess Life everlasting,* Mat. xix. 29.

Of *the* SPIRITUAL WORKS *of* MERCY.

2. WHICH are the spiritual Works of Mercy ? *A.* To admonish Sinners ; to instruct the Ignorant; to counsel the Doubtful; to comfort the Sorrowful; to bear patiently with the Troublesome; to forgive Injuries; to pray for the Living and the Dead. *2.* Why are these call'd spiritual Works of Mercy ? *A.* Because by them we do good to the Soul of our Neighbour.

INSTRUCTION. As the corporal Works of Mercy relate to the Body, Works of Mercy spiritual relate to the Soul: And as the immortal Soul far exceeds the Body ; so do these spiritual Works of Mercy surpass the others, and ought therefore to be more diligently practis'd, by those whose Charge and Office exact it, or in whose Power it is : And if a Reward is promised to those,

who

The CHRISTIAN DOCTRINE *Explained.*   263

who do the leaſt corporal Work of Mercy to others, what muſt be the Reward of ſpiritual ones? A far greater Degree of Glory will be their Recompence: Next to ſaving your own Soul, the beſt Thing you can do is, to co-operate to the Salvation of others.

The holy Scripture, in many Places, recommends theſe ſpiritual Charities. Of the firſt we read, Gal. vi. *If any one be overtaken in Sin, you that are ſpiritual, admoniſh ſuch a one, in the Spirit of Mildneſs.* Of the ſecond, in *Daniel,* (c. xii.) *They who inſtruct others unto Juſtice, ſhall ſhine like Stars, for all Eternity.* Of the third, in St. *James,* (c. v. 19.) *If any one of you ſhall ſtray away from the Truth, and ſome one ſhall convert him, he ought to know, that he who made him be converted from the Error of his Way, ſhall ſave his Soul from Death, and cover a Multitude of Sins.* Of the fourth, in St. *Paul* to the *Rom.* xii. 15. *Weep with thoſe that weep.* Of the fifth, in the Epiſtle to the *Romans,* (c. xv. 1.) *We, who are ſtrong, muſt ſupport the Weakneſſes of the Infirm.* Of the ſixth, in the Goſpel of St. *Luke* (c. vi.) *Forgive, and you ſhall be forgiven.* Of the ſeventh, in St. *James,* (c. v.) *Pray for one another, that you may be ſaved.*

EXHORTATION. Learn, O Chriſtian, to do all theſe Works of Mercy ſpiritual, according to your Ability, and as in your Power. 1. Do not fail to correct or admoniſh Sinners, when there is a Proſpect, that by ſo doing you can put a Stop to Sin; this may prevent many from damning their Souls, and what greater Charity? 2. Refuſe no Pains to inſtruct the Ignorant; by this many may be ſaved, and God eternally glorified. — Great is the Duty of Parents and Superiors, to correct and inſtruct others under them, as they muſt one Day give an Account of what was committed to their Charge. 3. Be not backward to give your Counſel and beſt Advice to others, chiefly to thoſe who are out of the way of Salvation, by their Errors or Vices: Be as an Agent for God; by admoniſhing and ſpeaking to thoſe that err or do wicked Things; *that they may forſake them, and believe in our Lord,* Wiſdom, xii. 2. When you ſhall ſee in the other World Souls delivered from ſuch Torments, as thoſe of Hell; and raviſh'd with ſuch Bliſs as that of Heaven, thro' your Endeavours under God, O how will you think your Charity beſtow'd !———4. Viſit thoſe in Affliction, and comfort them;

264   *The* Poor Man's Catechism : *Or,*

them ; the Comfort you give them, will return to yourfelf : You will find more Satisfaction in fuch Vifits, than
in all the bad Company you keep : *It is better to go to a
Houfe of Mourning, than to a Houfe of Feafting,* Ecclef vii. 3.
5. Bear the troublefome Manners of others, reflecting on
your own Failings.   6. Return not Evil for Evil, but forgive, and God will forgive you a Thoufand for one.
7. Pray daily for all Men, Friend and Enemy ; the latter
has more Need of your Prayers, and your Charity is
greater to him, the more he wants it : This is being a true
Difciple of *Jefus,* who prayed for his Crucifers.   Pray
in particular for Infidels and Sinners ; that God would
open their Eyes, to fee Truth from Error, and diftinguifh folid, from deceitful and deluding Joys : Through
fuch Prayers of devout Chriftians, many are converted.
Pray alfo for the Dead, for your deceafed Brethren ; 'tis
the laft and greateft Charity you can do for them : Remember this Truth ; that as we are ftill in the fame
Church with them, though in a different State, they
partake of our Prayers : There is ftill Communion between us ; *for Charity never ceafes.*

Of S I N.

Q. WHAT is Sin ? *A.* 'Tis *an Offence againft God ;*
as being a wilful Tranfgreffion of his Law,
either by Thought, Word, or Deed.   By the Law of
God, here is meant, all that God has commanded or forbidden, whether by himfelf, or by his Church, and by
all lawful Superiors.

INSTRUCTION.   As we are now treating of Sin and
Vice, we muft diftinguifh thefe two.   *Vice* is the Habit of
Sin ; *Sin* is the Act committed : By often repeated Tranfgreffions, Sin grows into Habit ; and what more difficult
to overcome ?   How few habitual Sinners have we known
reclaim'd ? Sin grows into a Habit, through repeated Re-
lapfes, a Neglect of Repenting, and of Amending.   All
Sin is dreadful ; but the Habit of Sin, grown into Vice,
is moft dreadful ; becaufe Vice takes off, by Degrees,
the Fear of God, or Senfe of Eternity : It makes us blind
to all Good : This was the Cafe of *Pharaoh,* and the
Jews ; they grew harden'd in Vice, through their repeated Tranfgreffions, Prefumption, and Ingratitude : Yet
it

The CHRISTIAN DOCTRINE *Explained.* 265

it is a certain Truth, that the Mercy of God never aban-
dons any one in this Life, *totally* and *finally* ; but preſſes
the moſt hardened to repent, and gives them ſufficient
Grace.

All Sin in general is of that Nature, that it brings the
greateſt Miſchief upon the Soul, and may be truly ſtyl'd,
the *only real Evil in Life,* the *Evil of Evils,* as all others
ſpring from it: It is an Evil not to be conceived; none
but thoſe who feel the eternal Effects of it, are ſenſible
how great it is : Faith tells us that it makes us hateful,
and Enemies to God ; deprives us of his Grace here,
and Glory hereafter ; that it cauſes a Separation between
us and God, and ſo brings Death to the Soul, and makes it
guilty of Hell's Torments: But what that Glory is, which
Sin deprives us of, or what Hell's Torments are, no one,
in this mortal Body, can fully ſee : But as no Tongue can
expreſs, or Mind conceive, what God has prepar'd for
thoſe who love him ; ſo 'tis alike inconceivable, what
Puniſhment he has prepar'd for thoſe who hate him ; to
which ill Diſpoſition, Sin at length brings the Sinner :
The imperfect Enjoyment of God here, is only known by
the Sweets we find in Virtue, and thoſe Refreſhments of
Soul, in his ſecret and divine Impulſes, in the Hearts of
good Men ; ſo likewiſe, Men may feel and know, in
Part, the Torments of Hell, through that terrible Remorſe of Conſcience, that ariſes from Sin and Vice, which
is a Worm that never dies, as long as Sin continues.

Of ORIGINAL SIN,

Q. WHAT is original Sin ? *A.* 'Tis the Sin in which
we are all born, by Means of *Adam's* Fall.

INSTRUCTION. *Orignal Sin* was the firſt Sin committed by Man, and by the firſt Man *Adam* ; when, contrary to the expreſs Command of God, drawn away
through the Deluſion of the Devil, and in Compliance
to his Wife, he conſented to eat of the forbidden Fruit ;
and from thence enſued the fatal Curſe on all Mankind :
Duſt thou art, and into Duſt thou ſhalt return. This had
been follow'd with an everlaſting Excluſion from Heaven,
and Deprivation of the Sight of God, had he not, thro'
pure Mercy, promiſed the Coming of a Redeemer, to
reſcue us from this immenſe Evil. This Redeemer was

N no

266 *The* POOR MAN's CATECHISM : *Or,*

no other than God the Son, the second Person of the Bleſſed Trinity, made Man. None but an infinite Being could atone for an Offence againſt an infinite Being; none but an infinite Mercy could ſatisfy an infinite Juſtice.

This is the Sin in which we are all born, as Sons of ſinful *Adam*. Through his Sin, we loſt original Juſtice, and are born out of the Grace and Favour of God;——— *Children of Wrath*, with a corrupt Nature, that carries us to all kind of Sin : *As by one Man, Sin enter'd into the World, and by Sin, Death ; ſo unto all Men Sin did paſs, in whom all have ſinned*, Rom. v. 12. The only Remedy at preſent, to take off the Guilt of this Sin, is the Means which our Redeemer has left in Baptiſm ; whereby we have the Merits of his Blood and Paſſion applied to our Souls ; without which there can be no Remiſſion of any Sin, according to that Maxim, *Without Blood ſpilt, there is no Remiſſion*, Heb. ix. 22. Therefore Baptiſm is now commanded for all : *Go teach all Nations, baptizing them in the Name of the Father, and of the Son, and of the Holy Ghoſt*. None of the Children of *Adam* ſhall now enter Heaven, without it ; no, not even Infants ; for the Redeemer of the World has ſaid it, *Unleſs one be re-born of Water and the Holy Ghoſt, he cannot enter into the Kingdom of God :* Theſe unbaptized Infants will never enter Heaven ; but are carried to a Part of Hell, call'd *the Limbus of Children* ; where they endure *the Pain of Loſs*, that is, will never ſee God ; tho' they do not endure *the Pain of Senſe*, according to the Tradition of all the Fathers, very few excepted.

Tho' our bleſſed Redeemer frees us from the eternal Puniſhment, and Guilt of original Sin ; yet the Penalties of it, which were to afflict *Adam* and his Poſterity in this World, ſtill remain ; and theſe are the Evils that will reign in us till Death : Our Bodies ſubject to all Kinds of Infirmities and Death ; our Souls ſubject to *Ignorance*, of what is right; to *Weakneſs*, in doing Good, and reſiſting Evil ; to *Concupiſcence*, which inclines us to Sin; and to *Malice*, or Perverſeneſs of Will ; hence proceed all our Diſorders. But ſtill our Remedy againſt theſe, is the Grace of God, through Jeſus Chriſt, whereby *we can do all Things, through him that ſtrengthens us*.

EXHORTATION. Let not this Inſtruction on original Sin paſs, without ſome Profit to your Soul. Behold, in
that

The CHRISTIAN DOCTRINE *Explained.* 267

that firft Sin, the infinite Perverfenefs of Man; behold, in that Inftant, the infinite Goodnefs of God: Man finning, and God forgiving, with the Promife of a Redeemer, to crufh the Head of the Serpent. As often then as you read this, reflect, with the greateft Gratitude, on your Redemption, and fay, *What fhall I return to our Lord for all he has given to me?* Greater was the Mercy of God to Man, than to the very Angels; *The Angels that finned he did not fpare*, but left them without Redemption; Man finned, and he caft an Eye of Pity upon him: *So God loved the World*, Jo. iii. 16.

Great Bleffing, to have original Sin forgiven you in Baptifm, thro' the Merits of Chrift's Paffion and Death, and thereby to be reftor'd to your primitive Innocence; to become the Children of God, intitled to Glory!——— Renounce the Devil, his Works, and Pomps now, as you did then: You were made Chriftians for greater Things, than to make yourfelves Slaves again to *Satan*, to Flefh and Blood, and to the Follies of the World. You were then, by Grace, made Partakers of the divine Nature, beware how you degenerate; you were once Children of Darknefs, now Sons of Light: Once Slaves of the Devil, now Servants of God, Chriftians and Followers of Chrift; with this *Character* you were mark'd in Baptifm; if you live up to it, it will remain to your Glory; if otherwife, to your Confufion. You were then intitled to Glory, ufe now the Means, that may bring you to the Enjoyment of it; *Seek the Things above, not thefe below*, Col. ii. 12. Things that will make your Soul happy, not thofe Things that will render it again miferable. While your Body is on Earth, let your Soul be in Heaven, by Prayer, Reading, Contemplation. O what is a Soul without God, without the Grace, the Love of God! the moft wretched of all Creatures on Earth. Preferve then, by all Means, the Love and Grace of God in your Heart: Abhor whatever deftroys or leffens it, as does all Sin and Iniquity. Reflect often on the Sin of your firft Parents; and if fo great Miferies follow'd it, what muft be the End of your manifold Sins and Offences? O my Soul, repent *and fin no more, left fome worfe Thing befal you.*

Of

[Francis Petre], *Instructions and Regulations for Indulgences Allowed to the Faithful in the N. District* (1753)

The quickening maturation of the English Catholic community's ecclesiastical structures in the eighteenth century allowed an ever-increasing degree of authority to the episcopal Vicars Apostolic appointed by the Holy See, with titular dioceses, to administer the Church in England and Wales in four regional 'Districts'.[1] Working increasingly in concert and generally supported in their aims by the Holy See, the Vicars were centralizing what had been the long-standing diffuseness, not to say fragmentation, of post-Reformation English Catholic ecclesiastical organization and were also notching up victories for their own authority over the religious Orders.

Part of the regulatory task that the Vicars Apostolic took in hand, in the generally quieter times of the eighteenth century, was that of bringing post-Reformation English Catholicism closer into line with the decrees and spirit of the Council of Trent. This policy is evident in the current document in the control of indulgences, which corresponds with the Council's restrictions on abuses in those devices whose mishandling had seemed to many to have given rise to the Protestant Reformation: *Instructions and Regulations* warn, for example, against 'spurious and apocryphal' indulgences 'such as that pretended to have been found in the Sepulchre of our Lord' (p. 393).

These directions, issued in December 1753, were given out by 'F. A.' – Francis Petre, Vicar Apostolic and Bishop of Amoria *in partibus infidelium* – the official diocesan, that is to say, of that ancient extinct bishopric. Francis Petre was born in 1692, at Writtle in Essex and was nephew of the Vicar Apostolic Bishop Benjamin Petre (1672–1758). Francis was admitted to Douai in 1718, ordained at Tournai in 1720 and sent on the English Mission in 1724. He inherited the family estate at Fidlers in Essex from his brother in 1729 and in 1735 was elected to the 'Old Chapter', the rather shadowy governing body of the English secular clergy. In 1750 Petre was designated by Benedict XIV (Prospero Lorenzo Lambertini, *r.* 1740–58), Bishop of Amoria and coadjutor in the Northern District to Bishop Edward Dicconson (1670–1752). He succeeded the latter as Vicar Apostolic in 1752, taking on responsibility for the pastoral care of the historic heartlands of post-Reformation English Catholicism. Petre lived on an estate he owned in Lancashire and died near Blackburn in 1775, leaving over £2,100 and a valuable library.

Not an author, but known for his enthusiastic application to his work, as well as for his 'great zeal, piety and learning',[2] Petre is considered by Bossy as 'a competent if not memorable bishop in the North.'[3] He clearly, though, left an impact as a disciplinarian amongst the secular clergy: in 1786 Robert Banister wrote to his fellow-priest Henry Rutter wishing that Petre's successor in the Northern District 'would publish again the Instructions set forth in 1752 by Bishop [Francis] Petre with injunctions and precepts drawn from the canons, to repress the pride, worldly spirit, continual dissipation and worldly manners of his missionary priests.[4]

1. Basil Hemphill, OSB, *The Early Vicars Apostolic of England 1685–1750* (London, Burns & Oates, 1954).

2. W. Mazier Brady, *The Episcopal Succession in England, Scotland and Ireland A. D. 1400 to 1875* (Rome, Tipografia della Pace, 1876), vol. 1, pp. 260–4.

3. Bossy, *English Catholic Community*, p. 213.

(1)

Inſtructions and Regulations for the Indulgences allowed to the Faithful in the N. Diſtrict.

1. INdulgences, according to the Catholick Acceptation of the Word, are not any Leave to commit Sin, as ſome have miſrepreſented the Doctrine and Practice of the Church, nor yet any Pardon for Sins to come ; nor indeed, properly ſpeaking, any Pardon of Sins at all, *viz.* as to the Guilt, or eternal Puniſhment due to that Guilt, but only a Releaſing to ſuch as are truly penitent, the Debt of temporal Puniſhment, which remained due to their Sins, after the Sins themſelves as to the Guilt, and eternal Puniſhment, had been already remitted by the Sacrament of Penance, or by perfect Contrition.

2. The Faith of the Catholick Church, as to this Article of Indulgences, is comprized in the Profeſſion of *Pius* IV. in theſe two Points : that there is in the Church a Power of granting Indulgences; and that the due uſe of them is moſt wholeſome to Chriſtian People : agreeably to the Declara-

A   tion

(2)

tion of the Council of *Trent, Seff.* 25. and the Commiffion given by our Lord himfelf, St. *Matth.* xvi. 19. and the perpetual Doctrine and Practice of the Church of God in all Ages.

Whatfoever thou fhalt bind upon Earth, it fhall be bound alfo in Heaven: and whatfoever thou fhalt loofe on Earth, it fhall be loofed alfo in Heaven.

3. But though the Faith of the Church, with relation to Indulgences, has been always the fame and invariable, the Difcipline of the Church has not been always the fame, but has varied, according to the different Circumftances of Times and Places, and the Exigences of the Faithful ; fo that in fome Ages the Church has been more referved in her Grants of Indulgences, in others more liberal ; and fometimes, upon juft Confiderations, has recalled or fufpended former Grants ; or exchanged them into others, as has feemed to her chief Paftors, all Circumftance confidered, moft expedient for the Glory of God, and the Good of Souls.

4. The Council of *Trent* in its Decree relating to Indulgences, not only order all Abufes to be retrenched in the ufe of them, but alfo recommends a *Moderation* in the Grant of them ; a Caution of fo much

(3)

much the greater Importance, as the multiplying of them without Neceffity would expofe them to Contempt, and endanger their being rendered ineffectual: it being the common Opinion of Divines, that where there is no juft Caufe or Motive for the Grant of an Indulgence, God Almighty will not ratify the Grant.

5. For the Validity of an Indulgence, befides the Neceffity of a fufficient Authority in him that grants it, and of a juft Caufe or Motive for the Grant; it is alfo neceffary on the Part of him that is to obtain the Indulgence, that he duly perform the Conditions perfcribed, fuch as going to Confeffion and Communion, Fafting, Prayer, Alms, &c. and that he have fincerely renounced his Sins, and be in the State of Grace; for it is in vain to expect the Remiffion of the Punifhment due to Sin, whilft a Perfon wilfully continues in the State of Sin.

6. Wherefore Indulgences, fo far from being a Licence to commit Sin, or any Encouragement to Sin, cannot be obtained by any but fuch as are truly penitent for their Sins, and fincerely determined to renounce them. And it is with this penitential Spirit, the Faithful ought to

A 2   apply

(4)

apply for the Benefit of Indulgences; as being fenfible of the great Debt they have contracted by their Sins, and humbly fuing to be difcharged from it, in Virtue of the Blood of Chrift, by the Power of the Keys committed to the Church.

7. The great Benefit of Indulgences confifts in the Difcharge of this Debt, which might otherwife hinder or retard the Soul from entering into the Joys of her Lord. Yet not fo, as to exempt Sinners from the Obligation of doing Penance for their Sins in this Life; this being, by divine Ordinance, an indifpenfible Duty. *Except you do Penance you fhall all perifh,* St. *Luke* xiii. 5. For the Treafure of the Church, out of which Indulgences are difpenfed by her chief Paftors, is intended by our Lord for the Relief of the Indigent, but not for the Encouragement of the Indolent, who refufe to labour for themfelves by Penance and Good Works.

8. Of Indulgences fome are called *plenary,* which releafe the whole Debt, that remained due on account of paft Sins. Others are Indulgences of a certain Number of Years, or Days; for Example, of feven Years, or forty Days; which allude to the Penances enjoined by the Canons

for

(5)

for certain Sins, for fo many Years, or Days, according to the Quality of the Sin : now thefe kind of Indulgences, when duly obtained, difcharge fo much of the Debt of Punifhment as correfponds to the Sins, which, by the Canons of the Church, would have required fo many Years or Days of Penance.

9. The Holy See Apoftolick, confidering the Neceffities of the Faithful in this Kingdom, amongft other extraordinary Faculties imparted to the Bifhops, the Apoftolical Vicars, as Delegates of the fame Holy See, has given them a Power to grant a plenary Indulgence three times a Year, to the Faithful committed to their Charge, in their refpective Diftricts, leaving to their Choice the Days they fhall think proper to appoint for this Purpofe ; and empowering them to communicate this Faculty to fuch paftoral Miffionaries, Secular or Regular, as they fhall think fitting. In confequence of this Power we have appointed, and do appoint for the obtaining thefe three Indulgences, 1. The Solemnity of *Chriftmafs* taking in the whole Octave and the following Days, till the Feaft of the *Epiphany* inclufively. 2. The

A 3   firft

(6)

firſt week in *Lent* beginning with the firſt
Sunday, and ending with the ſecond *Sunday* incluſively. 3. The Solemnity of
Whitſuntide with its Octave and all the in-
termediate Days to the end of the Octave
of *Corpus Chriſti*; ſo that as many of the
the Faithful as ſhall duly perform the Devotions and Conditions required, upon
ſome one Day, within the time Limited
abovementioned, ſhall, on that Day, obtain a plenary Indulgence; yet ſo that they
cannot obtain this Indulgence more than
once during the ſame Limited time.

10. The Conditions required on the
Part of the Faithful, for the obtaining any
of the three Indulgences above-named,
are, 1ſt, That they confeſs their Sins with
a ſincere Repentance, to a Prieſt approved
by the Biſhop. 2dly, That they worthily
receive the Holy Communion. 3dly, That
if their State and Condition allow it, they
give ſome Alms to the Poor, either on
the Eve, or the Day of their Communion.
4thly, That on the Day of their Communion they offer up ſome Prayers to
God; 1. For the whole State of the Catholick Church throughout the World.
2. For the bringing back all ſtraying
Souls to the Fold of *Chriſt.* 3. For the
gene-

(7)

general Peace of *Chriſtendom.* 4. For the
Bleſſing of God upon this Nation.

11. As for all ſuch as by ſome lawful
Impediment ſhall be prevented from performing the Conditions above required at
any of the three appointed Times ; that
they may not be deprived of the Benefit
of the Indulgences, we empower, by theſe
Preſents, their reſpective Paſtors, whether
Seculars or Regulars, to impart the ſaid
Indulgences to them afterwards. And in
general when any approved Miſſioner, by
reaſon of his ſerving two or more Congregations, or through the Multitude of his
Penitents, cannot ſerve them all within
the eight Days appointed, we allow him
to impart the aforeſaid Indulgences to the
People in the following Week or Fort-
night, as Circumſtances ſhall require.

12. As to the publiſhing either in publick or private Chapels any other Indulgences granted to Religious Orders, his
preſent Holineſs, Pope *Benedict* XIV. in
his late Regulations made for this Miſſion, has eſtabliſhed the following Rule,
which he will have to be religiouſly obſerved. ' For the good of the *Engliſh*
' Miſſion, ſaith he, (num. 23.) all Acts
' of Piety are approved, Prayers, Faſts,
' and

(8)

' and meritorious Works, which are ap-
' proved of by the Holy Roman Church.
' But as for the Indulgences, annexed to
' thefe Works, by Virtue of the Privi-
' leges, which have been granted by
' Popes to this or that Religious Or-
' der, they are fufpended. But to the
' end that the Faithful may both quietly
' and plentifully enjoy the Spiritual Ad-
' vantage of Holy Indulgences, a Power
' is granted to every Apoftolick Vicar,
' within the Bounds of his own Diftrict,
' to impart a plenary Indulgence four
' Times a Year, on fuch Solemnities as
' they fhall judge moft Convenient.'

13. Upon Occafion of this Grant, a
Doubt being raifed, whether the Power
of imparting the three former Indulgences ftill fubfifted; or whether they
were to be included in the Number of the
four, allowed by this new Grant? The
Holy See being confulted anfwered, *Octob.*
3. 1753. That the three former were
ftill to fubfift as before; and that the four
are entirely a new Grant, in lieu of thofe
formerly imparted by the Regulars, which
are now fufpended.

14. For thefe four Indulgences we appoint in this Diftrict the following Solemnities.

(9)

nities. 1. The Solemnity of *Easter*, including all the fifteen Days from *Palm Sunday* to *Low Sunday*. 2. The Feaft of St. *Peter* and St. *Paul* with its Octave. 3. The Solemnity of the *Assumption* of the *Blessed Virgin*, including the whole Octave. 4. The eight Days or Octave of the Feaft of *All Saints*. On thefe Solemnities we impart to the Faithful committed to our Charge, and to all their Paftors, a plenary Indulgence, once for each Solemnity, upon their performing the Conditions mentioned by his Holinefs in his Grant.

15. Thefe Conditions are, that after having confeffed their Sins to a Prieft approved by the Bifhop, and worthily received the Holy Communion, they vifit fome Chapel or Oratory where Mafs is celebrated, and there pray for the Peace and Welfare of the Church of God throughout the World, and efpecially in this Nation, and that they be in a Difpofition and Readinefs of Mind to affift the Poor with Alms according to their Abilities; or to be diligent in frequenting Catechifms and Sermons, when they can do it without great Inconvenience, or in vifiting, affifting, and comforting the Sick, or fuch as are near their End.
Where

(10)

Where it is to be noted, that it is not neceſſary for the gaining theſe four Indul-gences, that any of theſe Works of 'Mer-cy, corporal or ſpiritual; or this aſſiſt-ing at Catechiſm, or Sermon, ſhould be done on the ſame Day with the Commu-nion; but only that Perſons ſhould be in a Diſpoſition and Readineſs of Mind to comply with thoſe Duties, when Oppor-tunity ſhall offer; it being the Deſign of the Grant of theſe Indulgences, to ani-mate the Faithful to the Practice of all good Works, and to a diligent Attention to the Word of God.

16. As to the Sick, or others who are not able to perform any one or more of the Conditions required; the Biſhops are authorized by his Holineſs to exchange what they are not able to perform, into ſuch other Things as they are capable of, that ſo they may not be deprived of the Benefit of theſe Indulgences. Wherefore we deſire their reſpective Paſtors to con-ſider their Condition, and to Appoint them ſome Prayer or Alms which they are ca-pable of; and what they ſhall thus appoint, we, by the Authority committed to us, ſubſtitute in lieu of the other good Works, which they are not able to perform, in or-

der

(11)

der to their gaining thereby the aforesaid Indulgences.

17. His Holiness has also been pleased to authorize the Bishops, to give by themselves, or by other Priests, delegated by them, the solemn Benediction, with the plenary Indulgence annexed to it, the Form and Manner of which he has lately published for the Benefit of the Faithful who are at the Point of Death; which Faculty we also impart to all approved Missioners, Secular or Regular, who have been admitted by us to the Care of Souls; enjoining to them at the same time all possible Diligence, in attending on such as are apprehended to be near their End; in administring to them the Holy Sacraments in due time, and in instructing and disposing them to receive in a penitential Spirit, and with an humble Confidence in the Mercy of God, through the Death and Passion of *Jesus Christ*, this last Benediction.

18. Besides these Indulgences, that are common to all the Faithful of this District, there have been others granted by Pope *Clement* XII. which are still in force, in Favour of all such as duly assist at the teaching of the Catechism, or Christian Doctrine, whether in Churches, Chapels, or

Ora-

(12)

Oratories; in particular an Indulgence of seven Years, and as many *Quadragenæ*, or Indulgences of forty Days, which he grants to the Faithful, as often as having confessed their Sins with true Repentance, and worthily received the Holy Communion, they shall, on the same Day, devoutly assist at the Catechism ; and a pleanary Indulgence three times a Year, *viz.* *Christmas-Day*, *Easter-Day*, and the Feast of St. *Peter* and St. *Paul*, which he grants to all such as constantly frequent this holy Exercise, either in the way of teaching or learning the Christian Doctrine : provided they confess and communicate upon those Festivals, and pray for the usual Intentions of the Church.

19. The same Pope pressingly recommends to all such as have the Care of Souls, the Instruction, not of Children only, but of Persons grown up, of all Conditions of Life; and orders that such Instructions be never ommitted on Festival Days, by the Pastors, or others, who in Churches or Country Chapels say Mass to the People ; nothing being of greater Importance to the Salvation of Souls than Instruction ; and nothing more pernicious than the Ignorance of Christian Truths.
For

(13)

For which Reafon alfo in our late Mandate, dated *October* 11, 1753, we have ftrictly enjoined to all Miffioners, who have the Charge of any fettled Congregation, to give Catechifm in publick before the People on every *Sunday*, fo as to explain and inculcate to their Hearers the Meaning of the Chriftian Doctrine, and not the Words only, left otherwife thro' their Fault that of the Prophet come to be verified, *The little Ones have afked for Bread, and there was no one to break it unto them*, Lament. iv. 4. the Confequences of which would be moft dreadful, both to the Sheep and the Shepherds.

20. Let all then that have the Care of Souls, duly attend to their Inftruction; and by their Diligence herein encourage and affift them to gain fuch Indulgences as may be obtained by a regular affifting at the Chriftian Doctrine, as well as the other Indulgences allowed to the Faithful of this Diftrict: but as for fuch Indulgences as are now fufpended, let them not prefume to publifh them. And as for fuch as are fpurious and apocryphal, fuch, as that pretended to have been found in the Sepulchre of our Lord, or imparted by Revelation to St. *Bridget*; which, with many

others

(14)

others of the like Nature, have been rejected
and condemned by the See Apoftolick, in
a Decree publifhed *March* 7, 1678, and ordered to be abolifhed wherever they were
found : let all Paftors ufe their beft Diligence to remove them out the Hands of
the Faithful, as being full of Superftition,
and tending to delude them into a falfe
Security, with Danger of their Souls.
December 10, 1753.

F. A.

(15)

AS the Mortality among the Cattle, which for many Years paſt has raged in diverſe Parts of the Kingdom, has broken out again with great Fury in ſeveral Counties; in order to turn away this Scourge, we enjoin to all Prieſts of the *Northern* Diſtrict, whether Seculars or Regulars, to recite in their Maſs on all Days, except Feaſts of the firſt Claſs, the Collect appointed for that purpoſe *(pro peſte animalium)* with the Secreta and Poſtcommunion correſponding to it; and to all Paſtors to excite their People to join in Prayer for the ſame Intention: and particularly to call upon them to turn away from their Sins, by a ſincere Converſion to God, leſt otherwiſe if they ſhould continue incorrigible under theſe Scourges of Heaven, they draw upon their Heads more rigorous Judgments: it being no unuſual thing for a Mortality among the Cattle to be followed by the like Mortality among Men ; and that more eſpecially where the former Scourge produces no Amendment.

F. A.

[Dominique de Bouhours], *The Life of St Francis Xavier of the Society of Jesus, Apostle of the Indies and of Japan. Translated into English by Mr Dryden* (London, Jacob Tonson, 1688), pp. 203–24

John Dryden's translation of the *Vie de Saint François Xavier* (1648) by the French Jesuit, biographer and religious author Dominique de Bouhours (1628–1702) was published in London by Jacob Tonson – the present edition – in 1688.

Francis Xavier was born in 1506 in the castle of Xavero or Xavier near Pamplona in Navarre, the youngest son of a royal councillor. Following study at the University of Paris, he lectured on Aristotle at the Collège de Beauvais and was brought into contact with Ignatius Loyola (1491–1556), with whom he joined, along with a few others, in the initial launch of the Society of Jesus in Paris in 1534. He was ordained in 1537 and worked in Rome for the incipient Society, which was licensed by the papacy in 1540. In 1541 King John III (or João) of Portugal (1502–57), supported by Pope Paul III (r. 1534–49), sent him to missionize Portuguese dependencies in Asia. Francis Xavier he arrived in Goa, south of Bombay, in 1542, as a missionary both to the colonists and to the indigenous population.[1] Amongst Indians he won some sensational successes, as when in 1543 he baptized 10,000 people in Travancore in south-west India. He then embarked on an epic missionary tour taking in Malacca (modern Melaka) on the west coast of modern Malaysia, the Banda island group in modern Indonesia, the island of Amboina (modern Ambon), also in present-day Indonesia, the Moluccas Island (or 'Spice Island') chain between Celebes (Sulawesi) and western New Guinea (Irian Jaya) and the Philippines and East Timor. This ambitious sea-born mission climaxed in what is today Sri Lanka, where Xavier baptized the King of one of the island's three kingdoms, Kandy, along with many of his subjects. His next missionary endeavour, to Japan, in 1549, established what was to be a century of Christian presence in that country.[2] Returning to Goa in 1552, in the face of considerable local opposition he planned a further mission campaign, to China. He died in December 1552 within sight of the Chinese Empire, near Canton, and his body was returned to Goa where it lies as a focus of reverence in the city's Bom Jesus Cathedral. Acclaimed miracle-worker, mystic and ascetic, Francis Xavier was canonized in 1622.

The Pauline scale and heroism of Francis Xavier's missionary journeys, along with his tragic young death at the age of forty-six, made his story – that of an aristocratic academic who had become a *conquistador* for Christ – the focus of a species of hagiography combining drama, adventure and travel into an Asiatic world in which European Catholicism invested high hopes of growth, making up for losses in Europe itself. Xavier's odyssey offered visible instances of the emergence of the Catholic faith as a world religion, and while his religious sympathy for Asian faiths was severely limited, his outspoken Christian empathy for the sufferings of colonized peoples made him a model for generations of Catholic missionaries: he is, indeed, the patron saint of the Church's overseas missions.[3]

The account excerpted here, grounding Xavier on the pattern of Christ and on other New Testament exemplars, vividly describes his maritime expeditions as well as his land-based missionary work.

John Dryden's translation from the French represented the high point of empathy between his convert Catholicism and the royal family, with the dedication to the Queen pointing out that she had adopted Xavier as her patron and expressing the pious hope that prayer would give England a 'Son of Prayers': in September 1687 James II, on pilgrimage to the Catholic shrine at Holywell in north Wales, had prayed for a son, and a heir was born to him and Maria Beatrice in June of the following year. Dryden's version was reissued in 1743 and a publication of the work of 1837 was attributed to 'James' Dryden.

Dryden was born in his grandfather's Northamptonshire vicarage in 1631. He was taught at Westminster School and went on to Trinity College, Cambridge, graduating in 1654. He subsequently proceeded to London, where he associated himself with Cromwell's circle, leading to the production of his *Heroic Stanzas* of 1658 on the Protector's death. *Astrea Redux* and his *Panegyric*, both celebrating the Restoration, followed in 1660 and 1661 respectively. Dryden then embarked on a series of 'heroic' plays in verse, of which *The Indian Emperor* of 1665 was an example. His *Annus Mirabilis* commemorated the extraordinary events, including the Great Fire of London, of 1666, and in 1668 appeared his work of literary criticism, the *Essay on Dramatic Poesy*.

His life flourished in the 1660s: he became a Fellow of the Royal Society in 1663, married a daughter of the Earl of Berkshire in the same year, took his Master of Arts in 1668 and in 1670 was appointed Poet Laureate and Historiographer Royal, with a handsome salary. He issued his anti-Dutch *Amboyna* in 1673 and in 1678 a dramatic masterpiece in blank verse, *All for Love*, on the story of Antony and Cleopatra. In a series of brilliant political satires centring on the two parts of *Absalom and Achitophel*, 1681 and 1682, Dryden vilified the Whigs and their Exclusionist campaign to debar the Catholic Duke of York from the succession. He was made London collector of customs in 1683.

Dryden's own religious evolution was quite complex. *The Spanish Friar* of 1681 was anti-Catholic, and his *Religio Laici* of 1682 defended the Church of England, but in 1685 he became a Catholic and there followed his highly accomplished salute to his new religion, *The Hind and the Panther* of 1687, as well as the translated life of Xavier. That Dryden's conversion was genuine is shown by his persistence in the Catholic faith after James's fall, when he lost his laureateship, took up translations of the classics and produced his final work, *Fables, Ancient and Modern*, in 1699. John Dryden died in 1700. He was the leading figure, alongside his fellow-Catholic Alexander Pope (1688–1744), in English literary classicism.[4]

1.   Stephen Neill, *A History of Christianity in India. The Beginnings to 1707* (Cambridge, Cambridge University Press, 1985), ch. 7.

2.   C. R. Boxer, *The Christian Century in Japan 1549–1650* (Berkeley and Los Angeles, CA, University of California Press, 1967).

3.   See the lively biography by James Brodrick, SJ, *Saint Francis Xavier* (London, Burns Oates, 1952).

4.   An impression both of the quantity and versatility of Dryden's output can be gained from: *The Works of John Dryden*, general eds. Edward Niles Hooker and H. T. Swedenberg, Jr (20 vols, Berkeley and Los Angeles, CA, University of California Press, 1956–89). See also Hugh MacDonald, *John Dryden. A Bibliography of Early Editions and of Drydenia* (Oxford, Clarendon, 1939, and reissued London, Dawson of Pall Mall Reprint, 1966); John A. Zamonski, *An Annotated Bibliography of John Dryden: Texts and Studies 1949–1973* (Folkestone, Dawson, 1975), esp. no. 939. For Dryden and religion, see Sanford Budick, *Dryden and the Abyss of Light* (New Haven, CN, and London, Yale University Press, 1970) and Louis I. Bredvold, *The Intellectual Milieu of John Dryden. Studies of Some Aspects of Seventeenth-Century Thought* (Ann Arbor, MI, University of Michigan Press, 1966), esp. ch. IV. Good general accounts of Dryden include: David Hopkins, *John Dryden*, general ed. Isobel Armstrong (Tavistock, Northcote House in Association with the British Council, 2004), and Steven N. Zwicker (ed.), *The Cambridge Companion to John Dryden* (Cambridge, Cambridge University Press, 2004), esp. ch. 13.

Book III. *St.* Francis Xavier. 203

While the Ship that carried *Xavier* was croffing the Gulph of *Ceylan*, an occafion of Charity was offer'd to the Saint, which he wou'd not fuffer to efcape. The Mariners and Souldiers pafs'd their time, according to their cuftome, in playing at Cards. Two Souldiers fet themfelves to it, more out of avarice than pleafure, and one of them plaid with fuch ill fortune, that he loft not only all his own money, but the ftock which others had put into his hands to traffick for them. Having nothing more to lofe, he withdrew, curfing his luck, and blafpheming God. His defpair prevail'd fo far over him, that he had thrown himfelf into the Sea, or run upon the point of his Sword, if he had not been prevented. *Xavier* had notice of thefe his mad intentions, and execrable behaviour, and immediately came to his relief. He embrac'd him tenderly, and faid all he cou'd 'to comfort him : But the Souldier who was ftill in the tranfports of his fury, thruft him away, and forbore not even ill Language to him. *Xavier* ftood recollected for fome time, imploring God's affiftance and counfel; then went and borrow'd fifty Royals of a Paffenger, brought them to the Souldier, and advis'd

vis'd him once more to try his fortune.
At this the Souldier took heart, and
play'd fo luckily, that he recover'd all
his loffes with great advantage. The
Saint, who look'd on, took out of the
overplus of the winnings, what he had
borrow'd for him; and feeing the Game-
fter, now return'd to a calm temper,
wrought upon him fo fuccefsfully, that
he, who before refus'd to hear him, was
now overpowr'd by his difcourfe, never
after handled Cards, and became exemplary in his Life.

He arrives at Malacca, a digreffion concerning it.   They arriv'd at *Malacca*, the 25*th.* of
September. As this is one of thofe pla-
ces in the *Indies*, where the Saint, whofe
Life I write, had moft bufinefs, and whither he made many Voyages, it vvill
not be unprofitable to fay fomewhat of
it. 'Tis fcituate beyond the Gulph of
Bengale, towards the head of that great
Peninfula, vvhich from the mouth of
the *Ara*, is extended to the South, almoft to the Equinoctial Line; and is of
two Degrees and a half of Elevation, o-
ver againft the Ifland of *Sumatra*, which
the Ancients, who had not frequented
this Channel, believ'd to be joyn'd to
the Continent.

Malacca was under the Dominion of
the Kings of *Siam*, 'till the *Saracens*, who
traded

Book III. *St.* Francis Xavier.   205

traded thither, becoming powerful, firſt
made it *Mahometan,* then caus'd it to
revolt againſt the lawful Prince, and ſet
up a Monarch of their own Sect, call'd
Mahomet. There was not at that time,
any more famous Mart Town than this,
and where there was a greater con-
courſe of different Nations. For, beſides
the People of *Guzuratte, Aracan, Mala-
bar, Pegu, Sumatra, Java,* and the *Molucca's,* the *Arabs,* the *Perſians,* the *Chi-
neſe,* and the *Japonians,* traffick'd there:
and accordingly the Town lay extended
all along by the Sea ſide, for the convenience of Trade.

Amongſt all the Nations of *Aſia* there
is not any, more inclin'd to pleaſure;
and this ſeems chiefly to proceed, from
the mild temper of the air. For there
is an eternal Spring, notwithſtanding
the neighbourhood of the Line. The Inhabitants follow the natural bent of
their complexion; their whole buſineſs
is Perfumes, Feaſts, and Muſique; to
ſay nothing of Carnal Pleaſures, to
which they ſet no bound. Even the
Language, which they ſpeak, participates
of the ſoftneſs of the Country. 'Tis call'd
the *Malaya Tongue,* and of all the Orient,
'tis the moſt delicate, and ſweet of Pronunciation.

Don

206 *The LIFE of* Book III.

Don Alphonfo Albuquerque, conquer'd *Malacca,* in the year 1511, and thirty thoufand men, with eight thoufand pie-ces of Artillery, and an infinite number of Elephants and Ships were not able to defend it. It was taken by force, at the fecond Affault, by eight hundred brave *Portuguefes,* feconded by fome few *Malabars.* It was given up to pillage, for three days, and the *Moor King,* after all his endeavours, was forc'd to fly with only fifty Horfemen to attend him. The *Portuguefes* built a Cittadel, which the fucceeding Governours took care to for-tifie: yet not fo ftrongly, as to be proof againft the attempts of the *Barbarians;* who many times attacq'd it, and half ruin'd it.

As foon as *Xavier* came on fhore, he went to vifit the Governour of the Town, to inform him of his intended Voyage to *Macaffar.* The Governour told him, that he had lately fent thither a Prieft, of holy life, with fome *Portuguefe* Soul-diers; and that he expected to hear of them very fuddenly. That in the mean time he was of opinion, that the Father and his Companion, fhou'd ftay at *Malacca,* till the prefent condition of the Chrifti-ans in *Macaffar* were fully known. *Xa-vier* gave credit to the Governour, and retir'd

Book III. *St.* Francis Xavier. 207

retir'd to the Hoſpital, which he had choſen for the place of his abode. The People ran in Crowds to behold the countenance of that great Apoſtle, whoſe fame was ſpread through all the *Indies*; and over all the Eaſt. The Parents ſhow'd him to their Children; and it was obſerv'd, that the Man of God, in careſſing thoſe little *Portugueſes*, call'd every one of them by their proper names, as if he had been of their acquaintance; and were not a ſtranger newly come on ſhore.

For what remains, he found the Town, *In what condi-* in a moſt horrible corruption of man- *tion he found* ners. The *Portugueſes*, who liv'd there *the Town; and* at a diſtance, both from the Biſhop, and *what he did in* the Viceroy of the *Indies*, committed *order to reform* all manner of Crimes, without fear of *it.* Laws, either Eccleſiaſtical or Civil. A- varice, Intemperance, Uncleanneſs, and forgetfulneſs of God were every where predominant, and the Habit only, or rather the exceſs and number of their Vices, diſtinguiſh'd the Chriſtians from the Unbelievers.

This terrible Proſpect of a ſinful Town, gave *Xavier* to comprehend, that his ſtay in *Malacca* was neceſſary, and might poſſibly turn to a good account; but be- fore he wou'd undertake the Reformation

tion of a Town, fo univerfally corrupted, he employ'd fome days in ferving of the Sick: he pafs'd many nights in Prayer, and perform'd extraordinary Aufterities.

After thefe Preparatives, he began his publick inftructions according to the methods which he had frequently practis'd at *Goa*. Walking the Streets at evening, with his Bell in his Hand, he cry'd with a loud voice, *Pray to God for thofe who are in the ftate of Mortal Sin:* and by this, he brought into the minds of Sinners, the remembrance and confideration of their Offences. For feeing the ill habits of their Minds, and that the difeafe was like to be inflam'd, if violent remedies were apply'd, he temper'd more than ever the ardour of his Zeal. Though he had naturally a Serene Countenance, and was of a pleafing Converfation, yet all the charms of his good humour feem'd to be redoubled at *Malacca*, infomuch, that his Companion, *John Deyro*, cou'd not but wonder at his gayety, and foft behaviour.

He labours with fuccefs at Malacca. By this procedure, the Apoftle gain'd the Hearts of all, and became in fome manner, Lord of the City. At the very firft, he rooted out an eftablifh'd cuftom, which permitted the young Maids to go

in

Book III. *St.* Francis Xavier. 209

in the Habit of Boys, whenever they pleas'd, which occasion'd a world of scandal. He drove out of Doors, the Concubines, or turn'd them into lawful Wives, according to his former method. As for the Children, who had no knowledge of God, and who learnt Songs of Ribaldry, and Obsceneness, as soon as they began to speak, he form'd them so well in a little time, that they publickly recited the Christian Doctrine, and set up little Altars in the Streets, about which they sung together the Hymns of the Catholick Church. But that in which he was most successful, was to restore the practice of *Confession*, which was almost entirely lost. But now, Men and Women crowded the Tribunal of holy *Penitence*; and the Father was not able to supply the necessities of so many.

He labour'd in the knowledge of the *Malaya* Tongue, which is spoken in all the Isles beyond *Malacca*, and is as it were the Universal Language. His first care was to have a little Catechism translated into it, being the same he had compos'd on the Coast of *Fishery*: together with a more ample instruction, which treated of the principal duties of Christianity. He learnt all this without Book, and to make himself the better understood,

P stood,

ftood, he took a particular care of the Pronunciation.

With thefe helps, and the affiftance of Interpreters, who were never wanting to him at his need, he converted many *Idolaters*, as alfo *Mahometans* and *Jews*; amongft the reft, a famous Rabbi, who made a publick Abjuration of *Judaifm*. This Rabbi, who before had taken for fo many Fables, or juggling tricks, all thofe wonders which are reported to have been done by *Xavier*, now acknowledg'd them for Truths, by the Evidence of his own Eyes. For the Saint never wrought fo many Miracles as at *Malacca*. The Juridical Depofitions of Witneffes then living, have affur'd us, that all fick perfons, whom he did but touch, were immediately cur'd; and that his Hands had an healing vertue, againft all Diftempers. One of his moft famous cures, was that of *Antonio Fernandez*, a Youth, not above fifteen years of age, was fick to death. His Mother, a Chriftian by profeffion, but not without fome remainders of Paganifm in her Heart, feeing that all natural Remedies were of no effect, had recourfe to certain Enchantments frequently practis'd amongft the Heathens, and fent for an old Sorcerefs, who was call'd *Nai*. The Witch made her Magical Opeperations,

Book III. *St.* Francis Xavier.

rations, on a Lace brayded of many thrids, and ty'd it about the Arm of the Patient. But inſtead of the expected cure, *Fernandez* loſt his Speech, and was taken with ſuch violent Convulſions, that the Phyſitians were call'd again; who all deſpair'd of his recovery. It was expected every moment he ſhou'd breath his laſt, when a Chriſtian Lady, who happen'd to come in, ſaid to the Mother of the dying Youth, *Why do you not ſend for the holy Father? he will infallibly cure him.* She gave credit to her words, and ſent for *Xavier.* He was immediately there: *Fernandez,* who had loſt his Senſe, and lay gaſping in death, began to cry out, and make violent motions, ſo ſoon as the Father had ſet his Foot within the Doors: but when he came into the Room and ſtood before the Youth, he fell into howlings, and dreadful wreathings of his Body, which redoubled at the ſight of the Croſs, that was preſented to him. *Xavier* doubted not but there was ſomething of extraordinary in his Diſeaſe, nor even that God, for the puniſhment of the Mother, who had made uſe of Diabolical Remedies, had deliver'd her Son to the evil Spirits. He fell on his Knees by the Bed-ſide, read aloud the Paſſion of our Lord, hung his Reli-

P 2 quiary

quiary about the Neck of the fick perfon, and fprinkled him with Holy Water. This made the fury of the Devil ceafe : and the young Man, half dead, lay without motion as before. Then *Xavier* rifing up, *Get him fomewhat to eat,* (faid he) and told them, what nourifhment he thought proper for him. After which, addreffing himfelf to the Father of the Youth, *When your Son,* added he, *fhall be in condition to walk, lead him your felf, for nine days fucceffively, to the Church of our Lady of the Mount, where to morrow I will fay Mafs for him.* After this he departed, and the next day, while he was celebrating the Divine Sacrifice, *Fernandez,* on the fudden came to himfelf, fpoke very fenfibly, and perfectly recover'd his former health.

He revives a dead Maid.

But how wonderful foever, the cure of this Youth, appear'd in the Eyes of all Men, the Refurrection of a young Maid was of greater admiration. *Xavier* was gone on a little Journey, fomewhere about the Neighbourhood of *Malacca,* to do a work of Charity, when this Girl dy'd. Her Mother, who had been in fearch of the holy Man during her Daughter's ficknefs, came to him, after his return, and throwing her felf at his Feet, all in Tears, faid almoft the fame words to him, which

Book III.   *St.* Francis Xavier.   213

which *Martha* said formerly to our Lord, *That if he had been in Town, she who was now dead, had been alive: but if he wou'd call upon the name of* Jesus Christ, *the dead might be restor'd to life.* Xavier was overjoy'd to behold so great Faith in a Woman, who was but lately baptis'd, and judging her worthy of that blessing which she begg'd, after having lifted up his Eyes to Heaven, and silently pray'd to God some little space, he turn'd towards her, and said to her with much assurance, *Go ; your Daughter is alive.* The poor Mother seeing the Saint offer'd not to go with her to the place of Burial, reply'd betwixt hope and fear, *That it was three days since her Daughter was interr'd :* 'Tis no matter, answer'd *Xavier, open the Sepulchre, and you shall find her living.* The Mother, without more reply, ran full of Confidence to the Church, and in presence of many persons, having caus'd the Grave-stone to be remov'd, found her Daughter living.

While these things pass'd at *Malacca,* a Ship from *Goa* brought Letters to Father *Xavier* from *Italy* and *Portugal :* which inform'd him of the happy progress of the Society of *Jesus,* and what it had already perform'd in *Germany* for the publick service of the Church.   He was

He receives Letters from Europe, by the new Missioners, who are sent him.

P 3   never

never weary of reading thofe Letters, he kifs'd them, and bedew'd them with his Tears, imagining himfelf, either with his Brethren in *Europe*, or them prefent with himfelf in *Afia*. He had news at the fame time, that there was arriv'd a fupply of three Miffioners, whom Father *Ignatius* had fent him, and that *Don John de Caftro*, who fucceeded *Alphonfo de Sofa*, in the Government of the *Indies*, had brought them in his company. Thefe Miffioners were *Antonio Criminal, Nicholas Lancilotti*, and *John Beyra*, all three Priefts; the two firft *Italians*, and the laft a *Spaniard*: Apoftolical Men, and of eminent Vertue, particularly *Criminal*, who of all the Children of *Ignatius* was the firft, who was honour'd with the Crown of Martyrdom. *Xavier* difpos'd of them immediately, commanding by his Letters, *That* Lancilotti *fhou'd remain in the Seminary of holy Faith, there to inftruct the young* Indians *in the knowledge of the Latin Tongue, and that the other two fhou'd go to accompany* Francis Manfilla *on the Coaft of* Fifhery.

He defers the Voyage to Macaffar, and defigns another. For himfelf, having waited three Months for news from *Macaffar*, when he faw the feafon, proper for the return of the Ship, which the Governour of *Malacca* had fent, was now expir'd, and that

Book III.　*St.* Francis Xavier.　**215**

that no Veffel was come from thofe parts,
he judg'd, that Providence wou'd not
make ufe of him at prefent, for the inftruction of thofe people, who had a
Prieft already with them. Neverthelefs,
that he might be more at hand to fuccour them, when ever it pleas'd God to
furnifh him with an occafion, it was in
his thoughts to go to the Neighbouring
Iflands of that Coaft, which were wholly
deftitute of Gofpel Minifters.

God Almighty at that time, reveal'd *He foreknows,*
to him the Calamities which threatn'd *and foretels the*
Malacca; both the Peftilence and the *ruin of* Malac-
War, with which it was to be afflicted *ca.*
in the years enfuing; and the utter defo-
lation to which it fhou'd one day be reduc'd for the punifhment of its Crimes.
For the Inhabitants, who fince the arrival of the Father, had reform'd their
Manners, relaps'd infenfibly into their
Vices, and became more diffolute than
ever, as it commonly happens to Men of
a debauch'd life, who conftrain themfelves for a time, and whom the force of
ill Habits, draws backward into Sin.
Xavier fail'd not to denounce the Judgments of God to them, and to exhort
them to Piety, for their own intereft.
But his Threatnings and Exhortations
were of no effect: and this it was that
　　　made

made him fay of *Malacca,* the quite contrary of what he had faid concerning *Me-
liapore,* that he had not feen, in all the
Indies, a more wicked Town.

*He goes to Am-
boyna, and
what happens
to him in his
Voyage.*
He imbark'd for *Amboyna* the firft of
January 1546, with *John Deyro,* in a Ship
which was bound for the Ifle of *Banda.*
The Captain of the Veffel was a *Portuguefe,*
the reft, as well Mariners as Souldiers,
were *Indians;* all of them almoft of feveral
Countries, and the greateft part *Mahometans,* or *Gentils.* The Saint converted
them to *Jefus Chrift,* during the Voyage,
and what convinc'd the Infidels of the
truth of Chriftianity, was, that when
Father *Xavier* expounded to them the
Myfteries of Chriftianity in one Tongue,
they underftood him feverally, each in
his own Language, as if he had fpoken at
once in many Tongues.

They had been already fix weeks at
Sea, without difcovering *Amboyna;* the
Pilot was of Opinion they had pafs'd it,
and was in pain concerning it, not knowing how to tack about, becaufe they had
a full fore-Wind. *Xavier* perceiving the
trouble of the Pilot. *Do not vex your
felf,* faid he, *we are yet in the* Gulph;
*and to morrow at break of day, we fhall be
in view of* Amboyna. In effect, at the
time mention'd, the next morning, they
faw

Book III. *St.* Francis Xavier. **217**

faw that Ifland. The Pilot being unwilling to caft Anchor ; Father *Xavier*,
with fome of the Paffengers, were put
into a Skiff, and the Ship purfu'd its
courfe. When the Skiff was almoft ready to Land, two light Veffels of Pyrats,
which ufually cruis'd on that Coaft, appear'd on the fudden, and purfu'd them
fwiftly. Not hoping any fuccour from
the Ship, which was already at a great
diftance from them, and being alfo without defence, they were forc'd to put off
from Shore, and ply their Oars towards
the main Sea ; infomuch that the Pyrats
foon loft fight of them. After they had
efcap'd the danger, they durft not make
to Land again, for fear the two Veffels
fhou'd lye in wait to intercept them at
their return. But the Father affur'd the
Mariners, they had no further caufe of
fear : turning therefore towards the
Ifland, they landed there in fafety, on the
fixteenth of *February*.

The Ifle of *Amboyna* is diftant from *He arrives at*
Malacca about two hundred and fifty *Amboyna :*
Leagues, 'tis near thirty Leagues in com- *forms there.*
pafs, and is famous for the concourfe of
Merchants, who frequent it from all
parts. The *Portuguefe*, who conquer'd
it, during the time that *Antonio Galvan*
was Governour of *Ternata*, had a Garrifon

fon in it; befides which, there were in the Ifland feven Villages of Chriftians, Natives of the place, but without any Prieft, becaufe the only one in the Ifland was juft dead. *Xavier* began to vifit thefe Villages, and immediately baptis'd many Infants, who dy'd fuddenly after they were Chriften'd. *As if,* (fays he himfelf in one of his Letters) *the Divine Providence, had only fo far prolong'd their lives, till the Gate of Heaven were open'd to them.*

Having been inform'd, that fundry of the Inhabitants, had retir'd themfelves from the Sea-fide, into the midft of the Woods, and Caves of the Mountains, to fhelter themfelves from the rage of the *Barbarians,* their Neighbours and their Enemies, who robb'd the Coafts, and put to the Sword, or made Slaves of all, who fell into their Hands, he went in fearch of thofe poor Salvages, amidft the horrour of their Rocks and Forefts; and liv'd with them as much as was neceffary, to make them underftand the duties of Chriftianity, of which the greateft part of them was ignorant.

He converts the Idolaters and Moors of Amboyna.
After having inftructed the Faithful, he apply'd himfelf to preach the Gofpel to the *Idolaters* and *Moors,* and God fo blefs'd the endeavours of his Servant, that

Book III.   *St.* Francis Xavier.   219

that the greateſt part of the Iſland became Chriſtians.   He built Churches in
every Village, and made choice of the
moſt reaſonable, the moſt able, and the
moſt fervent, to be Maſters over the reſt,
till there ſhou'd arrive a ſupply of Miſſio-
ners.   To which purpoſe he wrote to
Goa, and commanded *Paul de Camerine*
to ſend him *Francis Manſilla, John Beyra,*
and one or two more, of the firſt Miſſio-
ners, which ſhou'd arrive from *Europe:*
He charg'd *Manſilla* in particular, to come.
His deſign was to eſtabliſh in one of
thoſe Iſles a Houſe of the Company,
which ſhou'd ſend out continual ſupplies
of Labourers, for the publication of the
Goſpel, through all that *Archipelago.*

While *Xavier* labour'd in this manner   *A* Spaniſh
at *Amboyna,* two *Naval* Armies arriv'd   *Fleet arrives*
there : One of *Portugal* with three Ships,   *at* Amboyna.
the other of *Spaniards* with ſix Men of
War.   The *Spaniards* were come from
Nueva Eſpagna, or *Mexico,* for the Con-
queſt of the *Molucca*'s in the name of the
Emperour *Charles* the Fifth, as they pretended; but them Enterpriſe ſucceeded
not.   After two years cruiſing, and long
ſtay with the King of *Tidore,* who receiv'd them, to give Jealouſie to the
Portugueſe, who were allyed to the King
of *Ternate,* his Enemy, they took their
way

way by *Amboyna*, to pafs into the *In-dies*, and from thence to *Europe*. They were engag'd in an unjuft Expedition, a-gainft the Rights of *Portugal*, and with-out Order from *Charles* the Fifth, for that Emperour, to whom King *John* the third addrefs'd his Complaints thereupon, difavow'd the Proceedings of his Subjects, and gave permiffion, that they fhou'd be us'd like Pyrates.

Yet the *Portuguefe* proceeded not againft them with that feverity. But it feems that God reveng'd their quarrel; in af-flicting the *Spaniards* with a contagious Fever, which deftroy'd the greateft part of their Fleet. It was a fad fpecta-cle to behold the Mariners and Souldi-ers, lying here and there in their Ships, or on the fhoar, in Cabins, cover'd only with Leaves. The Difeafe which confum'd them, kept all men at a diftance from them, and the more neceffity they had of fuccour, the lefs they found from the People of the Ifland.

He affifts the   At the firft report which came to
Spanifh Fleet, *Xavier* of this Peftilence, he left all
during the Con- things to relieve them: And 'tis fcarce
tagion amongft to be imagin'd, to what actions his Cha-
them. rity led him on this occafion. He was day and night in a continual moti-on, at the fame time adminiftring to
         their

Book III.   *St.* Francis Xavier.   221

their Bodies and their Souls; affifting the dying, burying the dead, and Interring them even with his own hands. As the Sick had neither Food nor Phyfick, he procur'd both for them from every fide; and he who furnifh'd him the moft, was a *Portuguefe* call'd *John d' Araus*; who came in his company from *Malacca* to *Amboyna*. Neverthelefs the Malady ftill encreafing day by day, *Araus* began to fear he fhou'd impoverifh himfelf by thefe Charities, and from a tender hearted man, became fo hard, that nothing more was to be fqueez'd out of him. One day *Xavier* fent to him for fome Wine, for a fick man who had continual faintings: *Araus* gave it, but with great reluctance, and charg'd the Meffenger to trouble him no more; that he had need of the remainder for his own ufe, and when his own was at an end, whither fhou'd he go for a fupply? Thefe words were no fooner related to Father *Francis*, than inflam'd with a holy indignation, *What*, fays he, *does* Araus *think of keeping his Wine for himfelf, and refufing it to the Members of* Jefus Chrift; *the end of his Life is very near, and after his death, all his Eftate fhall be diftributed amongft the Poor.* He denounc'd death to him with his own mouth, and the

the event verify'd the Prediction, as the
fequel will make manifeft.

Though the Peftilence was not wholly
ceas'd, and many Sick were yet aboard
the Veffels, the *Spanifh Fleet* fet Sail for
Goa, forc'd to it, by the approach of
Winter, which begins about *May*, in
thofe quarters. Father *Xavier* made Pro-
vifions for the neceffities of the Souldiers,
and furnifh'd them, before their departure, with all he cou'd obtain from the
Charity of the *Portuguefe*. He recommended them likewife to the Charity of
his Friends at *Malacca*, where the Navy
was to touch, and wrote to Father *Paul
de Camerine* at *Goa*, that he fhou'd not
fail to Lodge in the *Colledge of the Company*, thofe Religious of the Order of St.
Auguftin, who came along with the Army from *Mexico*, and that he fhou'd do
them all the good Offices, which their
Profeffion, and their Vertue claim'd from
him.

He paffes into　　After the *Spaniards* were departed,
divers Iflands. *Xavier* made fome little Voyages to places near adjoyning to *Amboyna* : and vi-
fited fome Iflands which were half un-
peopled, and defart, waiting the convenience of a Ship, to tranfport him to the
Molucca's, which are nearer to *Macaffar*
than *Amboyna*. One of thofe Ifles is
　　　　　　　　　　　Baranura ;

Book III. *St.* Francis Xavier. **223**

Baranura; where he miraculoufly recover'd his Crucifix, in the manner I am going to relate, according to the account which was given of it by a *Portuguefe,* call'd *Faufto Rodriguez,* who was a witnefs of the Fact, has depos'd it upon Oath, and whofe Juridical Teftimony is in the procefs of the Saints Canonifation.

We were at Sea, fays *Rodriguez,* Father *Francis, John Rapofo,* and my felf, when there arofe a Tempeft which allarm'd all the Mariners. Then the Father drew from his bofome a little Crucifix, which he always carri'd about him, and leaning over deck, intended to have dipt it into the Sea; but the Crucifix dropt out of his hand, and was carri'd off by the Waves. This lofs, very fenfibly afflicted him, and he conceal'd not his forrow from us. The next morning we landed on the Ifland of *Baranura;* from the time when the Crucifix was loft, to that of our landing, it was near 24 hours, during which, we were in perpetual danger. Being on fhore, Father *Francis* and I, walk'd along by the Sea fide, towards the Town of *Tamalo,* and had already walk'd about five hundred paces, when both of us beheld arifing out of the Sea, a Crab-Fifh, which carried betwixt

He recovers his Cruc fix, which was fallen into the Sea.

twixt his Claws, the fame Crucifix, rais'd on high. I faw the Crab-Fifh come directly to the Father by whofe fide I was, and ftop'd before him. The Father, falling on his knees, took his Crucifix, after which the Crab-Fifh return'd into the Sea. But the Father, ftill continuing in the fame humble pofture, hugging and kiffing the Crucifix, was half an hour praying with his hands acrofs his breaft, and my felf joyning with him in thankfgiving to God, for fo evident a Miracle: after which we arofe, and continu'd on our way. Thus you have the Relation of *Rodriguez*.

They ftaid eight days upon the Ifland, and afterwards fet fail for *Rofalao*; where *Xavier* Preach'd at his firft coming, as he had done at *Baranura*. But the Idolaters who Inhabited thefe two Iflands, being extreamly vicious, altogether brutal, and having nothing of humane in them, befides the figure, gave no credit to his words, and one only man amongft them, more reafonable than all the reft, believ'd in *Jefus Chrift*. Infomuch, that the Holy Apoftle, at his departure from *Rofalao*, took off his Shoos, and fhook off the duft, that he might not carry any thing away with him, which belong'd to that execrable Land.

Truly

[Edward Ambrose Burgis], *The Annals of the Church* (London, T. H., 1712), pp. 62–74

As well as drawing inspiration for what were for them the relatively recent adventures of Francis Xavier, English Catholic readers were also able to contemplate the continuity of their faith from that of the early Church. By doing so, they were able to counter the common Protestant allegation that the Roman communion represented a corruption of pristine Christianity. The record of persecution that marked Apostolic Christianity also had its parallels with the experience of the post-Reformation English Catholic community.

The Annals of the Church was printed in London in 1712 by 'T. H'. The author, the Dominican Edward (in religion: Ambrose) Burgis (1673?–1747) was born in Bristol, the son of a priest of the Church of England. Converted to Catholicism, he entered the Order of Preachers in Naples in 1696 or 1697 and was sent to Louvain to study Philosophy. In 1709 he lectured on morals at the English Dominican priory established by Cardinal Philip Howard (1629–94) at Bornhem in East Flanders, and from 1710 he taught in Louvain, where in 1718 he was chosen rector of the Dominicans' College of St Thomas Aquinas. In 1723 Burgis took the degree of Master of Sacred Theology and in 1724 was again appointed rector at Louvain. He was elected English Provincial in 1730, taking up residence in London; in 1735 he was again installed as rector at Louvain and subsequently may have served on the Mission in Yorkshire. He was elected Prior of Bornhem in 1741, was director to Dominican nuns in Brussels in 1745 and Vicar General for the Southern Netherlands in 1746. Burgis died in Brussels in 1747.

Alongside his distinguished work in the administration for the Dominican Order, Burgis was a leading scholar and author. In 1709 he brought to completion *An Introduction to the Catholick Faith. By an English Dominican* – the prior (1705, 1708, 1718, 1725) and historian of Bornhem Thomas Worthington (1671–1754). The 1712 *The Annals of the Church* covered the period AD 34–300 and in the preface 'To The Reader' the author announced his intention eventually to bring the history down to his own time. Seven Latin theological and historical treatises followed, and between 1737 and 1738 *The Annals of the Church from the Death of Christ* (4 volumes, including one volume of notes, London; Thomas Meighan took the story forward to AD 500. Then a five-volume version was published by Meighan in 1738).

THE

ANNALS

OF THE

CHURCH.

LONDON:

Printed by *T. H.* and ſold by the Book-
ſellers of *London* and *Weſtminſter.* 1712.

62   *The Annals of the Church.*

Of CHRIST 65, 6, 7. *Of* NERO 10, 11, 12.
      Of PETER 20, 22, 23.

1. SAINT *Jofeph* of *Arimathea* and his 12
      Companions fettled in the Monaftery
of *Glaftenbury* in *Somerfetfbire*, which they had
lately finifh'd. They embrac'd the moft perfect State of Religion, and were fo entirely
taken up with the Delights of an afcetick Life,
that nothing was to divert 'em from it, but
the good of their Neighbor. Their Lives
were fo many Leffons to Piety, and their Sermons replete with fo many authentick Proofs
of the Doctrin they preach'd. This Monafte-
ry in fucceeding Ages was endow'd with large
Revenues, and fo fruitful of Saints, that tis to
be doubted if the *Chriftian* World can produce its equal. Kings and Princes have always
had it in the higheft Veneration, and made
frequent Pilgrimages to pay their Vows to fo
facred a Place.

2. About this Year S. *Lazarus* dy'd. He
was exil'd from his native Soil (in 44) with
his Sifters *Martha* and *Magdalen* for beingSer-
vants to *Jefus Chrift*. In this Banifhment they
every Day made Advances towards the heavenly *Jerufalem*. *Martha* foon follow'd her
Brother thither. *Magdalen* retir'd into a fo-
litary Grot at *Baume* in the Southern Part of
France; where having fpent thirty Years in the
Contemplation of Heaven, fhe went thither
to take a full Poffeffion of thofe joys of which
fhe had here receiv'd a Foretaft. Her Body
                                              lies

lies in this Grot which belongs to the *Domini-tans:* who are not wanting to keep this ſacred Treaſure with due Reſpect, and emulate the Mortification of this fair Penitent. *

3. The Goſpel made a great progreſs in the Capital City of the World, and the Faithful enjoy'd a perfect Calm, when all on a ſuddain Divine Providence permitted a Storm to riſe to try the Conſtancy of their Faith. *Nero* had an ambition of calling the City after his own Name, and thinking the narrow Streets and antiquated Buildings unworthy his Imperial Majeſty was reſolv'd to ſet it on fire. Whilſt *Rome* was in Flames he went to the Top of a Tower, and dreſt like a Comedian play'd the Burning of *Troy*, and feaſted his inhuman Sight with a Spectacle which cou'd not but draw Tears from all Perſons Eyes, and touch the Hearts of every Beholder. The Fire laſted 6 days together, and of 14 Parts of the City only 4 eſcap'd. 'Tis impoſſible to conſider the Waſt and Ravage it made: thouſands of Perſons were loſt in it, and the magnificent Temples of the Gods, the Triumphal Arches, Pyramids, Columns, and all the other Trophies and Spoils of conquer'd Nations were reduc'd to Aſhes. He thought to diſcharge himſelf from the imputation of ſo horrid a Crime by caſting the odium of it upon the *Chriſtians.* A great number of 'em periſh'd on this account by Torments that mov'd the compaſſion of their very Enemies. For every Body knew that the Emperor was Author of the Crime as well as the Puniſhment. Some were

64 *The Annals of the Church.*

were cover'd with the Skins of Wild Beaſts, to be baited and torn in pieces by ravenous Dogs. Others were anointed with Gum, Roſine, Wax and other combuſtible Matters, had a Stake put under their Chin, to keep 'em from bending, then were ſet afire, that they might ſerve for Torches and Flambeaux to expel the Evening Darkneſs, according to that of *Juvenal* :

Death was their Doom, on Stakes impal'd upright,
Smear'd o'er with Wax, and ſet on Fire to light
The Streets, and make a dreadful Blaze by Night.

4. He was not content to puniſh 'em at *Rome* but put out his Proclamations againſt 'em every where. *Gervaſius* and *Protaſius*, *Nazarius* and *Celſus*, *Vitalis*, *Urſicinus* and *Valeria* ſuffer'd at *Milain* and *Ravenna*. The Names of the greateſt Part of the other Martyrs are blotted out of the Annals of Fame by the Envy of *Dioclefian*, but are preſerv'd in Heaven and tranſcrib'd in the Book of Life. Thus the firſt Perſecution was begun by the moſt finiſh'd Prodigy of Wickedneſs : But we glory, ſays *Tertullian*, in being firſt devoted to Deſtruction by ſuch a Monſter ; for whoever is acquainted with that Enemy to all Goodneſs, will have the greater Value for our Religion, as knowing that *Nero* cou'd hate nothing exceedingly, but what was exceedingly good.*

5. *Plautius Lateranus*, *Seneca* and *Lucan* were dipt in *Piſo*'s Conſpiracy againſt the Emperor, and put to death for't. Succeeding Ages chang'd *Lateranus*'s Houſe into a Church, to this day call'd S. *John Laterans*. Tis very likely

ly *Seneca* was acquainted with S. *Paul* ; but as for the Letters that go under their Names, they contain grofs Anacronifms and other Things unworthy of the Doctor of Nations and the Moral Philofopher.

Of CHRIST 68. *Of* NERO 13. *Of* PETER 24.

1. THE Punifhment of the Confpirators diverted the Perfecution from the *Chriſtians.* S. *Peter* and *Paul* return'd to *Rome* to comfort them, and oppofe the fpreading Errors of *Simon* the Magician, who had gain'd a ftrange afcendant over the Emperor, by being fo well verft in his darling Studies of Magick. His turning himfelf into different fhapes, and the other wonders which he feem'd to perform by the illufions of this abominable Art, made way for his more abominable Doctrin, which magnify'd all forts of Impurity, even thofe that are againft Nature, and taught it lawful for all Women to proftitute their Bodies, and be common to every one. S. *Peter* often difputed with him, but he was bound too faft by the charms he made ufe of, and too deeply engag'd in the fervice of Hell to repent. At length the Prince of the Apoftles confounded him whom he cou'd not convert. For this Magician appointed the Emperor a Day, when he fhou'd fly up to Heaven in his Prefence. The Novelty of the Spectacle brought all *Rome* to it; accordingly, by the Devils affiftance, he was carry'd up to the Clouds, when S. *Peter* made this new *Icarus*

F   fall

66   *The Annals of the Church.*

fall headlong down by the Efficacy of his
Prayer. The Wounds he receiv'd from the
Fall, join'd with the Difgrace of it, foon put
an End to his Life, and freed the Church from
fo formidable an Enemy. He left Succeffors of
his Impiety behind him, and was outdone by
the Impurity of the *Nicolaits* his Cotempo-
raries. Some refer their Original to *Nicolaus*
one of the feven Deacons : The Fathers are
divided upon this point, and I fhall not undertake to determin it. S. *Peter*, about this time,
wrote his fecond Letter, as a Spiritual Antidote
againft this unchaft Doctrin of the Flefh. S.
Jude's Epiftle is much upon the fame occafion,
and often in the very fame words.

2. The Emperors lewd life correfponded ex-
actly with the deteftable leffons of his Magician ; he violated the Chaftity of the *Roman*
Matrons, and glory'd more in the deflowring
Virgins then in conquering Armies. At his
Court the name of Chaftity was odious, and
therefore the Apoftles who extoll'd the Vertues
of it, cou'd not but incur his indignation. He
loft his Favourite Magician by the Prayers of
S. *Peter* : And the Perfuafions of S. *Paul*
wrought upon one of his Miftreffes to flie his
wanton Embraces, and adhere to the unfpot-
ted Purity of the Gofpel. They were both,
upon this, imprifon'd in the *Mamertin* Dungeon, and the Emperor fet forward to *Achaia*,
to fee the *Ifthmus* he had order'd to be cut.

3. Above three hundred thoufand Perfons
came to celebrate the Solemnity of the Paf-
over in *Jerufalem*. It happen'd the Eighth of
April

The Firſt Age. 67

April, and was attended with frequent Prodigies, and Portents. A Cow that was deſtin'd a Victim for the Sacrifice, brought forth a Lamb at the Altar. In the dead of the ſucceeding Night ſo great a Blaze of Light appear'd in the Skies, that for the ſpace of half an hour it ſeem'd broad Day. The Eaſtern brazen Gate of the Temple which twenty Men were ſcarce able to ſhut, burſt of it ſelf wide open. The 21 of *May* in the dusk of the Evening, Fiery Chariots, Armies and Embattl'd Squadrons were beheld in the Clouds. On the Feaſt of Pentecoſt a confus'd Noiſe diſturb'd the Prieſts Devotions in the Interior Temple, and then a lamentable Voice cry'd out ; *Let us depart, let us depart from hence.* Theſe Signs were the fore-runners of the *Jewiſh* Calamities, and portended the Deſtruction of that unhappy Nation, which happen'd ſoon after. For,

4. They who thus long had only murmur'd and complain'd of the hard uſage they met with from the cruelty and avarice of their Governors, now break out into open Rebellion againſt *Florus, Albinus*'s Succeſſor. He had ſeis'd upon the ſacred Treaſure of the Temple, and took from thence ſeventeen Talents : This occaſion'd variety of Paſquinades ; one of 'em, that touch'd him moſt, was, the begging Alms about the Street in his Name. Their moſt ſubmiſſive excuſes cou'd not allay his deſire of revenge, to gratify which he gave orders to the Soldiers to plunder the Market-place, and kill all they met in the way. The chief

F 2 Nobi-

68   *The Annals of the Church.*

Nobility of the Town were brought before
him; fome of 'em were enroll'd in the order
of *Roman* Knights, but being *Jews* by extraction, *Florus* caus'd 'em to be whipt, without
having regard to their Quality.   This caus'd
a popular Infurrection, which King *Agrippa*
endeavour'd to quell, perfuading them to wait
with patience the arrival of a new Governor.
The People inftead of thanking him for his
wholfom advice, affronted and pelted him with
Stones, infomuch, that he was forc'd to fly out
of the City for fecurity.   The Factions encreafing, their number form'd a Body together and
headed by *Eleazar* attack'd a Fort call'd *Maf-
fada*, wherein was a *Roman* Garrifon, took it
by Storm and put 'em all to the Sword.   *Agrippa* fent three thoufand Soldiers to put a Stop
to the Tumults in *Jerufalem*, but the Factious
Party prevailing, they burn'd *Agrippa*'s Palace,
the High Prieft's Houfe, the Archives where
all the publick Regifters were depofited, and
flew the High Prieft, and his Brother *Ezechias*:
and put to the Sword a Garrifon of *Roman* Soldiers, after Capitulation and Promife of Quarter.

5.   The fame day, and, as 'tis thought, the
very fame hour, the *Gentiles* that inhabited the
City of *Cefarea* flew the *Jews* there, to the number of twenty thoufand.   All *Paleftine* was engag'd in this Civil War, and there was fcarce
a little Village but was divided in two Parties,
the *Syrians* and the *Jews*, without giving one
another Quarter.   In thefe diforders thirteen
thoufand *Jews* perifh'd at *Scythopolis*; Two
Thoufand

The Firſt Age. *69*

thouſand Five hundred in *Aſcalon*, in *Ptolemais*
Two Thouſand, and Fifty thouſand in *Alexandria*. *Ceſtius* Preſident of *Syria* entred into
Paleſtine with a powerful Army, ravag'd the
Country, and ſack'd or burn'd all the Towns
in his way, among which was *Joppe*, where
Eight thouſand *Jews* were deſtroy'd. Thence
he ſet forward to lay ſiege to *Jeruſalem*; miſ-
ſing his Stroke he turn'd back, and the *Jews*
cut of Six thouſand of his Men in the Rear.
Nero receiving an account of this in *Achaia*,
ſent *Veſpaſian* to force the Seditious to their
duty. The *Jews* made great preparations for
defence, elected *Ananus*, the Father of *Eleazar*
their General, High Prieſt, that he and *Joſephus Gorion* might govern, and provide for the
Common Good. The *Chriſtians* foreſeeing the
calamitous Circumſtances *Jeruſalem* was like
to fall under, and mindful of the advice our
Saviour gave when he convers'd on Earth, a-
bandon'd this criminal City, and ſought their
habitations in *Pella* and other places on the
farther ſide of the River *Jordan*.

Of CHRIST 69. *Of* NERO 14. *Of* PETER 25.
Of LINUS 1.

1. VESPASIAN entring *Paleſtine* laid all
the Country waſt, and ſpar'd neither
Man, Woman nor Child. In the City of *Aſcalon* alone he put Ten thouſand *Jews* to the
Sword. After a Siege of two Months he took
the Strong Town of *Jotapata*, Forty thouſand
were kill'd in't, and Twelve hundred taken

F 3 Pri-

70 *The Annals of the Church.*

Priſoners, of which number was *Joſephus* the Hiſtorian. In *Japha* he kill'd Fifteen thouſand, and Eleven thouſand Six hundred *Samaritans* in the attack of *Garizim.* In conclusion, all *Galilea* the ſtrongeſt Province of the Kingdom was ſubdu'd by his victorious Arms, and became a Theatre of Blood and Slaughter; thoſe who eſcap'd with Life, loſt their Liberty, and others, to ſecure both, took refuge in *Jeruſalem.*

2. That City was miſerably torn in pieces by different Factions: The New-comers increas'd the diſorders there, rifl'd the Inhabitants, and choſe by lot one *Phanus* an ignorant Fellow of a baſe extraction for High Prieſt. *Ananus* willing to maintain his Poſt, had frequent Skirmiſhes with theſe ſtrangers (who call'd themſelves the *Zealots,*) and always came off with ſucceſs. They had been entirely defeated, had not one *John* of *Giſcala,* a great Stickler in appearance for *Ananus*'s Party, and Sworn of his Privy Council, betray'd all his Secrets, and ſpread a rumor abroad that he had contriv'd to give up the Town to the *Romans.* To prevent this they call'd the *Idumeans* in; who committed all manner of violence and diſorder with ſo little remorſe, that one may juſtly ſay, they had extinguiſh'd all the ſoftneſs of human nature, and were fleſh'd in blood and cruelty. Twelve Thouſand of the Nobility and a World of vulgar Citizens periſh'd in the Common Slaughter. The Prieſts cou'd not eſcape; *Ananus* was ſtrangl'd in the Market-place, and *Zacharias* the Son of *Baruch* ſlain in the Temple

The Firſt Age. 71

ple. The Town ſeem'd the Shambles of Men, the
Temple appear'd like a Lake of Bloud, and the
Sacred Altar, to which even the *Gentiles* and
Barbarians paid an awful reſpeĉt, was beſmear'd
with human Gore, and polluted with the un-
buried Carcaſſes of ſlaughter'd Citizens. Theſe
were the heavy puniſhments they ſuffer'd,
which yet were light in compariſon of thoſe, divine vengeance inflicted on 'em afterwards,
when it determin'd utterly to exterminate and
overturn ſo ungrateful and diſobedient a People.

3. The Apoſtles had been almoſt nine
Months in priſon, when the Sentence of death
was pronounc'd againſt them. The Faithful
were loath to be depriv'd of their Paſtor, and
therefore entreated S. *Peter* to make his eſcape
out of the Priſon, and City, and ſave himſelf
elſewhere. There was no great hazard in the
attempt, ſince he was favour'd by *Proceſſus*
and *Martinian* the Keepers of the Priſon, and 47
Soldiers of the Guard, who were all converted
by the Apoſtles, and chriſten'd in a Fountain
of Water that ſprung up miraculouſly in the
Dungeon, and remains to this day without
diminiſhing or encreaſing. Yielding at laſt to
their holy violence and going out of the City,
he met our Saviour, and ask'd him where he
was a going, to whom the Son of God reply'd :
I am going to *Rome* to be crucify'd again. The
Apoſtle underſtood his Divine Maſter's Will
by this, and return'd back to Priſon. Before
the Apoſtles were put to Death, they were
ty'd faſt to two Pillars and whipt ; the crime
of Impiety was laid to their charge, and there-

fore

72   *The Annals of the Church.*

fore S. *Paul* though a Citizen of *Rome* receiv'd this difgraceful punifhment as well as S.
Peter that was a Stranger. However they were
diftinguifh'd in their death ; for the Head of
the Church was Crucify'd, and the Doctor of
Nations Beheaded ; who converted three of
the Soldiers that led him to Martyrdom, and
made them Partakers of it.   From his Neck
Milk gufh'd out in abundance ; after his head
was divided from his body, it made three
Bounds upwards, and as many Fountains rofe,
which remain to this day as facred Monuments
of his Paffion.   S. *Peter* was crucify'd, and he
defir'd it might be with his Head downwards,
that even in Death a diftinction might be made
betwixt the Mafter and the Servant.   Thus
the 29th of *June* thefe glorious Saints finifh'd
their Courfe, nor cou'd Death feparate thofe
whom the Functions of Apoftlefhip had fo
clofely united.   Their Tombs remain'd inviolate in all the heats of Perfecution, and in every Age Devotion has brought Pilgrims of all
States and Conditions thither.   Kings and
Emperors have come to kifs the Feet of thofe
Servants of *Chrift*, who for his fake appear'd fo
contemptible when alive : And laying afide the
pomp and greatnefs of Majefty, have with bend-
ed knees beeen humble Suppliants before the
Shrines of the Fifher and Tent-maker.

    4. *Linus* a Native of *Volterra* in *Tufcany*, and
the fame mention'd by S. *Paul* in his 2d. Epift.
to *Timoth.* c. 4. v. 21. fucceeded S. *Peter* in
the government of the univerfal Church, at a
time when *Nero*'s perfecution was at the high-
                                                        eft.

eft. His own Domesticks *Torpetes* and *Evellius*, with many others, suffer'd under it. *Lucina* and *Perpetua* Ladies of the first Rank were officious in paying the last Rites to their memory, and burying them; and receiv'd the Crown of Martyrdom for their reward. His cruelty extended it self to distant Countries, and the most exquisite Torments were invented every where to make the *Christians* revolt from their Faith; but while he thus wag'd War with Heaven, his Generals in different provinces threw off their Obedience to him, which oblig'd him to think rather of defending his Sovereignty, than of abusing it by tormenting the Faithful.

Of CHRIST 70. *Of* NERO 15. *Of* GALBA 1.
       Of LINUS 2.

1. NERO had a thousand different thoughts at once, upon the news of *Galba*'s revolt in *Spain*. First he was for taking poyson, now for flying, then for going suppliant to *Galba*, to stop him by his promises and intreaties, and next moment again for begging pardon of the People in publick; but after all cou'd resolve on nothing. He appear'd an execrable Monster to all Mankind, on the account of his Barbarity and Lasciviousness. He made it his boast, that he had banish'd Chastity from every part of his Body: His common Debauches were beyond number, but the too just grounds he gave the World of suspecting incestuous dealings with his own Mother, and his publick taking to Wife one of his own Sex with all the

74   *The Annals of the Church.*

Rites and Ceremonies of a lawful Marriage render'd him univerfally odious. He poifon'd his Confort *Octavia*, the Daughter of the Emperor *Claudius*, and her Brother Prince *Britanicus* : His Mother, Preceptor and the beft part of the *Roman* Senate fell by his Fury ; and his darling Miftrefs *Poppea Sabina* died, with a kick he gave her, when fhe was big with child. To fay he was bloudy, barbarous, inhuman wou'd be kittle : all is fum'd up in a word when I call him *Nero*. He fled to avoid the indignation of the People, and lay hid fome time in a Grot four Miles from *Rome*, but finding himfelf upon the point of being difcover'd, he kill'd himfelf by the affiftance of his Eunuch *Epaphroditus*. He was unworthy of a death from nobler hands; and he cou'd not have a more infamous Executioner than himfelf. He died the 10th of *June* after a long Tyranny of 13 years, 8 Months, and odd days.

2. *Galba* his Succeffor deriv'd his Pedigree from an ancient *Roman* Family, and retain'd the rigid Severity of ancient *Rome* in his Difcipline and Conduct. His perfonal good Actions were nothing extraordinary, and his bad ones very few in Number. But entirely giving himfelf up to be abus'd and flatter'd by three Favourits, in whom Vices of various Natures impetuoufly rag'd, he was never his own Man, but when his darling Sin of Covetoufnefs exerted it felf. This loft him the Affections of the Soldiery, who were highly exafperated at his refufing 'em a Donative, and faying that 'twas his Cuftom to chufe out Soldiers and not to buy 'em.

Of

Notes

Robert Parsons, *A Christian Directory*

p. 6, l. 5: *let*: hindrance.

p. 6, l. 18: *The Noble-men of Jewry*: John 12:42–3.

p. 6, ll. 23–4: *Demas that forsook St Paul in his bands*: Demas, once one of Paul's 'fellow-labourers' (Philemon:24) abandoned him in his final imprisonment.

p. 7, ll. 1–2: *that most excellent Parable*: 'the parable of the sower'.

p. 7, l. 32: *holy conversation*: righteous conduct.

p. 9, ll. 5–6: *as the words of Christ are*: as the words of Christ indicate they are.

p. 10, margin (i): *2 Par. 9.*: 2 Chronicles 9: The Vulgate uses the Greek term for the Books of Chronicles, *Paraleipomena* – 'things omitted' (concerning the Kings of Judah).

p. 10, margin (ii): *30 cori similæ & 60 cori farinæ*: thirty measures of the finest wheat flour and sixty measures of meal.

p. 10, margin (iii): *3 Reg. 4. 3 Reg. 11.*: The account of Solomon's wealth is also adapted from I Kings (otherwise known as 'the Third Book of the Kings' – 3 Regorum), 4:22–8, as well as from I Kings 10.

p. 10, margin (iv): *Eccles. I.*: This, on the basis of Ecclesiastes 1:1, accepts the attribution of the book to Solomon (see I Kings 4:32) and cites Ecclesiastes 1:2.

p. 10, ll. 36–7: *as St Hierom interpreteth*: St Jerome's (see vol. 1, *Pope Pius. His Confession of Faith*, Notes, p. 399) commentary on Ecclesiastes.

p. 11, margin (i): *Solomon's saying of himself*: Ecclesiastes 1:12–14.

p. 11, margin (ii): *Cap. 2. Ibid.*: a free version of Ecclesiastes 2:1–11.

p. 11, margin (iii): *I John 2.*: St John's First Epistle 2: 17.

p. 12, l. 6: *Whatsoever is in this world*: I John 2:16.

p. 13, ll. 5–6: *a Samaritan, and had a Devil*: John 8: 48.

p. 13, l. 7: *for that he kept not the Sabbath-day*: e.g. Luke 13:14; John 5:16, 7:23, 9:14–16.

p. 13, ll. 9–10: *there was a schism or division among them*: John 9:16.

p. 13, margin (v): *Mark 27.*: Mark 15 or Matthew 27.

p. 13, margin (ix): *I Cor. 4.*: I Corinthians 4:3.

p. 13, margin (x): *Luke 12.*: Mark 10:46–8.

p. 14, margin (i): *Dan. 31.*: Daniel 3.5.

p. 14, margin (ii): *Prov. 27.*: Proverbs 27:21.

p. 14, margin (iv): *Psal. 9.*: Psalm 9 (enumeration in Authorized Version [AV] and Douai–Rheims [DR]): 14. DR reads 'Have mercy on me, O Lord: see my humiliation *which I suffer* from my enemies.'

p. 14, margin (v): *Psal. 140.*: In the DR enumeration and version, Psalm 140:5 reads 'The just man shall correct me in mercy, and shall reprove me: but let not the oil of the sinner fatten my head.'

p. 14, l. 27: *Is not all this vanity?*: In the DR enumeration and version, Psalm 39:5 reads: 'Blessed is the man whose trust is in the name of the Lord; and who hath not had regard to vanities, and lying folly.'

p. 14, margin (vii): *Apoc. 4.*: Revelation 4:10.

p. 14, margin (viii): *Psal. 14.*: not identified.

p. 15, margin (i): *Eccl. 23.*: Ecclesiastes 2:3 reads 'I sought in my heart to give myself unto wine, yet acquainting mine heart with wisdom; and to lay hold on folly.'

p. 15, l. 16: *travel*: labour, travail.

p. 15, margin (iii). *John II.*: see John 11:46.

p. 15, margin (iv): *John 19.*: John 19:38–9.

p. 15, l. 22: *Agrippa and Festus*: Acts 25–6.

p. 15, margin (vi): *I Cor. 14.*: I Corinthians 14:20.

p. 16, margin (ii): *Phil. 3.*: Philippians 3:8.

p. 17, margin (ii): *Job 17.*: Job 17:14.

p. 17, margin (iii): *Osee 9.*: Hosea 9:10–11.

p. 18, ll. 1–2 and margin (i): *being descended himself of Kings ... Mat. 8. 20, 24. 26.*: The references are to Jesus's impoverishment, the royal genealogy of Jesus Christ appearing in Matthew 1:1–17.

p. 18, margin (iii): *I Reg. 9. I Reg. 16.*: I Samuel (otherwise known as I Kings): 8–11 recounts the rise of Saul. I Samuel:16 recounts the choice of David.

p. 18, margin (iii): *Mat. 4. Psal. 49. I. Cor. I.*: Matt. 4:18–21; Psalm 49 (AV): 2; I Corinthians 1:26.

p. 18, margin (iv): *I Cor I. I Reg. 9.*: I Corinthians 1:20; I Samuel 9:21.

p. 19, margin (i): *I Cor. 3.*: I Corinthians 1:26.

p. 19, margin (ii): *I Cor. 3.*: I Corinthians 3:18.

p. 19, margin (iii): *Sap. 9.*: not identified.

p. 19, margin (iv): *Prov. 31. Pal. 118. Psal. 4.*: Proverbs 31:30; Psalm 119 (AV):37; Psalm 4:2 (AV) reads 'how long will ye love vanity, and seek after leasing?'.

p. 21, margin: *The vanity of apparel, Eccl. II.*: Ecclesiasticus, or The Wisdom of Jesus the Son of Sirach (Apocrypha) 11:4.

p. 22, margin (i): *I Tim. 6.*: I Timothy 6:8 – Timothy, who had may have had responsibility for one of Paul's congregations, being represented as a 'Bishop'.

p. 22, margin (ii): *Luke 7.*: Luke 7:24–8.

p. 22, margin (iii): *Luke 16.*: Luke 16:19.

p. 22, margin (iv): *4 Reg. I.*: 2 Kings I:4.

p. 22, margin (v): *Gen. 3.*: Genesis 3:21.

p. 22, margin (vi): *Heb. 12.*: Hebrews 11:37 (accepting the attribution of the Epistle to the Hebrews to Paul).

p. 23, margin (i): *Psal. 77*: not identified.

p. 23, ll. 22–3: *Pride of life …Concupiscence of the eyes*: First Epistle of John 2:16.

p. 23, margin (ii): *I Tim. 6.*: I Timothy 6:17.

p. 23, margin (iii): *Prov. II.*: Proverbs 11:4.

p. 23, margin (iv): *Sap. 5.*: The Wisdom of Solomon (Apocrypha 5:8).

p. 24, margin (i): *Psal. 75.*: Psalm 75 (DR): 5: 'They have slept their sleep; and all the men of riches have found nothing in their hands.'

p. 24, margin (ii): *the Prophet Baruch …Bar. 3*: Baruch (Apocrypha) 3:18: '[Where are they] that hoard up silver and gold … and there is no end of their getting?'

p. 24, margin (iii): *Jam. 5.*: James. 5:1–3.

p. 25, margin (i): *Psal. 61.*: Psalm 61 (in DR enumeration and version) 61:11: 'Trust not in iniquity, and covet not robberies: if riches abound, set not your hearts upon them.'

p. 25, margin (ii): *Eccl. 31.*: Ecclesiasticus, or The Wisdom of Jesus the Son of Sirach (Apocrypha) 31:5: 'He that loveth gold shall not be justified.'

p. 25, margin (iii): *Zach. I. Matt. 19.*: Zechariah 1:15; Matthew 19:24.

p. 25, margin (iv): *Luke 6.*: Luke 6:24.

p. 25, margin (v): *I Tim. 6.*: 1 Timothy 6:9.

p. 26, ll. 21–2: *called by St John, Concupiscence of the flesh*: First Epistle of John 2:16.

p. 26, margin (i): *Luke 6.*: Luke 6:25.

p. 27, margin (i): *John 16.*: John 16: 20.

p. 27, margin (ii): *Job 21.*: Job 21:12–13.

p. 27, margin (iii): *Job 5. Job. 9.*: Job 3:24; Job 9:28.

p. 27, margin (iv): *Eccl. 9.*: Ecclesiastes 9:1.

p. 27, margin (v): *Tob. 5.*: Tobit (Apocrypha, DR) 5:12: 'And Tobias said: What manner of joy shall be to me, who sit in darkness, and see not the light of heaven?'

p. 27, margin (vi): *I Cor. 2. 2. Cor. 7. Phil. 2. Job 2. John 16.*: 1 Corinthians 2:3; 2 Corinthians 7:5; Philippians 2:12; Job 2:12; John 16:20.

p. 27, margin (vii): *Rom. 8 Ephes. 4. Mat. 24.*: Romans 8:23; Ephesians 4: not identified; Matthew 24:8–12, 15–42.

p. 28, margin (i): *2 Cor. 5 & 7.*: 2 Corinthians 5:2, 4; 2 Corinthians 7:11, 15.

p. 28, margin (ii): *Eccl. 7.*: Ecclesiastes 7:2.

p. 28, margin (iii): *Mich. 6.*: Micah 6:8.

p. 28, margin (iv): *John 10. Luke 19.*: John 11:35; Luke 19:41.

p. 29, margin (i): *Prov. 14*: Proverbs 14:13.

p. 30, margin (i): *Amos I. Tob. 2.*: Amos 8:10; Tobit (Apocrypha) 2:6, repeating Amos.

p. 30, margin (ii): *Apoc. 18.*: Revelation 18:7.

p. 30, margin (iii): *Psal. 39.*: Psalm 39:6 (AV): 'Surely every man walketh in a vain shew.'

p. 30, margin (iv): *Esay 56.*: Isaiah 5:18.

p. 30, margin (v): *Psal. 3.*: not identified.

p. 30, margin (vi): *I Reg. 17.*: I Kings 16:1–4 (AV).

p. 30, margin (vii): *Psal. 39.*: Psalm 39:5 (DR).

Nicholas Cross, *A Sermon Preach'd before her Sacred Majesty the Queen*

p. 36, l. 1: *THESE Inventions of Antiquity*: Cross's overture dealt with an ancient Egyptian cult representing nature in human form.

p. 36, l. 7: *says the Psalmist*: Psalm 36:8.

p. 36, l. 21: *Quia non sunt condignæ*: Romans 8:18.

p. 37, l. 3: *Eye hath seen*: 1 Corinthians 2:9.

p. 37, ll. 4–5: *The Royal Prophet insinuates as much*: Psalm 17, one attributed to King David, v. 15: 'I will behold thy face in righteousness: I shall be satisfied when I awake with Thy likeness.'(AV)

p. 39, l. 14: *as St Paul says*: Acts 17:28.

p. 39, l. 16: *St Austin expresses this*: St Augustine, not identified.

p. 40, l. 14: *Vanitas vanitatum*: 'Vanity of vanities, saith the Preacher': the second verse of Ecclesiastes, claimed to be by 'the son of David, king in Jerusalem' – King Solomon.

p. 40, ll. 25–6: *the third Heaven*: 2 Corinthians 12:2.

p. 41, l. 5: *to be dissolved*: Philippians 1:23.

p. 41, l. 26: *Amari potest*: In bk viii, ch. IV of 'On the Trinity' St Augustine wrote: 'Even he therefore who is not known, but yet is believed, can be loved (*amari potest*).'

p. 42, ll. 11–12: *Similes ei erimus*: First Epistle of John 3:2.

p. 42, ll. 21–2: *for above these five thousand Years*: since the Creation.

p. 43, l. 25: *formally in God*: in God's own form or essence.

p. 44, l. 17: *his mysterious Book*: Revelation 21:27.

p. 45, ll. 4–5: *St Thomas gives it to the Operation of the Understanding*: In his discussion of 'The Original State with Respect to Man's Mind', in the *Summa Theologiae*, 1a, 94, I, Thomas Aquinas wrote: 'Now the loftier a creature is and the more it resembles God, the clearer is the sight of God to be obtained through it.'

p. 45, l. 14: *SCOTUS*: known as the 'subtle doctor', Cross's fellow-Franciscan, the Oxford and Paris Scholastic John Duns Scotus (1265–1308) was born at Duns, about fifteen miles west of Berwick-on-Tweed. Duns Scotus taught, against the tradition of Aquinas, that the human will was superior to the intellect, could choose freely to love or hate good – in contrast to the intellect, which was bound to assent to truth – and exercised love where the intellect grasped understanding, the will then aiming at happiness in the love of God.

p. 48, l. 7: *Antepast of heaven*: foretaste of heaven.

p. 48, ll. 16–17: *as St Peter terms it*: in AV and DR 1 Peter 1:3 has 'a lively hope'.

p. 49, l. 22: *length of Days*: Psalm 21:4.

p. 51, l. 16: *John xvi*: John 16:22.

p. 51, l. 4: *St Austin*: St Augustine, not identified.

p. 51, l. 7: *St Gregory stiles it*: not identified.

p. 51, ll. 12–13: *that unfortunate rich Man*: Luke 16:24.

p. 51, ll. 25–6: *the fifth Chapter of St Matthew*: Matthew 5:10.

p. 52, ll. 11–12: *Holy Job*: Job 7:1 (the DR version reads 'The life of man upon earth is a warfare'; the AV reads 'Is there not an appointed time to man upon earth?').

p. 52, l. 23: *sweaty Brows*: Genesis 3:19.

p. 56, l. 2: *he should not touch upon his life*: Job 2:6.

p. 56, l. 11: *Seneca*: Lucius Annaeus Seneca, known as 'the Younger' (*c.* 5 BC–AD 65), Roman poet, statesman and philosopher; his *dialogi* on ethical questions included the *De constantia sapientis*.

p. 56, l. 17: *the Delay our Blessed Saviour made*: Mark 4:37.

p. 59, l. 2: *Quia oportebat Christum pati*: Luke 24:26: 'Ought not Christ to have suffered these things, and enter into His glory?' (AV).

p. 59, l. 31: *Hebr. Cap. xi*: Hebrews 11:38.

p. 60, l. 11: *Tim. Cap. ii*: 2 Timothy 2:5.

p. 60, l. 14: *Matt. xi*: Matthew 11:12.

p. 60, l. 20: *a position of Aristotle*: not identified.

p. 61, l. 21: *St Hierom*: see the observation of the Church father St Jerome (*c.* AD 342–420) in his Homily 73, on Psalm 96, 'In martyrdom … blood is shed that the soul may be delivered from temptations … that it may leave all persecution behind'.

p. 62, l. 11: *Tristitia vestra vertitur*: John 16:20.

John Persall, *A Sermon Preach'd before the King and Queen*

p. 69, ll. 9–10: *he wrote fifteen learned Books*: St Augustine's best-known work on this subject was his *De Trinitate*.

p. 72, ll. 8–9: *to obey the Apostle, making reason stoop to faith*: see, for example, 1 Corinthians 1:19 ff., 1 Corinthians 2.

p. 75, ll. 18–19: *a Paralogism*: a conclusion not following from its own premises.

p. 78, ll. 21–2: *St Vincent in a Bed of Roses*: The martyr St Vincent of Sara-
gossa was put to death in AD 304 during the persecution of Diocletian.
Elaborate tales came to be embroidered around his execution: imprisoned and starved, he was ordered to sacrifice to the gods and, on his
refusal, was put on the rack, roasted, and put in the pillory; just prior
to his execution, his fellow-Christians were allowed to prepare a bed of
rest for him.

p. 78, l. 23: *St Laurence in a Bed of Flames*: The Roman deacon Laurence was
put to death in AD 258, supposedly as a punishment for refusing to surrender the Church's property; tradition recounted that he was roasted to
death on a gridiron.

p. 78, l. 15: *Quam bonus*: see Psalm 143:10 (AV): 'Thy spirit *is* good; lead me into
the land of uprightness.'

p. 84, l. 16: *if Charity be wanting*: 1 Corinthians 13:1–4.

p. 85, l. 2: *Come you Blessed*: Luke 25:34.

p. 86, l. 11: *as we read in Tertullian*: for Tertullian, see vol. 1, *Pope. Pius His Profession of Faith*, Notes, p. 399. In his *Apologeticum* (*c.* AD 197–8) Tertullian
showed how the Christians were blamed for all misfortunes.

p. 87, l. 13: *ejice ancillam*: 'throw out this low and unworthy affection.'

p. 88, ll. 13–14: *the World, Flesh and Devil*: 'from all the deceits of the world,
the flesh, and the devil' – from the litany following morning prayer in the
Book of Common Prayer.

Mr Gother's Spiritual Works … Instructions on the Epistles and Gospels of the Sundays from Advent to Trinity Sunday

p. 96, ll. 7–9: *not only, what is lawful, but likewise what is expedient*: I Corinthians 6:12.

p. 98, l. 6: *but a Hireling*: John 10:12.

p. 98, l. 17: *I know my Sheep*: John 10:14.

p. 98, l. 26: *And hence S. Augustine says*: for example, in his Sermon 263, on
the Ascension, Augustine explained that 'the manifestation of the human
nature of Christ is necessary for the faithful in this life so that they may
make their way toward the Lord'.

p. 98, l. 32: *Love one another*: John 15:12, 17.

p. 99, l. 2: *Learn of me*: Matthew 11:29.

p. 99, ll. 4–5: *Bear with one another*: Colossians 3:13.

p. 99, ll. 10–11: *if they have called the Master …Beelzebub*: Matthew 10:25.

p. 99, ll. 13–14: *The Servant is not above the Master*: John 15:20, 18.

p. 99, l. 26: *This is Life Everlasting*: John 17:3.

p. 99, ll. 29–30: *as St Paul said to the Ephesians*: Ephesians 4:17.

p. 109, ll. 16–17: *This St Chrysostom observes particularly in St Joseph*: for Chrysostom see vol. 1, *Pope Pius. His Profession of Faith*, Notes, p. 398. His *Homilies*

included a commentary on Mathew's Gospel, where Joseph's 'Disquiets' and their resolutions are narrated in ch. 1:19–24 and ch. 2:1–23.

p. 111, ll. 9–10: *Dixi in abundantia mea*: Psalm 30:6: 'And in my prosperity I said, I shall never be moved.'(AV)

p. 112, ll. 10–11: *Christ here in express terms foretold his Apostles*: John 16:20.

p. 112, ll. 23–4: *the Death of the Old Man*: Romans 6:6.

[Thomé de Jesus], *The Sufferings of our Lord Jesus Christ*

p. 143, ll. 9–10: *to declare thrice that that man was innocent*: Luke 23:4, 14, 22.

p. 143, l. 13: *away with him, crucify him*: Matthew 27:22, 23; Mark 15:13,14; Luke 23:18, 21; John 19:6, 15.

p. 144, l. 21: *John xix. 6*: John 19:7.

p. 145, ll. 3–4: *He therefore went back into the judgment-hall*: John 19:9.

p. 145, ll. 30–1: *Our Saviour answering nothing*: Matthew 27:14; Mark 15:3; Luke 23:9; John 19:9.

p. 146, l. 1: *speakest thou not to me?*: John 19:10.

p. 146, l. 8: *thou wouldst not have any power at all*: John 19:11.

p. 148, ll. 12–13: *If thou dost release this man*: John 19:12.

p. 148, ll. 27–8: *behold your king. But they cried out immediately*: John 19:14–15.

p. 148, ll. 29–32: *What, replies Pilate … we have no king but Cesar*: John 19:15.

p. 149, l. 8: *called for water*: Matthew 27:24.

p. 149, ll. 13–14: *his blood be upon us and upon our children.*: Matthew 27:25.

p. 150, ll. 16–17: *having delivered Barabbas at the desire of the Jews*: Matthew 27:26; Mark 15:15; Luke 23:25.

p. 150, l. 18: *and a herald published*: Matthew 27:37; Mark 15:26; Luke 23:38; John 19:19.

p. 151, l. 33: *This makes St Paul say*: The traditional attribution of the Epistle to the Hebrews to Paul is accepted here.

p. 154, l. 9: *O my resurrection and my life*: John 11:25.

p. 155, l. 1: *complacence for*: acquiescence in.

p. 158, ll. 8–9: *against the advice of his wife*: Matthew 27:19.

p. 158, ll. 10–15: *And he released to them him …but delivered Jesus up to their will!*: Matthew 27:16–17, 20–1, 26; Mark 15:7, 11, 15; Luke 23:18–19, 25; John 18:39–40.

p. 161, ll.. 29–30: *and put him on again his own garment*: Matthew 27:31; Mark 15:20.

p. 164, ll. 14–15: *children of wrath*: Ephesians 2:3.

p. 166, l. 19: *and fell with his face on the ground*: The tradition that Jesus fell three times under the weight of his cross became part of the Franciscan-sponsored devotion known as the Stations of the Cross.

p. 166, l. 26: *a man of Cyrene, called Simon*: Matthew 27:32; Mark 15:21; Luke 23:26.

p. 167, ll. 8–10: *to receive Alexander and Rufus into the number of his disciples, both Simon's sons*: Mark 15:21: Mark introduces these two men into his text in such a way as to indicate that they were known to his Christian readers; for a Rufus, whom Paul wished to 'salute', see Romans 16:13.

p. 167, ll. 15–16: *There were also some devout women*: Luke 23:27.

p. 167, ll. 23–5: *daughters of Jerusalem .. and over your children*: Luke 23:28.

p. 167, l. 28 to p. 168, ll. 1–2: *for behold the days shall come … if they do these things in the green wood*: Luke 23:29–31.

p. 168, l. 6: *what will be done in the dry*: Luke 23.31.

p. 168, l. 14: *(Luke xxiii. 28.)*: Luke 23:28–31.

p. 168, ll. 32–3: *when he was going to Jerusalem, amidst the applauses*: Matthew 21:8–9; Mark 11:8–10; Luke 19:36–8; John 12:12–13.

p. 169, ll. 1–2: *he wept bitterly over that unhappy city*: Luke 19:41–4.

[Nicholas Caussin], *Entertainments for Lent*

p. 173, l. 1: *ENTERTAINMENTS*: Considerations.

p. 173, ll. 8–9: *The Delight of Sin is momentary, the Torment eternal.*: not identified.

p. 175, l. 10: *for your Majesty's happy return*: Faced with parliamentary impeachment, Henrietta Maria left England for Holland in February 1642 and collected funds abroad for the King's cause. In February 1643 the Queen returned, landing on the Yorkshire coast, and then rejoined Charles.

p. 175, ll. 15–16: *in the solitude of a prison*: During the period of the Queen's visit until her return to the Continent in June 1644, Brook was in prison in the Tower (from January 1644).

p. 176, l. 14: *some of that gall*: Matthew 27:34.

p. 176, l. 18: *mount Tabor*: A tradition dating from the second century made this mountain the site of Jesus's transfiguration (Matthew 17:2, Mark 9:2).

p. 176, l. 28: *beadsman*: a person commissioned to pray for another or for others.

p. 177, l. 7: *Gen. 3.*: Genesis 3:19.

p. 177, l. 16: *a kind of Proteus*: in Greek mythology the sea god who had the gift of prophecy and who could change his shape as he wished.

p. 178, l. 26: *St Paulinus saith*: The bishop and poet Paulinus of Nola (AD 353–431) wrote extensively on Scripture.

p. 179, l. 22: *a plant call'd Naple*: not identified.

p. 180, l. 1: *Cynocephales*: in mythology, a race of dog-headed men.

p. 180, ll. 16–17: *this caitiff dust*: despicable dust.

p. 181, l. 2: *Matthew vi.*: Matthew 6:16–21.

p. 182, l. 10: *Tertullian saith*: for Tertullian, see vol. 1, *Pope Pius. His Profession of Faith*, Notes, p. 399.

p. 183, ll. 21–2: *as St Clement saith*: Clement of Alexandria (*c.* AD 150–*c.* 215) had his name deleted from the Roman catalogue of sainted martyrs (the 'Martyrology') in 1586 on the grounds of some alleged theological unsoundness, though his saint's day of 4 December continued to be observed in Caussin's France.

p. 184, l. 18: St Matthew xviii.: Matthew 8:5–13.

p. 184, ll. 23–4: *my boy lieth at home*: like the Greek of the original in the New Testament text, *pais*, the Latin *puer*, a boy, could mean either 'son' or 'servant'. In the reflection on the reading, the choice of the interpretation 'servant' seems to emphasize the centurion's altruism.

p. 187, l. 11: *by the Words of saint Augustine*: not identified.

p. 188, ll. 2–3: *as the Israelites were with manna*: Numbers 11:6.

p. 189, l. 9: *St Matthew v.*: Matthew 5:43–8.

p. 190, l. 18: *like another Cain in the world*: Genesis 4:14.

p. 191, ll. 17–18: *When David wept for Saul*: 2 Samuel 1:12.

p. 193, l. 2: *St Matthew vi.*: Matthew 14:23–36.

p. 193, ll. 24–5: *incontinent, they knew him*: They recognized him straight away.

p. 194, l. 12: *intricate*: perplexed.

p. 197, l. 5: *St Matthew iv.*: Matthew 4:1–7.

Mr Gother's Spiritual Works ... Prayers for Every Day in Lent

p. 216, l. 25: *this Acceptable Time*: In the lesson set for the Sunday following Ash Wednesday, from 2 Corinthians 6:10, Paul quoted Isaiah 49:8: 'In an acceptable time have I heard thee'.

p. 217, ll. 24–5: *to whom Moses was well pleasing*: Exodus 24:18, 34:28; Deuteronomy 9:9, 9:25, 10:10.

p. 217, l. 28: *who didst deliver Hezechias*: 2 Kings 19:1, 20.

p. 218, l. 1: *who didst spare the Ninivites*: Jonah 3:5–10.

p. 218, ll. 5–6: *who didst shew Mercy to Judith*: Judith (Apocrypha) 9:1, 13:18.

p. 218, ll. 9–10: *who didst spare Esther and her people*: Esther 4:16, 8:7, 16.

p. 218, ll. 13–14: *who didst mercifully assist the Macchabees*: 2 Maccabees (Apocrypha)13:12, 15–17.

p. 218, ll. 17–18: *who, by thy Prophets, didst call*: e.g. Ezra 8:21.

p. 218, ll. 21–2: *by whose Holy Will thy only Son*: Matthew 4:2.

p. 219, l. 15: *By that bitter Cup*: Matthew 26:39, 42; Mark 14:36; Luke 22:42; John 18:11.

p. 219, ll. 18–19: *By that bitter Cup, which was given thee*: Matthew 27:34; Mark 15:23.

p. 222, l. 4: *By thy own Ordinance*: e.g. Matthew 16:18–19.

p. 224, ll. 24–8: *Let the wicked Man forsake his Way ...full of Mercy to forgive.*: Isaiah 55:7.

p. 224, l. 30 to p. 225, l. 9: *thy Dislike of all such Fasts ... thou wilt have no regard to them*: Isaiah 58:4–5.

p. 230, ll. 14–15: *who wilt not the Death of a Sinner*: Ezekiel 18:23.

p. 231, ll. 6–7: *our sins have been multiplied above the Hairs of our Head*: Psalm 40:12, 69:4.

p. 233, ll. 4–5: *who didst bring Adam, after his Fall*: Genesis 3:12.

p. 233, ll. 7–8: *who didst cast Cain, despairing of thy Mercy*: Genesis 4:14.

p. 233, ll. 10–11: *who didst mercifully deliver Noah*: Genesis, ch. 6–9.

p. 233, ll. 13–14: *who didst pardon the Israelites*: Leviticus 26:40; Nehemiah 1:6.

p. 233, l. 16: *who didst forgive David*: 2 Samuel 12:13.

p. 233, l. 19: *who didst spare Achab*: I Kings 21:29.

p. 233, ll. 21–2: *who shew'dst Mercy to Manasses*: 2 Chronicles 33:12–13.

p. 233, ll. 24–5: *who cam'st into this World to save Sinners*: I Timothy 1:15.

p. 233, ll. 26–7: *who cam'st into the World to seek the Lost-Sheep*: Matthew 15:24

p. 233, ll. 28–9: *who cam'st into the World to call Sinners to Repentance*: Matthew 9:13; Mark 2:17; Luke 5:32.

p. 233, ll. 30–1: *who call'dst Matthew from a Publican*: Matthew 9:9.

p. 234, ll. 1–2: *who forgav'st Mary Magdalene, and became her Advocate*: Luke 7:37–50: Gother accepted the tradition of identifying as Mary Magdalene the anonymous repentant woman who anoints Jesus with oil and whose actions he defends.

p. 234, ll. 3–4: *who didst pardon Peter, having thrice denied thee*: Matthew 26:69–75; Mark 14:66–72; Luke 22:55–62; John 18:16–18, 25–7; John 21:15–17.

p. 234, ll. 5–6: *who promis'd Mercy to the Thief*: Luke 23:39–43.

p. 235, ll. 7–8: *we may put off the old Man*: Ephesians 4:22; Colossians 3:9.

p. 235, ll. 9–10: *we may not live according to the Flesh*: 2 Corinthians 10:2.

p. 235, ll. 11–12: *having put on the Armour of God*: Ephesians 6:11, 13.

p. 235, l. 13: *the Snares of the Enemy*: 1 Timothy 3:7; 2 Timothy 2:26.

p. 235, l. 14: 'dead to Sin': Romans 6: 11.

p. 236, ll. 12–14: *shall be accepted ... like Incense in thy Sight*: The prayer at the incensing of the offering at High Mass – 'Let my prayer, O Lord, be directed as incense in Thy sight: the lifting up of my hands as an evening sacrifice.' – was based on Psalm 141:2.

p. 236, l. 23: *no iniquity has Power over them*: Psalm 119:133.

p. 238, l. 27: *the Robe of Justice*: Isaiah 61:10.

p. 239, l. 30 to p. 240, ll. 30–1: *We confess, O Lord ... the Fast, which thou hast chosen.*: Isaiah 58:4–7.

p. 242, l. 1: *put on the New Man*: Ephesians 4:24; Colossians 3:10.

p. 242, ll. 6–7: *to keep the Unity of the Spirit in the Bond of Peace*: Ephesians 4:2.

p. 242, l. 9: *That we return none Evil for Evil*: I Thessalonians 5:15.

p. 242, ll. 12–13: *to bear one another's Burthens*: Galatians 6:2.

p. 242, ll. 20–1: *we may strive to make our Election sure*: 2 Peter 1:10.

p. 242, ll. 23–4: *we may not faint or be tir'd*: Hebrews 12:3.

[Anon.], *The Primer, or, Office of the B[lessed] Virgin Mary*

p. 248, l. 8: *O Lord, make haste to help me.*: Psalms 38:22, 40:13, 70:1, 71:12.

p. 248, l. 11: *The Anth. O Admirable Intercourse*: not identified.

p. 248, l. 12: *PSALM 92*: Psalm 93 in the DR version.

p. 249, l. 6: *The Anth. When thou wast unspeakably*: not identified.

p. 249, l. 6: *PSALM 99*: Psalm 100 in DR.

p. 249, l. 25: *The Anth. The Bush which Moses saw*: not identified.

p. 249, l. 26: *PSALM 62*: Psalm 63 in DR.

p. 250, l. 28: *PSALM 66*: Psalm 67 in DR.

p. 251, ll. 19–20: *The Anth. The Root of Jesse has Budded.*: not identified.

p. 251, l. 20: *The Song of the Three* Children, Dan. 3.: The apocryphal interpolation between Daniel 3:23 and 3:24, the song of praise of Azariah and his companions, delivered form the fiery furnace.

p. 252, l. 27: *Ananias, Azarias, Misael*: the original names –Hananiah, Mishael and Azariah (AV) – of the singers of the 'Song of the Three Children' (or 'Song of the Three Young Men'), Shadrach, Meshach and Abednego respectively (Daniel 1:6–7). This canticle, known as the *'Benedicite'*, in praise of the creation was recited at Lauds on Sunday, the first day of the making of the universe.

p. 253, l. 8: *The Anth. Behold Mary*: not identified.

p. 253, l. 9: *PSALM 148*: Psalm 148 in DR (AV's Psalm 147:12–20 became a new Psalm 147 in DR, so that the remaining Psalms in DR and AV shared the same numbering).

p. 254, l. 11: *PSALM 149*: Psalm 149 in DR.

p. 255, l. 3: *PSALM 150*: Psalm 150 in DR.

p. 255, l. 23: *The Chapter, Cant. I.*: a Scripture reading – from the Song of Songs 6:9.

p. 255, l. 28: *The HYMN, O gloriosa Virginum*: The hymn *'O gloriosa virginum'* in the Roman Breviary of 1632 – 'Most glorious of virgins, thou! / supreme among the ranks of blest …' – was sung on festivals of Mary.

p. 255, l. 29 to p. 256, l. 12: *O Mary! Whilst thy Maker blest … The Father, Son and Holy Ghost*: a translation from *O gloriosa virginum*.

p. 256, l. 15: *The Anth. A Wonderful Mystery*: *Mysterium mirabile*: not identified.

p. 256, l. 16: *The Song of Zach.*: the prophecy of Zacharias, in Luke 1:69–79: 'Blessed be the Lord God of Israel'.

p. 257, ll. 24–5: *V. Lord hear my Prayer./ R. And let my Cry come to thee*: Psalm 102:1.

p. 257, ll. 27–8 to p. 258, ll. 2–3: *O God, who by the Fruitful Virginity of the Blessed Virgin Mary … who liveth and reigneth one God with thee, &c.*: the collect for commemorations in honour of the Blessed Virgin Mary at Masses between 30 December and the feast of the Purification, 2 February.

p. 258, l. 4: *The Anth. All ye Saints of God*: not identified.

p. 258, l. 11: *Protect, O Lord, thy People*: not identified.

p. 258, ll. 31–2: *V. Bless we our Lord. / R. Thanks be to God*: the words of dismissal in the Tridentine rite for Masses in the penitential seasons.

p. 259, l. 5: *The Anthem. Alma Redemptoris Mater*: This antiphon, whose opening was sometimes translated in vernacular versions as 'Blest Mother of our Lord!', attributed to Hermannus Contractus (d. 1054), was recited between Advent and the feast of the Purification, in honour of Mary's maternity. A translation of it follows in the text.

p. 259, l. 25: *The Anthem. Ave Regina Cælorum*: This anonymously authored antiphon in honour of Mary's queenship of heaven, sometimes translated in vernacular versions as 'Hail Mary, queen of heav'nly spheres', was sung at Compline and Lauds between the feast of the Purification and Maundy Thursday: a translation follows in the text.

p. 260, l. 7: *Strengthen us, O God of Mercy*: not identified.

p. 260, l. 22: *The HYMN. Memento rerum conditor*: This anonymously composed hymn, given this title in the Roman Breviary of 1632, and from the Christmas anthem *Jesu, redemptor omnium*', was incorporated in the Little Office of the Blessed Virgin Mary. Its opening was sometimes translated in vernacular versions as 'Divine redeemer, bear in mind': a variant translation follows in the text.

p. 261, l. 6: *PSALM 53.*: Psalm 54 (DR).

p. 261, l. 24: *PSALM 84.*: Psalm 85 (DR).

p. 262, l. 30: *PSALM 116.*: Psalm 117 (DR).

p. 263, l. 9: *The Chapter. Cant. 6*: a Scripture reading – from the Song of Songs 6:10.

Mr Gother's Spiritual Works … Instructions for Particular States and Conditions of Life

p. 272, l. 1: *289*: this page is misnumbered and the original pagination misses out pages 289 and 290.

p. 272, l. 22: *the Broad Way*: Matthew 7:13.

p. 275, ll. 14–16: *the Apostle gives Directions .. to do all in the Name of … Jesus Christ*: Colossians 3:17.

p. 276, ll. 23–4: *And not favour themselves in his Wrong, who employs them*: and not advantage themselves to the disadvantage of their employer.

p. 286, l. 22: *Children, as the Scripture Terms them*: Leviticus 25:55.

p. 299, ll. 7–9: *the Post … makes them Remarkable*: their positions draw attention to all they do.

Mr Gother's Spiritual Works … A Practical Catechism

p. 306, ll. 6–7: *For tho' Cain was Afflicted for his Sin*: Genesis 4:11–16.

p. 306, ll. 7–8: *and Pharaoh*: Exodus 7–12, 14.

p. 306, ll. 8–9: *and the Children of Israel in the Desert*: Exodus 15–17.

p. 306, l. 9: *and Saul and David*: 1 Samuel 16:14, 18:10, 19:9; 1 Samuel 24:5; 2 Samuel 6:9; 2 Samuel 12:19–23.

p. 306, l. 14: *as Abraham*: Genesis 22:1–9.

p. 306, l. 14: *Elias*: I Kings 17:20.

p. 306, l. 14: *Job*: Job, ch. 1–3, 6–7, 10, 16–17, 19, 29–-0.

p. 306, l. 14: *Toby*: Tobit (Apocrypha), ch. 2–3.

p. 306, l. 15: *the Man born Blind*: John 9:1–3.

p. 308, ll. 2–3: *Did not Jacob lament*: Genesis 37:34.

p. 308, l. 4: *and Joseph his being Falsly Accus'd*: Genesis 39.

p. 311, l. 31: *Rom. 5.*: Romans 5:3.

p. 313, ll. 21–2: *Casting his whole Care upon God*: 2 Peter 5:7.

p. 314, ll. 6–7: *why should Christ call upon all, who Labour*: Matthew 11:28.

p. 333, ll. 27–8: *Thou shalt love the Lord thy God with thy whole Heart.*: Deuteronomy 6:5, 10:12, 11:13, 30:6; Mark 12:30.

p. 336, ll. 7–8: *A. …Q.*: The roles of questioner and answerer have become mixed up.

p. 342, ll. 21–2: *I cannot but admire at*: I can only wonder at.

[John Anselm Mannock], *The Poor Man's Catechism*

p. 353, ll. 1–2: *How many Cardinal Virtues are there?*: In the classification of the virtues ('habits of right conduct') by St Thomas Aquinas into the intellectual (for example, wisdom, knowledge and understanding), theological (faith, hope and charity) and moral virtues, the moral virtues, originally identified by Aristotle in the *Nichomachian Ethics*, were classed as cardinal or 'hinge' virtues because of the dependence of other virtues on them.

p. 354, l. 19: *Eccles. xxxii. 24.*: Ecclesiasticus, or the Wisdom of Jesus the Son of Sirach (Apocrypha, AV), 32:19.

p. 354, l. 25: *Ephes. v. 15.*: Ephesians 5:15–16.

p. 354, l. 31: *Kings and Magistrates rule*: Proverbs 8:15.

p. 356, ll. 30–1: *Justice and Peace have embrac'd each other*: Psalm 85:10.

p. 356, ll. 31–2: *Give unto every one his Due*: The *Institutiones* (AD 533), part of the comprehensive legal code, the *Corpus Juris Civilis* of the Emperor Flavius Amicius Justinianus ('Justinian', *c.* AD 482–565), in bk I, ch. 1, par. 1 state: 'Justice is the constant wish to render to every one his due.'

p. 357, l. 2: *loves Justice*: Psalm 33:5.

p. 357, l. 5: *the Just shall live for ever*: Psalm 37:29.

p. 357, ll. 39–40: *and St John Baptist, for reprehending the Sin of Adultery*: Matthew 14:1–12; Mark 6:17–29.

p. 358, l. 20: *Eph. v. 12*: Ephesians 6:12.

p. 358, ll. 37–8: *My Help is only from our Lord*: Psalm 121:2.

p. 359, ll. 37–8: *He that is abstinent, shall taste Life*: not identified.

p. 361, l. 1: Of the GIFTS of the HOLY GHOST: In the Vulgate version of Isaiah 11:2–3 seven gifts of the Spirit, including fear of the Lord, come down on the Messiah. In the traditional teaching of the Catholic Church, these gifts were fully revealed in Christ at his baptism and subsequently to his disciples at Pentecost and they allow the faithful to respond to the promptings of the Holy Spirit.

p. 361, l. 6: *the Prophet Isaiah, (c. lxi. I)*: Isaiah 61:1–3 announces the mission of the Messiah, the Spirit being upon him.

p. 362, l. 11: *Lord give me Understanding to know thy Ways*: Psalm 119:73, 119:125.

p. 362, ll. 36–7: *the Blind leading the Blind*: Matthew 15:14; Luke 6:39.

p. 362, ll. 37–8: *Of whom St Barnard rightly says*: the Cistercian monastic leader and writer Bernard, Abbot of Clairvaux (1090–1153), known as the 'last of the Fathers'; quotation not identified.

p. 363, l. 1: *Prov. ii. 10.*: Proverbs 2:10–11.

p. 363, ll. 6–7: *The Fear of our Lord is the Beginning of True Wisdom*: Psalm 111:10.

p. 363, l. 21: *Pierce, O Lord, my Flesh with thy Fear*: not identified.

p. 363, l. 24: *Of the FRUITS of the HOLY GHOST*: The fruits of the Spirit, in Galatians 5:22 (AV), counteracting the 'works of the flesh' (Galatians 5:19–21), are love, joy, peace, long-suffering, gentleness, goodness and faith' – the Latin Vulgate added modesty, continence and chastity. The schedule eventually assembled in Catholic doctrine reads: 'charity, joy, peace, patience, longanimity (long-suffering), goodness, benignity, mildness, fidelity, modesty, continence and chastity'.

p. 363, ll. 30–2: *the Description of the celestial Jerusalem … that bringeth twelve Fruits, (c. ult.)*: The final chapter of Revelation, 22, v. 2, featuring the tree of life, which provides a numerical convergence with the twelve fruits of the Spirit.

p. 365, ll. 1–2: *A good Tree cannot bear bad Fruit, nor a bad Tree good Fruit.*: Matthew 7:18.

p. 365, ll. 12–18: *God will not be laughed at …Life everlasting, Gal. viii. 6*: Galatians 6:7–8.

p. 368, l. 9: *(Luke vi. 24, &c.)*: Luke 6:24–6.

p. 368, ll. 31–2: *Solomon … confess'd it*: Ecclesiastes 1:2, 14, 18 and *passim*.

p. 368, l. 39: *live not as Dives did*: Luke 16:19.

p. 370, l. 18: *Mat. xxv.*: Matthew 25:34.

p. 370, l. 33: *Isaiah lvii. 7.*: Isaiah 58:7.

p. 370, l. 34: *much practised by Job, Toby*: Job 29:12–17; Tobit (Apocrypha) 1:3.

p. 371, ll. 5–6: *of the seventh much is said in the Book of Toby*: Tobit (Apocrypha) 2.

p. 371, ll. 11–12: *Let not your Left Hand see what your Right Hand does*: Matthew 6:3.

p. 371, l. 13: *God loves a chearful Giver.*: 2 Corinthians 9:7.

p. 371, ll. 20–1: *who opens his Hand, and fills every Creature with Blessings*': not identified.

p. 372, ll. 5–6: *laid up Treasures in Heaven*': Matthew 6:20.

p. 372, l. 21: *and with him all Things*': John 3:35, 13:3.

p. 372, l. 28: *of the SPIRITUAL WORKS of MERCY*: The medieval concept of the spiritual works of mercy in parallel with the corporal works was assembled from scriptural sources including: (1) to admonish sinners: Matthew 18:15–20, Colossians 3:5–17, 1 Thessalonians 5:12, 2 Thessalonians 3:15; (2) to instruct the ignorant: Romans 11:25, 1 Corinthians 10:1, 1 Timothy 4:6–12, 2 Timothy 4:1–5, 1 Thessalonians 4:13; (3) to counsel the doubtful: Luke 24:36–53, John 20:26–9; (4) to comfort the sorrowful: John 11:19, 1 Thessalonians 4:13–18; (5) to bear wrongs patiently: Matthew 16:24, James 5:7–11; (6) to forgive all injuries: Matthew 6:15, Matthew 18:21–35, Colossians 3:13; (7) to pray for the living and the dead: James 5:16, Colossians 1:3, 9; 2 Maccabees (Apocrypha) 12:45.

p. 373, l. 7: *Gal. vi.*: Galatians 6:1.

p. 373, l. 10: *in Daniel, (c. xii)*: 12:3.

p. 373, l. 12: *St James, (c. v. 19)*: James 5:19–20.

p. 373, ll. 19–20: *in the Gospel of St. Luke (c. vi)*: Luke 6:37.

p. 373, l. 21: *in St James, (c. v.)*: James 5:16.

p. 373, l. 39: *Wisdom, xii. 2.*: The Wisdom of Solomon (Apocrypha) 12:2.

p. 374, l. 3: *Eccles vii. 3.*: Ecclesiastes 7:2.

p. 374, l. 21: *for Charity never ceases*: 1 Corinthians 13:8.

p. 375, l. 37: *Dust thou art*: Genesis 2:19.

p. 376, ll. 2–3: *None but an infinite Being could atone for an offence against an infinite being*: the interpretation of the Atonement put forward by St Anselm (1033–1109) in his *Cur Deus Homo*.

p. 376, l. 8: *Children of Wrath*: Ephesians 2:3.

p. 376, ll. 18–20: *Go teach all nations … and of the Holy Ghost.*: Matthew 28:19.

p. 376, ll. 22–4: *Unless one be re-born of Water …he cannot enter into the Kingdom of God*: John 3:5.

p. 376, ll. 25–6: *a Part of Hell, call'd the Limbus of Children*: The Latin term *limbus*, meaning 'fringe', was used from the Middle Ages both to indicate the place of waiting for the righteous who had died before Christ until his resurrection (*limbus patrum*) and for the stationing in the '*limbus infantium*' of unbaptized children who, as St Augustine taught, without christening could not enter paradise. While some theologians maintained that the Almighty would confer baptism on infants by his own means – St Bernard, for example, proposing that their parents' faith availed such children of salvation –, most medieval theologians, including Peter Lombard (1100–64) and Thomas Aquinas, followed St Gregory Nazianzen (*c.* AD 328–90) in teaching that unbaptized children, though experiencing the loss of heaven, underwent none of the 'pain of sense' of the damned in hell and indeed enjoyed 'natural happiness' in limbo.

p. 376, ll. 40–1: *we can do all Things, through him that strengthens us.*: Philemon 4:13.